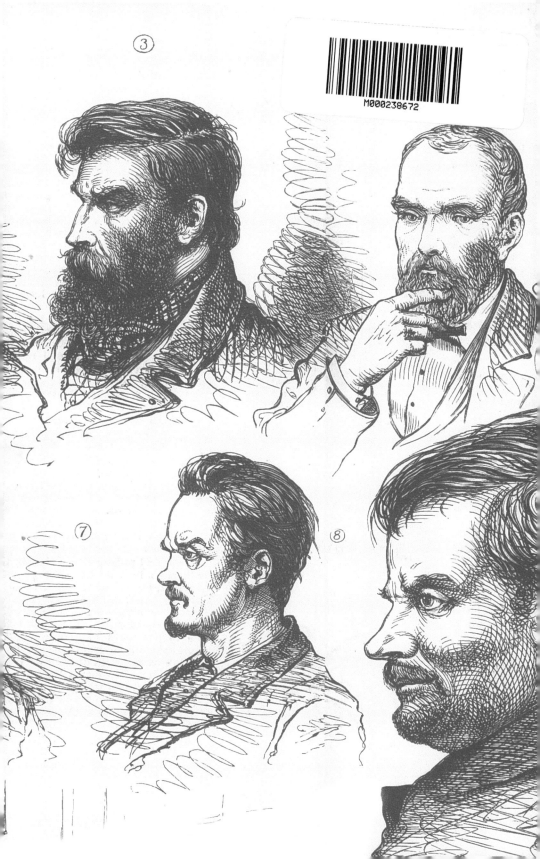

THE INVINCIBLES

Dr Shane Kenna, born in 1983, was a lifelong resident of Old Bawn in Tallaght, south Dublin. A history graduate of Trinity College, Shane cemented his research interests there in Irish political history and militant Irish republicanism, with an emphasis on late-nineteenth-century Ireland. His completed PhD was the basis of his first book, *War in the Shadows: The Irish-American Fenians who Bombed Victorian Britain* (Merrion, 2013). During his career as a historian, Shane lectured and gave talks across Ireland and further abroad, and was frequently interviewed by broadcasters including RTÉ, TV3 and BBC. Shane was also a prolific tour guide, working at sites such as Dublin Castle and Kilmainham Gaol, and on the 1916 Rebellion Walking Tour.

Shane's published output also includes *16 Lives: Thomas MacDonagh* (O'Brien, 2014), *Jeremiah O'Donovan Rossa: Unrepentant Fenian* (Merrion, 2015), *Conspirators: A Photographic History of Ireland's Revolutionary Underground* (Mercier, 2015), and numerous articles, both in print and online. Tragically, in 2017 at the age of thirty-three, Shane died after a brave battle with cancer. He is survived by his fiancée Edel Quinn, his mother Olive and brother John, and his extended family and close friends.

The Invincibles is the last completed text from this talented historian of Irish history, and its publication is a fitting tribute to Dr Shane Kenna's legacy in Irish historiography.

THE
INVINCIBLES
THE PHOENIX PARK ASSASSINATIONS
— AND THE —
CONSPIRACY
THAT SHOOK AN EMPIRE

DR SHANE KENNA

THE O'BRIEN PRESS
DUBLIN

First published 2019 by
The O'Brien Press Ltd,
12 Terenure Road East, Rathgar, D06 HD27, Dublin 6, Ireland.
Tel: +353 1 4923333; Fax: +353 1 4922777
E-mail: books@obrien.ie
Website: www.obrien.ie
The O'Brien Press is a member of Publishing Ireland.

ISBN: 978-1-78849-060-3

1 3 5 7 9 10 8 6 4 2

19 21 23 22 20

Printed and bound in Poland by Białostockie Zakłady Graficzne S.A.
The paper in this book is produced using pulp from managed forests.

Published in

Picture credits:

Front cover picture: Pictorial Press Ltd / Alamy Stock Photo

Aidan Lambert: pages 1, 8, 17, 38, 44, 60, 68, 69, 70, 71, 72, 77, 79, 80, 81, 84, 87, 90, 92, 103, 104, 130, 133, 134, 135, 144, 147, 148, 149, 158-159, 161, 172, 209, 268-269, 284, 285 and 291; National Library of Ireland: pages 49, 51, 58, 76, 105, 110, 124, 154, 178, 197, 208, 221, 232, 244, 248, 254, 258 and 262; Mícheál Ó Doibhilín: pages 157 and 241.

Dedicated to the love and passion my dear Shane had for Irish history, to Shane's fiancée Edel Quinn, to my dear husband Jimmy who passed away twelve years ago, to my son John and his wife Lisa, to my two granddaughters Darcy and Lily, and to all of Shane's friends and colleagues.

Olive Kenna

CONTENTS

THE EXECUTIONS

THE AFTERMATH

REMEMBERING DR SHANE KENNA

There are so many words I could use to describe Dr Shane Kenna: academic, historian, accomplished author, historical advisor, lecturer, mentor and one of the best tour guides in Dublin, among other things.

For his family and friends, Shane was all of these things and more. From the moment you met Shane, it was impossible to ignore his love of history, especially nineteenth-century Irish history. We, his friends who worked alongside Shane in Kilmainham Gaol, got to witness that passion every day, and got to hear Shane talk about Charles Stewart Parnell or the Invincibles. We became a small, tight-knit group and, although we all moved on from Kilmainham, the friendships that had started there went from strength to strength.

Over the years, we watched Shane achieve so many wonderful things. He wrote a number of books, including *War in the Shadows: The Irish-American Fenians Who Bombed Britain*, *Conspirators: A Photographic History of Ireland's Revolutionary Underground*, *Jeremiah O'Donovan Rossa: Unrepentant Fenian* and *16 Lives: Thomas MacDonagh*. He gave lectures on the national and international stage, and organised conferences on forgotten chapters in Irish history.

Shane was determined. Once he got an idea about a project into his head, he would put his all into making it a reality, as this book proves.

Shane left an impression on everyone he met. His passion for history, as well as his smile and great laugh, was infectious. He had an amazing ability to bring people together from different parts of his life, because the one thing that united us all was Shane.

There is no doubt that Shane dedicated himself wholly to his work. He was serious about the stories he wanted to tell, stories which had long been forgotten or had never before been discovered. However, although a serious historian, he did not take himself too seriously. He had a wonderful sense of humour, and with a gesture, a quote from Jean-Luc Picard or – and this may surprise some – a dance move entitled the 'Fenian Flick', Shane could lift the darkest mood.

He loved *Star Trek, Doctor Who, Batman* and *Indiana Jones*. In fact, it was seeing the professor/action hero Indiana Jones when Shane was a child that set him on the path to pursuing history as a career.

Shane was a tower of a man, over six feet tall. His stature was matched by his personality. He was kind-hearted, generous and a gentle soul, who did not refuse to help anyone with their queries, be they history students only starting out in college or relatives of those he wrote about.

I still remember the first day I met Shane, a nineteenth-century Fenian living in the twenty-first century. He was smiling from ear to ear, happy in the knowledge that he was going to be talking about Irish history every day.

This personal introduction to Shane's book has been very difficult to write, but it has also been an honour. A huge void has been left in the lives of Shane's family and friends with his passing, but if there is any solace to be found, it is that we have so many wonderful memories of him. Shane has left a legacy not just for future historians, but for those who loved him. He was a beloved son, brother, fiancé, uncle, nephew and friend, and an 'unrepentant Fenian historian'.

Liz Gillis, author and historian, 2017

INTRODUCTION

Even by the standards of violent secret societies, the story of the Irish National Invincibles has been clouded in mystery and warped by misinformation. It has also been notably neglected, for a body that created international news in May 1882, when it assassinated two of the most senior government officials in Ireland in the Phoenix Park. Fundamental details, such as the precise name of the organisation that coalesced in Dublin in 1881, have been debated, as well as the question of its role and relationship within the broader Irish Republican Brotherhood. While the identities of the main Invincibles have been ascertained, their names have never loomed large in the popular imagination. This is surprising, given that they had members executed in 1883. These men never attained the veneration accorded to the 'Manchester Martyrs'. In all probability, the exclusion of the Invincibles from the top tier of the republican pantheon derived in part from the magnitude of the killings they committed, coupled with the studied reticence of their associates in Ireland, Britain and the United States of America.

The revival and extremity of the physical force tradition in Ireland owed much to An Ghorta Mor (The Great Hunger) of 1845–50. The IRB's founders were among those who held the British Government culpable for the catastrophic death toll. The malign agency of Westminster, the sole parliamentary authority in Ireland since the Act of Union took effect in 1801, was detected in the dangerous mismanagement of the pre-'Famine' economy, and paltry efforts to stave off mass excess mortality, eviction and forced emigration. Veterans of the desperate Young Ireland revolt of 1848 consequently built a trans-Atlantic 'Fenian' organisation from 1858, in order to establish a sovereign Irish Republic outside the British Empire. There seemed to be no viable constitutional path to this progressive objective, as efforts by moderates working within the proto-democratic electoral system proved time and again.

In March 1867, the Fenians in Ireland promised adult suffrage and an equitable land system, in a country slowly recovering from the privations of An Ghorta Mor and without adequate security of tenure. Attempts to achieve such ambitious objectives by force of arms were contained that year by a programme of pre-emptive 'police' actions and effective counter-insurgency. The triumph of Dublin Castle, seat of the British interest in Ireland, aggrieved militant republicans, who endured damaging schisms on both sides of the Atlantic. Adversity spurred restructuring and new strategic thinking.

The most dramatic expressions of such multi-faceted processes were the resumed, albeit increasingly token, armed attacks on British North America from the USA. Irish-American Fenians, reorganised as Clan na Gael, humiliated London by conveying six escaped political prisoners from Western Australia to New York in 1876. In 1881–85, others mounted a sophisticated bombing campaign in England that badly shook the British establishment. Yet in 1884, the IRB was central to the creation of the Gaelic Athletic Association, a sporting and cultural national body, unconnected to political violence.

Quasi-legal Fenian initiatives included much deeper engagement in the day-to-day issues of the rural poor, and the discrete extension of logistic support to those attempting to convince the House of Commons to legislate in a manner favourable to Ireland. The revolutionary underground, however, was very much alive and, due to its temporary derailment in 1867, more keenly attuned to the threats posed by infiltration and agents provocateurs. The necessity of maintaining a credible, versatile paramilitary challenge to Dublin Castle, while guarding against its well-resourced counter-measures, ultimately spawned the Invincibles.

As is comprehensively detailed in this volume, the Invincibles surfaced when the newly formed Irish National Land League was deemed by the IRB to require robust underpinning. Liaison between leading Fenians and the Irish Parliamentary Party, not least Charles Stewart Parnell, preceded the October 1879 foundation of the Land League. A de facto alliance was by no means a foregone conclusion. Agitation for far-reaching land reform, rather than preparations to achieve an independent republic, did not appeal to all IRB and CnG figures, but significant grassroots aid was nonetheless provided. To a much greater extent than previously experienced, Fenians in Ireland generated support for the Land League and engaged in agrarian activism under its banner.

Dublin Castle resorted to coercion in its attempt to limit the influence of this dangerous compact. In so doing, it incurred severe reprisals from the Fenian hardcore. Men chosen for their willingness and capacity to carry out assassinations and bombings were grouped into the Invincibles in Dublin in 1881. Finance from the USA and input from senior Land League advocates in the UK formed part of preliminary arrangements. A number of Dublin-based IRB 'centres' drew volunteers into a cadre responsible for internal security; persons detected in acts of treachery were liable to be killed. Their name evoked the Fenian phrase 'beir bua', as well as the Phoenix symbol used by the IRB, to assert confidence in the inevitability of final victory.

The Invincibles made several attempts to kill Chief Secretary William E Forster, Britain's most senior political representative in Ireland, as a response to his introduction of repressive legislation used to jail Parnell and other constitutionalist leaders. A bitter opponent of Irish self-determination,

Forster resigned to protest Prime Minister WE Gladstone's release of Parnell from Kilmainham Prison, and was succeeded by Lord Frederick Cavendish. Gladstone evidently wished to negotiate with Parnell on terms that many Tories found objectionable.

Events in Dublin soon altered the situation. On 6 May 1882, Cavendish was in the presence of Permanent Undersecretary Thomas Burke, a prime target of the Invincibles for his perceived political apostasy and landlordism, when the assassination squad struck. Both men were knifed to death in broad daylight, the culmination of an elaborate plan that spanned the Irish Sea. Their deaths had major repercussions for Anglo-Irish affairs in the 1880s, and these are outlined in full in this authoritative volume.

Author Dr Shane Kenna has amassed and skilfully evaluated much important new information on the Invincibles, who, for the first time, are located in their appropriate context. His PhD dissertation from Trinity College, Dublin, was published in revised form as *War in the Shadows: The Irish-American Fenians Who Bombed Victorian Britain* (Irish Academic Press, Dublin, 2013), and immediately established him as a major new voice on the subject. A renowned history tour guide and public lecturer, the prolific Dubliner has published additional books on Irish republicanism, including the well-received biographies *16Lives: Thomas MacDonagh* (O'Brien Press, Dublin, 2014) and *Jeremiah O'Donovan Rossa: Unrepentant Fenian* (IAP, Dublin, 2015). Despite the onset of grave health problems, Kenna persevered with his research into the Irish National Invincibles, and drafted the manuscript now issued by O'Brien Press. He passed away, aged thirty-three, in February 2017. While this publication comprises a fitting tribute to a respected and popular young historian, it stands on its own considerable academic merit.

Dr Ruan O'Donnell

History Department, University of Limerick

1

BACKGROUND TO
THE INVINCIBLES

Traditionally, there had been much poverty on the island of Ireland, where a large tenant farming class existed. The place of the tenant farmer was quite insecure, as the system of landlordism in Ireland was far more favourable to the Irish landlord than to his English counterpart. Landlords had the ability to increase rents whenever they saw fit, and were entitled to evict tenants from their farms at their desire and on non-payment of rent.

It was against this backdrop that tenant farmers were faced with bad harvests in 1878 and 1879, the worst on record since the Great Famine. Parallel to this bad harvest, the situation for Irish farmers was weakened by a fall in the value of Irish agricultural produce, which decreased from about £50 million in 1876 to £37.5 million in 1879,[1] as the market favoured cheaper imports from America, Argentina and Australia. Many tenant farmers could not now afford to pay rent to their landlords, and increasingly the prospect of starvation and eviction loomed, on a scale not seen since the Famine. There was a massive increase in evictions, rising from 406 in 1877 to 1098 the following year,[2] the area worst affected being the impoverished west of Ireland. Emigration was witnessed on a scale not seen since the Famine, with sizable numbers of Irish people making for America and Britain.

With the Famine less than a generation behind them, tenant farmers were not prepared to allow tragedy to strike again, many this time organising as a movement seeking fairer rights on their farms and lands. And what made this 'new confluence of discontents so much more formidable than before was the existence of an effective tenant leadership on the tenant side'.[3] This was represented by the establishment of the Mayo Tenants' Defence Association at Castlebar on 26 October 1878, to defend the rights of the tenant farmer.

Increasingly, the Irish political agenda was dominated by the crisis on the land. By August 1878, John Devoy, a leading American-based Fenian already thinking of aligning the national question with the land question, was visited by Michael Davitt. Davitt, a member of the Supreme Council of the IRB, had been released on a ticket of leave from prison. Davitt, like many within Fenianism, had been impressed by a rising star in the Irish Party at Westminster, Charles Stewart Parnell, MP for Meath.

In Parliament, Parnell associated with Joseph Biggar MP, himself a former member of the IRB Supreme Council. Parnell was no fool; he knew exactly what connections Biggar enjoyed to Fenianism, and how extreme his republican views were. Biggar had developed a policy of obstruction, using the rules of the House of Commons to hold up its business if it would not consider the best interests of Ireland. Parnell subscribed rigidly to this policy, proponents arguing that the use of obstruction would blackmail Parliament to grant an Irish legislature, proving that politically both nations would be better facilitated separately, with a British parliament looking over British interests, and an Irish parliament doing likewise for Ireland. It is not credible to argue that Parnell did not give Biggar the sense that he did not support his politics and revolutionary connections, and it is even less credible to imagine that Biggar did not keep his revolutionary colleagues informed of Parnell's progress and attitudes.

This illustrates how any relationship Parnell had with Fenianism was ambiguous to say the least. He had won their attention when he declared in favour of an amnesty for Fenian prisoners, and declared in the House of Commons in relation to the Manchester Martyrs and the killing of a police sergeant during a Fenian rescue attempt in Manchester in 1867, 'I wish to say publicly as directly as I can that I do not believe and never shall believe that any murder was committed at Manchester.'[4] Parnell was obviously angling for the support and trust of Fenianism.

Charles Stuart Parnell in Westminster Parliament, during a reading of the land bill, from the *Illustrated London News*, 1881.

This is further illustrated by the recollections of veteran Fenian John Daly, a travelling organiser for the IRB and former member of the Supreme Council. At a meeting in Lower Abbey Street, Dublin, a summit arranged by Charlie Fay, a Home Rule MP for Cavan, Parnell informed Daly:

> ... that he was very much interested in Irish affairs, and that he understood I was taking an active part in the advanced movement. At that time the Home Rule party were getting sick and tired of old ... parliamentary humbugging ... and that he was thinking of going into Parliament himself and assuming a more advanced policy, and if he did so – did I think he might hope to get the support of the advanced or Fenian party?[5]

As a result of Parnell's perceived sympathy for physical-force nationalism, Fenianism kept a keen eye on the parliamentarian, and followed his progress with interest.

Michael Davitt persuaded Devoy that working with Parnell on the land question would by no means 'be used to hurt Fenianism or to decry Fenian ideals, but rather as a means of broadening the scope of the people to a more advanced programme than that put forward by Isaac Butt's federal Home Rule movement.'[6] Davitt's role in Devoy's conversion was aided by his coming to the conclusion that Victorian nationalist demands for political independence were not enough, and that real independence could only be achieved alongside socio-economic independence; this in turn required the end of landlordism, as 'the best friend of the national cause ... is the man who ... does his best to lift his countrymen out of the slough of poverty, degradation and despair'.[7] This could only be achieved with 'the abolition of landlordism'.[8] Devoy had also concluded that a mere conspiracy to establish a rebellion could not achieve independence. He argued that independence could only be achieved through public policy; Davitt's proposal offered him a course of action towards this end.

Devoy was not the only source of support for the 'new departure'. John Breslin also declared in favour, finding that it:

> ... is necessary to prevent Ireland from being misrepresented before the world by men who claim to speak in the name of their country. I would like to see a union effected between the advanced nationalists and the more earnest of the Home Rulers for this purpose, and I consider that it is only by such a union we can defeat those who now 'misrepresent Ireland'.[9]

Breslin, evidently aware of fears among elements of the physical-force movement, went on to note that the new departure would not divert from the real object of Irish liberation and national self-determination. Militants, he said, should therefore not 'relax their preparations for active work for one moment; for it is by active aggressive work alone that we can ultimately succeed'.[10] Thomas Bourke echoed Breslin in his support for a new departure. However, he warned that, 'I believe now as I have ever believed that nothing but force can ever free Ireland.'[11] Thus, while the style of the new departure deviated from the traditional demands of physical-force Irish nationalism, its substance was essentially the same. This was not a strategy for an agricultural revolution – this was a strategy for a political revolution.

Such an alliance was well understood by the Irish Party, who recognised that alignment with advanced nationalists could improve their electoral prospects in Ireland, providing increased funding and an existing operational base throughout the Irish countryside. Furthermore, it was regarded by Parnell as a means of rapidly securing power as the head of a national movement. Parnell, accompanied by Biggar, met a delegation of the Clan, including John O'Leary of the IRB, on 7 March 1879 in France. For Devoy, 'all were absolutely in accord as to absolute separation as the end'[12] of any programme they could come to regarding the national question. Parnell had seemingly given the impression that he was 'prepared to go more than half way to meet'[13] the demands and aspirations of physical-force nationalists. Understanding that Parnell was more than willing to associate with Fenianism if necessary, Devoy came to the conclusion that an alliance with Parnell would lead to 'some sort of practical nationalist climax, if possible to coincide with the centenary of the 1782 meeting of the Protestant Volunteers at Dungannon. It also seems fairly clear that Parnell ... to further immediate political advantage encouraged Devoy to think in such ambitious terms.'[14]

Devoy was not the only physical-force nationalist Parnell had stressed such views to. William Mackey Lomasney[15] and John O'Leary were equally fooled, the latter being told Parnell had agreed that 'as soon as he secured the means he would start in business with us and smash up the opposition firm'.[16]

This testimony was seemingly corroborated by British spy Henri Le Caron, who stated that Parnell had informed him his ultimate goal was not just Home Rule, but total separation from Britain.[17] Le Caron would later tell the Times special commission that he had had a conversation with Parnell in the lobby of the House of Commons, where Parnell explicitly told him that 'there need be no misunderstanding. We are working for a common purpose – for the independence of Ireland, just as you are doing; I have long ceased to believe that anything but force of arms will ever bring about the redemption of Ireland.'[18] While this was political manoeuvring on the part of Parnell, working to secure the support of American Fenianism and its valuable finances, it is evident that Parnell did indeed say this to the British spy. It can be taken as a given, however, that Parnell was being insincere in making this statement, given as his brother noted: 'with the Fenian doctrine itself, and with the Fenian methods, [Parnell] was never really in sympathy'.[19]

Seeking the support of Fenianism for political reasons and to secure his place as the leader of a unified national movement, the earlier French summit paved the way for a further meeting in Dublin in April 1879, at the

Morrison Hotel opposite Trinity College, with leading Fenians including Davitt and Devoy. According to historian FSL Lyons, Parnell found himself under pressure from two directions – Davitt urged him to lead a mass movement of tenants against landlords, while Devoy dangled before him once again the more sophisticated allure of the new departure.[20]

Parnell was as evasive and vague as ever. Politically, his mind was preoccupied. Should he represent tenants' interests at the head of an agrarian movement against landlordism, it could descend into violence; this could be politically dangerous to his ambitions of establishing Home Rule, an ambition requiring the support of moderate nationalism and public opinion. Parnell had talked himself into an alliance with extremists and a burgeoning militant agrarianism, to be organised largely by the Fenians. While he would have preferred to maintain a level of ambiguity, events were increasingly pushing him into the fold. It was becoming increasingly difficult to avoid commitment, as the countryside was moving toward a tremendous upheaval. Davitt and Devoy were in the process of establishing a broad social movement, uniting Fenians, ribbon men, priests, tenant farmers and the middle class. Parnell calculated that if he did not subscribe, this movement would rival and overtake his political ambitions, undermining his claim to be the leader of a great national movement in Ireland.

Davitt and Devoy didn't seem to recognise this, and continued to believe that only under Parnell could a movement be reunited. Fenianism would work with a broad political coalition to overthrow landlordism and, having done so, the coalition would come behind the Fenian banner, demanding separation from Britain and a resolution to the national question. By pressing for Parnell's involvement, however, Devoy was inflicting harm on his strategy, as he would begin the process of enthroning Parnell among the people, given that Parnell would be most associated with the struggle in the public mind. Fenian leaders would remain secondary to the public faces of the Land League.

At the Morrison Hotel meeting, an alliance was established between Parnell, Davitt and Devoy. At this Dublin summit, Devoy notes that Parnell agreed 'that the Home Rule and land movements should not be detrimental to Fenianism and furthermore, that preparation for an armed uprising should go forward'.[21] Meanwhile the Land League, functioning as an open organisation, would continue its agitation, in order to address the national question. Furthermore, Devoy claims that a compact was agreed whereby:

1.   Parnell would lead a public movement that would not be disadvantageous to the aims of physical-force nationalism.

2.   The movement would press for nothing less than a national parliament with full legislative power over all national interests, with an Irish executive accountable to the body.

3.   It would be accepted that the land question could only be solved by peasant proprietorship, this to be achieved by compulsory land purchase.

4.   Irish MPs under Parnell's leadership would sit, act and vote together as an independent Irish party in the House of Commons, accepting no paid or honorary parliamentary work.

Devoy's testimony is weak, and we have only his word, and both Parnell and Davitt denied that any such agreement was made. For Parnell this was understandable, particularly in the future proceedings of the Special Commission into his relations with physical-force republicanism. It does not align with Parnell's character to make any such agreement; it is more than likely that, as usual, he gave Devoy the understanding that he supported his aims. As a result, Fenians were duped once more into believing that an understanding existed with an enterprising politician. Equally, Devoy's testimony ignores the reality of Parnell not committing himself to the land question until September 1879. This sheds serious doubt on Devoy's recollection.

This established, the Clan, believing it could do business with Parnell, forwarded a telegram for Parnell to Charles Kickham, President of the Supreme Council of the IRB. It had asked Kickham for his blessing and to forward it to Parnell. Kickham refused this request, remaining committed to the Fenian principle that nothing could be gained through constitutionalism and land agitation. Kickham's opposition, however, was not strong enough to kill the proposal to work with Parnell. The Clan went ahead and published its terms, informing Parnell that 'nationalists here will support you', [22] providing he set upon:

First: Abandonment of the federal demand, and substitution of a general declaration in favour of self-government.

Second: Vigorous agitation of the land question on the basis of peasant proprietorship, accompanied by concessions tending to abolish arbitrary eviction.

Third: Exclusion of all sectarian issues from the platform.

Fourth: Irish members to vote together on all Imperial and Home Rule questions, to adopt an aggressive policy and to energetically resist coercive legislation.

Fifth: Advocacy of all struggling nationalities in the British Empire and elsewhere.[23]

The timing of the telegram to Parnell was no coincidence. On the motion of John Barry, the Fenian-controlled Home Rule Confederation of Great Britain unanimously conferred on Parnell the presidency of the organisation.[24] Parnell was now destined to become leader of the Irish Party, waiting in the wings for conferral.

This so-called 'new departure' had mammoth implications. For the first time, the forces of militant Irish nationalism would inextricably be linked to constitutional politicians. In the minds of militants, this new strategy would be a combination of secret and overt work, taking 'the shape of a combination between the advocates of physical force and those who believe in constitutional agitation, such as will leave the former free to prepare for active work, while in the meantime, giving a reasonable support to a dignified and manly demand for self-government on the part of constitutionalists'.[25]

The weakness of Fenianism was exposed in its inability to do anything to remedy the immediate political grievance – the land. While it could contend that it was British rule that had caused landlordism, and its abolishment would abolish landlordism and its failings, improving the position of tenant farmers, it could not provide amelioration of the land question in its own right. Equally, while many supported the concept of Irish self-determination, on its own it was not an effective means of agitating the people. Thus, by establishing land agitation as a principal issue of an open policy, the national question could be coupled to the land, both broadening its appeal and its political base.

Conditions continually worsened, particularly in the west. It was at this stage, in 1879, that a remarkable man, Michael Davitt, the son of an evicted Mayo family, arrived back in Mayo. What Davitt saw horrified him. He personally inspected and noted the distress in the county, talking with 'priests, farmers and local Fenian leaders, and everywhere he encountered the same story: the harvests of 1877 and 1878 had failed badly, all the small farmers and cottiers were in debt to landlords and shopkeepers and it was feared there would be a famine before 1878 was out'.[26]

That a cadre of leadership existed on the tenant side made it no surprise that by October 1879, the Irish National Land League was established, to stop evictions, seek a significant reduction of rent, improve the place of the tenant farmer and establish as an ultimate goal peasant proprietorship. Home Rule MP AM Sullivan recalled:

On that day was founded the most powerful political organisation Ireland has known for half a century; probably for a much longer period of history. Mr Parnell was selected as President, Mr Patrick Egan, Treasurer, Mr Michael Davitt and Mr Thomas Brennan as honorary secretaries.[27]

This would set the scene for a major social revolution on the island of Ireland – the Land War. For three years, between 1879 and 1882, there would be social conflict between two opposing forces, that of power and privilege against that of poverty and marginalisation. The outcome would ultimately be a shift in the ownership of the land on the island of Ireland. In this social revolution, tenant farmers were organised as a mass movement under an effective leadership. The Land League provided a rallying point for tenant farmers and their supporters, with effective leadership provided both at local and national levels. Men who had borne the experience of landlordism provided able county leadership, in parallel with a national leadership that was vocal and articulate.

According to AM Sullivan, while Parnell and Davitt were well-known figures in the public eye, associated with the development of the League, Patrick Egan was next only to Davitt as a principal organiser, a man with an almost mechanical mind accompanied by indomitable energy and vigour. Egan acted as 'a joint strategist of the whole campaign, and perhaps, excluding Davitt, the most resolute and Invincible spirit'.[28] A former member of the IRB Supreme Council, he had resigned with John O'Connor Power, Joseph Biggar and John Barry over the traditionalist IRB policy of refusing to have any truck with the Home Rule constitutionalist movement. This resignation did not mark an abandonment of republican principles – Egan remained steadfast in his belief in the principle of a republican form of government, and was well connected to Dublin and American Fenianism. Such was Egan's belief in this principle that though he was nominated twice as a candidate to the British Parliament for Queen's County and for Meath, he refused on each occasion to run for election, as he would not sit in the British Parliament and give an oath of allegiance to the British Queen. Egan argued that to do so only gave legitimacy to British rule in Ireland. Despite this view, Egan was willing to send decent men to the British Parliament to vocally represent Irish interests and, in line with the new departure policy, to withdraw from Parliament to Dublin when the time was right.

The social revolution then taking place was underlined by an understanding on both sides that landlordism was a key pillar of British rule in Ireland. If landlordism collapsed, it would be a significant blow to British interests in Ireland. Thus, much of the Land League's philosophy on landlordism focussed on its nature as a foreign system imposed upon the people, facilitating the conquest of Ireland. While for much of the grassroots, the national question was far from people's minds as a practical issue, for advanced nationalists within the League there was strong potential to use it as a tool for recruitment to the cause of republicanism, and for stirring revolutionary fervour. This undoubtedly explains the presence of so many high-ranking Fenian officials within the League's ranks, and the unprecedented support it received from Irish America, particularly Clan na Gael, against the wishes of the Supreme Council of the IRB.

Given this support from advanced nationalists for the Land League, a continual accusation was levied against the organisation that it was simply a disguised form of Fenianism. Associating the Land League with secret conspiracy was calculated to win the opposition of the Catholic hierarchy, and to scare off moderate nationalists from associating with the organisation:

> The allegation so constantly made against the League that it was 'veiled Fenianism,' obviously had its origin in the fact that men known to possess the confidence of an influential section of the 'Nationalist' party were put in posts of confidence, and were amongst the most active in the real direction of affairs.

But in one respect, at all events, this course was the most obvious conceivable, and was exceedingly serviceable. The dominant idea of the whole scheme was to bring in to this open movement men, from each and all of the various schools of political action, constitutional or unconstitutional, hitherto working in isolated or antagonistic formations. 'The Land' was a strong card for any one of them to hold.[29]

In this conflict of wills, landlordism had the powerful backing of the British Government, and all of the resources at its disposal. Landlordism would also be supported by the vast majority of members of the British Parliament, securing it a kind of legitimacy in the eyes of political elites. Parliamentarian support for landlordism was no surprise – aside from the necessity of Irish landlordism as a firm means of consolidation of British hegemony in Ireland, the social make-up of Parliament, made support for the tenant farmer unlikely. Parliament was dominated by political elites, and was a body of privileged and wealthy gentlemen. To be a Member of Parliament, one required a personal income, as there were no Parliamentary salaries or expenses.

The British Government's Irish policy would be represented by the Irish Chief Secretary, William Forster, a Liberal Member of Parliament and a Quaker. Forster had been given the Irish portfolio by William Gladstone upon his return to office in 1880, and was ill-prepared for the task ahead of him, which, given the increasing difficulty in Ireland, was by no means a trivial one. In some respects, Forster's term as Irish Chief Secretary proved to be a monolithic challenge, the most difficult for any Chief Secretary in the late nineteenth century. While initially averse to coercion and prone to favour relief schemes and conciliation, the increasing disturbances in Ireland led the Chief Secretary to turn to draconian policies for Ireland's pacification, to such an extent that he recommended the arrest of Land League officials for inciting violence, and the abolition of habeas corpus.

On 2 November, as the social revolution intensified, Parnell and thirteen others were arrested and charged with seditious conspiracy. This represented an attempt by the Government to break the Land League. Alongside Parnell, Matthew Harris, John Dillon, TD Sullivan, Patrick Egan, JW Nally, Joseph Biggar, John W Walshe, Thomas Sexton, PJ Sheridan, PJ Gordon, Thomas Brennan, MP Boyton and Michael M O'Sullivan would be tried in January 1881, in what became known as the Traversers' Trial:

> *The indictment charges these persons with a conspiracy; first to impoverish and injure the owners of farms let to tenants for rent; secondly conspiracy to impede and frustrate the administration of justice and the execution of legal writs for the levying of moneys due for rent or for recovery of land on non-payment of rent; thirdly, conspiracy to prevent the taking of any farm from which a tenant has been evicted; fourthly and lastly, conspiracy to excite discontent and disaffection among the Queen's subjects, with ill will and hostility between different classes – that is to say landlords and tenants in Ireland.*[30]

Against the Government's best aspirations, the jury could not reach a verdict, and the case was thrown out of court. This was certainly an embarrassing result for the Government. Now, determined to break the conspiracy, it was decided that special powers were required to dismantle the Land League. This would come through coercion.

By December 1881, the British Cabinet had met in camera, discussing the Irish crisis. Forster's suggestions were taken on board, and it was decided to follow a dual-headed policy of simultaneous coercion and conciliation. They sought to defeat the Land League using all of the resources of the State, while appeasing its main clientele with favourable legislation, side-lining extremists while appealing to moderates. For the former, Forster would be heavily associated with coercion. He was given the duty of introducing and guiding the passage of a coercion bill through the British Parliament at its next session, in effect associating Forster with draconian policy body and soul. For the latter policy of conciliation, Gladstone would set to work on his first Land Act, seeking to build on what was previously given. Forster would privately advise the Prime Minister on this programme of land reform.

This powerful backing for landlordism and the Government's intention to introduce coercion was graphically illustrated on the first day of Parliament in January 1881. Through the medium of the Queen's speech, it was announced:

> *I grieve to state that the social condition of* [Ireland] *has assumed an alarming character ... I have deemed it right to put in use the ordinary powers of the law ... but a demonstration of their insufficiency, amply supplied by the present circumstance of the country, leads me now to appraise you that proposals will be immediately submitted to you for entrusting me with the additional powers necessary, in my judgement for the vindication of order and public law, but likewise to secure on behalf of my subjects protection for life and property.*[31]

It was highly unlikely that this policy of coercion could work in Ireland. The introduction of coercion would only inflame the social revolution, alienating moderates and serving to radicalise the people. It would consolidate the legitimacy of the objectives of the Land League, and the illegitimacy of British hegemony in Ireland. From America, veteran Fenian John Devoy would contend:

> *The people, goaded into frenzy by studied injustice, may rise against some constituted authority. A local eviction, a collision with soldiers may ensue, and our people be shot down in multitudes. It is here that the offices of the American land league will be called into requisition. Will we then stand idly by and see our people and country devastated ... shall we desert them in the hour of peril?*

No; for every Irishman murdered we will take in reprisal the life of a British
minister. For every hundred Irishmen murdered we will sacrifice the lives of
the entire British ministry. For a wholesale massacre of the Irish people we will
make England a smouldering ruin of ashes and blood.[32]

In Parliament, the Irish vote would be represented by the Irish Party, who found themselves the unlikely defenders of the Irish tenant farmer and civil liberties. Forster was becoming an odium of hatred and a byword for tyranny, something personally rejected by the Chief Secretary, who viewed the introduction of coercion as a painful but necessary evil. In the course of Parliamentary debates regarding the introduction of the coercion bill, Forster met unprecedented criticism and personal abuse from the Irish Party, which much affected his mental health.

By February 1882, the British Government, by means of Chief Secretary Forster, had introduced its Coercion Act to Parliament. Entitled The Protection of Person and Property (Ireland) Act, it was an extremely draconian piece of legislation, which when passed would give the British Viceroy the power to arrest and imprison without trial individuals suspected of complicity in the agrarian conflict.

From the Government benches, Forster announced that the powers granted under the Coercion Act would allow for the placing of 'village ruffians and outrage mongers' under lock and key.[33] This drew the wrath of the incensed Irish Party. They strenuously fought the coercion bill, through an unprecedented use of obstructive tactics, forcing the House of Commons to sit for forty-one consecutive hours:

The debate was prolonged all day and all night, and on through the dull, grey
hours of the morning of the 1st of February, and still on all night without
ceasing, till the enraged and exhausted House found itself at nine in the
morning of the 2nd of February still in session with no prospect of release.

Then the Speaker interfered saying that it was clear to him the bill had been wilfully obstructed for forty-one hours. In order to vindicate the honour of the House, whose rules seemed powerless to meet the difficulty, he declared his determination to put the main question without further debate. This was done amidst loud shouts of 'privilege' from the Irish members, who left the House in a body, and the motion for leave to bring in the bill, a motion rarely obstructed by any debate, was carried by a vote of 164 to 19. For the first time in the history of Parliament, a debate had been closed by the personal authority of the speaker.[34]

Such were the feelings of outrage that the Irish Party debated withdrawing from the House, to assemble in Dublin as a convention in contravention of the British Parliament. Parnell, despite his courting of the Fenians, was against such a move. He insisted on working through Westminster, on the basis that he could not guarantee that the majority of the Irish Party would follow him, which would thus split the party and weaken its potential. Parnell further understood – and this has been largely overlooked in the study of this period – that alongside coercion, the British Government had intended to apply a policy of conciliation through a resolution to the land question. If outside Parliament, Parnell reasoned that he could not challenge the British response, and so he chose the constitutional path.

Returning to the House of Commons, the Irish Party were outraged to learn of the arrest of Michael Davitt on 3 February 1881, the State having revoked his parole from prison. Taken briefly to Kilmainham Gaol, he was quickly shuffled off to Milbank, Portland and Dorset prisons respectively. On the same day as Davitt was arrested, sensing that the Government was moving against the Land League organisation, treasurer Patrick Egan left for France with League funds, taking them outside of British jurisdiction. Byrne would also continue Land League activities from the relative safety of France, before making for America. Of Parnell's lieutenants, John Dillon reacted ferociously to the news of Davitt's arrest, and had to be removed from the Chamber of the House of Commons. Soon after Dillon, thirty-four others, including Parnell, would be ejected from the Chamber, such was the uproar from the Irish Party:

> *Mr Parnell readily accompanied the Sergeant-at-Arms, bowed respectfully to the Speaker, and left the House, amid the indignant exclamations of his supporters. Posing or posturing is a passion with these impulsive Irish members. It is needless therefore to state how they gloried in posing as martyrs until the last of them was removed by 'superior force.*[35]

By 2 March 1881, the Coercion Act was passed. The British Parliament had now given the Dublin Castle administration the power to withdraw habeas corpus. Another bill was introduced by William Vernon Harcourt, Secretary of State for the Home Department, allowing Irish police to search Irish homes for suspected arms.

The Dublin Castle administration wasted little time before using its draconian powers of arrest and detention. Some 900 members of the Land League were arrested and interned in various prisons, as Ireland descended further into anarchy. The arrests of these leading Land League figures did nothing to quell the disquiet in the country – in fact, the Chief Secretary had arrested many men of moderation and restraint, leaving the movement in the hands of men with more violent instincts. Open agitation was replaced with secret societies and night-time violence, while the Irish bourgeoisie and constitutionalist leaders were jailed.

Running parallel to coercion, the Government had sought some degree of conciliation through a resolution to the land question. This was represented by Gladstone's Land Act (1882), which, while far from resolving the land question, recognised a principle of co-partnership, giving the tenant farmer the much sought after three 'F's: Fixity of tenure; Fair rent; and Free sale.

To undercut the influence of the Land League, a Land Court was to be established, allowing tenant farmers to air grievances against their landlords within the confines of the law. It was envisaged by Gladstone that this court would fix payable rent prices between landlord and tenant for a period of fifteen years, and allowed a land commission to grant a loan of seventy-five percent of the sum needed for a farmer to buy out their holdings. Tenants were also to be compensated if they improved their holdings.

The Land Act was a good bargain, the Government establishing for the first time a principle of dual ownership between landlord and tenant, signalling a shift in the long-established governmental support for the rights of landlords. However, it excluded tenant farmers in arrears, particularly those who could not possibly afford to pay their rent. While the Land Act would please moderate supporters, it would draw the outrage of those to the left of Parnell, including Davitt, John Dillon and Irish America.

Parnell was thus troubled: If he accepted the Land Act, he would have moderate opinion on his side; if he rejected it, he would lose the moderates and be left with intransigent men who he would happily imprison if he were a Home Rule Prime Minister. He chose the middle ground, denouncing parts of the Land Act that he found disagreeable, while prepared to save it in its entirety if it encountered problems in Parliament. Parallel to this, he positioned himself as the defender of tenants in arrears. His moderate wing was horrified, but for them he offered a positive formula: 'the testing of the land act'. This policy would be agreed upon by a National Convention of the Land League at the Rotunda in Dublin, underlined by a moderate Parnell and a gathering enraged by coercion:

> *In a huge assembly, apparently in a fever of revolutionary enthusiasm, where not a single speaker was heard to advocate anything but the rejection of the Act, neck and crop, and where Parnell, when he rose to speak at the end of the debate, was received with a frozen silence and seemed to have scarcely a partisan left in the*

national convention, none even of his parliamentary lieutenants presenting himself
to say a word in favour of testing the unpopular act, the great leader in a speech of
prosiest good sense, brought the whole turbulent assembly all but unanimously to his
own conclusion. The 'Kilmainham party,' who at one moment seemed to dominate
the convention, when the tellers were named for a division accepted in silent
submission the overwhelming show of hands that declared for Parnell's Policy.[36]

Parnell endorsed a strategy whereby a number of test cases would be established by the Land League, to see how the Government courts would reduce the tenant farmers' rents, and at what cost. This he hoped would stop an exodus of wealthier farmers to the Land Court, greatly weakening the potential of the Land League. Thus, while condemning the Land Act and somewhat endorsing its benefits, they would essentially place the onus for the success or failure of the Act on the Government. Parnell's calls for testing the Act were not universally accepted, however, and big farmers flocked to the courts, while the excluded small farmers were forced to increasingly agitate – the League was breaking up fast, and Parnell's grip was loosening.

Parnell's strategy was anxiously watched by Irish-America, who were beginning to baulk at what they perceived to be a softness and growing weakness in his attitude. Irish-America firmly believed that only one strategy could successfully solve the land question: the withholding of rents. Parnell knew that without the support of Irish-American extremist backers, the Land League could not function and his entire campaign would collapse. He shifted further towards militant attitudes in his handling of the land question, making increasingly inflammatory speeches and denunciations of the Gladstone administration, to appease his militant wing.

While Parnell campaigned to solidify his base, Gladstone was working to rally English support for his cause. Gladstone reacted with increasing denunciations of Parnell, speaking in biblical terms, asserting that Parnell like Moses stood between life and death. In an obvious reference to violence and land agitation, he accused Parnell, unlike Moses, of wanting 'to extend the plague'. He denounced him as an uncompromising opportunist with questionable militant backers, acting unfairly and callously toward those of private property:

> Now the land act has passed into law, and now that Mr Parnell is afraid lest the people of England, by their long continued efforts should win the hearts of the whole Irish nation, he has a new and enlarged gospel of plunder to proclaim. He says that whereas the rental of Ireland is seventeen millions pounds of money, the landlord is entitled to nothing, but the original value of the land before the spade was put into it; and that the rental he may justly claim is not seventeen millions, but possibly about three millions of money ... is it possible to describe proceedings of this kind as any words more just than the promulgation of the doctrine of sheer plunder? [37]

Parnell's response, addressing a rally in Wexford, was uncharacteristically militant. Giving his opinion of the Land Act, he noted how:

> You have gained something by your exertions in the last twelve months; but I am here today to tell you that you have gained but a fraction of that to which you are justly entitled. And the Irishman who thinks he can throw away his arms, just as Grattan disbanded the volunteers in 1783, will find to his sorrow and destruction when too late that he has placed himself in the power of a perfidious, cruel and unrelenting English enemy. [38]

In uncompromising language, Parnell denounced Gladstone's policy of coercion, and his blatant hypocrisy in claiming to be on a mission to pacify Ireland and yet introducing coercion. He attacked the British Prime Minister personally, asserting that Gladstone was exceedingly unscrupulous and dishonest in his dealings with Ireland:

You have had an opportunity of recently studying the utterances of a very great orator, the person who till recently desired to impress upon the world a great opinion of his philanthropy and hatred of oppression; but who stands the greatest coercionist, the greatest and most unrivalled slanderer of the Irish nation that ever undertook that task. I refer to William Ewart Gladstone ... a man who by his own utterance is prepared to carry fire and sword into your homesteads, unless you humble and abase yourselves before him, and then before the landlords of this country.[39]

For Parnell, Gladstone was 'a masquerading Knight errant', [40] whose policies had failed Ireland and only served to injure, maim and cajole the Irish people. Parnell asserted that Gladstone's failure proved that Ireland had a natural right to govern herself, by laws made on Irish soil. Drawing on a speech made by Gladstone, in which the Prime Minister had stated that his Land Act had finally solved the Irish question by means of sustained efforts by the British Government to resolve Irish grievances, Parnell asked:

Long sustained efforts in what? Was it in evicting 2,000 tenants since the 1st of January last? Was it the putting of two hundred honourable and brave men into Kilmainham and the other gaols of the country? Was it in the issuing of a Police circular of a more infamous character than any which has ever been devised by a foreign despot? Was it in sending in hundreds of rounds of ball cartridges to his Bashi-Bazouks throughout the Country? Was it in sharpening the bayonets of the latest issue to the Royal Irish Constabulary? And if it was not, if all these sustained efforts which Mr Gladstone has taken up nobly and well from his predecessor in the title of misgoverning Ireland, I should like to know what were the efforts of which William Ewart Gladstone talks, when he speaks of the sustained efforts, which he is making for the people of Ireland.[41]

Gladstone's patience had finally snapped, and he resolved to use the Coercion Act to imprison Parnell for inciting violence. Yet before Gladstone could do this, he needed to publicly reply to the Irish leader, and he chose the London Guildhall as his venue.

Gladstone had been invited to address the London Guildhall on Thursday, 13 October 1881. The Prime Minister delivered a standard political address, referencing the political questions of the day, including condemning the Land League and the activities of Parnellite MPs. As Gladstone was speaking of his desire to achieve a lasting settlement in Ireland, a young man was seen approaching the stage with a telegram and, in a choreographed moment, handed it to the Prime Minister mid-speech. The room drew silent as Mr Gladstone carefully read the letter. He then continued his address to the wealthy audience, informing them that Parnell had just been arrested in Dublin and taken to Kilmainham Gaol:

> *I have just been informed, that, towards the vindication of law, of order, and the right of property, of the freedom of the land, of the first elements of political life and the resources of civilisation, the first step has been taken in the arrest of the man, who unhappily from motives which I do not challenge, which I cannot examine, and with which I have nothing to do, has made himself beyond all others prominent in the attempt to destroy the law.*[42]

Arrested by Inspector John Mallon of the Dublin Metropolitan Police, on 13 October 1881, for having 'tended to interfere with the maintenance of law and order', for Parnell, his imprisonment could not have happened at a better time. According to RV Comerford, his Kilmainham sojourn had a profound effect on his political career. [43] An astute politician, he knew the Land League coalition was fragile, and that his policy of condemning and testing the Land Act could not hold out for long. Furthermore, 'to his already great popularity there was added an aura of martyrdom'.[44] Dublin newspaper *The Freeman's Journal* lamented:

The arrest of Parnell at Morrison's Hotel, as depicted in the *Illustrated London News*, 22 October 1881.

A great and powerful sensation thrilled the metropolis ... when the news spread with astonishing rapidity that Mr Charles Stewart Parnell, MP, had been arrested. It is not too much to say that every man received the intelligence with bated breath, and it is nothing but the truth to add that in the minds and hearts of many, who wish our country well, the amazement was mixed with alarm ... The citizens were on their way when Parnell was on his way to Kilmainham, and the latter went as contently to his Bastille as did the others to their respective avocations.[46]

Making his way down Nassau Street in the city centre, Parnell passed by Trinity College, and by the Parliament house-cum-Bank of Ireland:

> *In Foster Place there was a force of one hundred policemen in readiness in case of any emergency ... When the party reached the Bank of Ireland ... four or six Metropolitan Police jumped upon two outside cars and drove in front of the party. On reaching the quays at the foot of Parliament Street, a number of horse policemen joined the procession at the rear. In this order the four vehicles made their way to Kilmainham ... At half past nine o'clock Mr Parnell appeared in front of the dark portals of Kilmainham.*[47]

Writing to his lover Kitty O'Shea, Parnell revealed his innermost feelings. He had concluded that the Land League had now outlived its purpose. Gladstone's Act had been a significant blow to the movement, and the League was breaking up fast. Parnell realised that politically, his arrest was quite opportune, allowing the public to perceive him as a martyred defender of tenants' rights:

> *Politically it is a fortunate thing for me that I have been arrested, as the movement is breaking fast, and all will be quiet in a few months, when I shall be released.*[48]

Parnell was soon followed by his parliamentary lieutenant John Dillon, MP, who was arrested at the Imperial Hotel on Dublin's Sackville Street. Unlike the arrest of the parliamentary leader, however, Dillon's arrest was the scene of a horrendous attack by the Dublin Metropolitan Police against members of the public who had gathered around the hotel. Drawing up in a semicircle to protect the doorway of the hotel and facilitate the removal of the MP for Tipperary, the police were grossly outnumbered by the public, who, upon realising that Dillon was to be arrested, began shouting abuse at them. Surrounding the carriage taking Dillon to Kilmainham Gaol, the crowd abated somewhat, but continued to angrily shout curses at Gladstone and watching police.[49] The crowd had shrunk, but by eight o'clock that evening, existing police monitoring the street were reinforced as a detachment of equestrian policemen under a Colonel Connolly arrived on the scene from O'Connell Bridge, causing serious indignation amongst the crowd. The foot police formed in companies and patrolled the street, up and down. Within an hour, a nationalist band had arrived in support of the gaoled Dillon and other suspects incarcerated under the Coercion Act:

> And with drawn batons [the police] charged a portion of the crowd standing between the Imperial Hotel and Sackville Place. Without discriminating between the respectable and the disorderly, the people were attacked, the batons being used with much more effect on the heads and faces and bodies of all so unfortunate as to meet the charge. Many fell from the blows they received and others, among them a couple of women, were thrown down by the force of the onset. The people, without the least thought of resistance fled terrified down Sackville Lane and along the Street and then only did the attack cease. But not only had batons been employed by the defenders of the lives and property of the citizens, but they kicked and cuffed indiscriminately all they succeeded in overtaking … the sole offence committed lay in the disorderly cries and groans of a few men and boys.[50]

The Irish Times, which reported the scene, was by no means a friend of the nationalist cause, but expressed outrage at the brutality of the police in dispersing the crowd. The newspaper firmly accused the police of inciting the crowd, and was horrified at what it saw as provocative behaviour on their part. Having dispersed along Sackville Lane and further up the street, the crowd now returned, bigger and louder, buoyed for a fight. Constables charged the returning crowd with batons, or 'merely relying on the strength of arm'.[51] Such was the brutality employed by the Dublin Metropolitan Police, The Irish Times reported:

Their conduct was such as to appear almost incredible to all who did not happen to witness it. After every charge they made men – among them respectable citizens – were left lying on the street with blood pouring from the wounds they received on the head from the batons of the police, while others were covered with severe bruises from kicks and blows of clenched fists delivered with all the strength that powerful men could exert.[52]

Successfully clearing Sackville Street of all persons,[53] large numbers of police withdrew from the scene. The crowd made for Prince's Street, near the General Post Office, loudly denouncing the police and the State. A man making a speech at Nelson's Pillar was approached by a constable, fighting through the crowd. Realising he could not get to the speaker, the constable made a hasty retreat, followed by the crowd. At O'Connell Bridge, the crowd were met by police reinforcements of one hundred uniformed officers. *The Irish Times* reported:

The police drew their batons, and the scene that follows beggars description. Charging headlong into the people, the Constables struck right and left, and men and women fell under their blows. No quarter was given. The roadway was strewn with the bodies of the people. From the Ballast Office to the Bridge to Sackville Street, the charge was continued with fury. Women fled shrieking and their cries rendered even more painful the scene of barbarity which was being enacted. All was confusion and nought could be seen but the police mercilessly kicking and batoning the people. Some few of the people threw stones … but with this exception no resistance was offered … When the people were felled they were kicked on the ground, and when they again rose they were again struck down by any Constable who met them.

Having carried all before them the police marched quickly down the quays and some of the bystreets but in a few minutes afterwards reappeared near Nelson's Pillar, where a dense crowd was congregated listening to the utterances

of an orator who was standing on the top most step. Unheeding the fact that
many of those who formed the gathering were merely attracted by curiosity
and innocent of any thought or act of disorder, the Police charged them with
an impetus and violence that soon cleared the ground. One Constable, a tall,
stalwart fellow – rendered himself especially conspicuous – right and left he
felled any man he saw near him. The people simply dropped around him.[54]

One man was set upon by several officers, kicked as if he were a foot-ball,[55] and was later taken unconscious to the nearby Jervis Street Hospital. By twelve o'clock, Sackville Street was deserted, occupied only by heavy detachments of police patrolling both sides of the street.

The following evening, similar scenes would be repeated when Dublin Metropolitan Police gathered opposite the General Post Office, at the Imperial Hotel. This action was met with boos and hissing from the crowds of onlookers who had gathered, many curious to see what the police had arrived for. The DMP came under considerable vocal attack, with verbal expletives and general disgust directed toward them. There were cries of 'Buckshot', a derogatory nickname for Chief Secretary Forster. Clearing the street, the police were equally aggressive with bystanders,[56] and 'far from discriminating between respectable persons and those of the corner boy class, bestowed their rough treatment in a remarkable number of cases'.[57] Frank Hugh O'Donnell, a maverick Member of Parliament for Dungarvin, County Waterford, and a member of the Irish Party, witnessed the distur-bance. Trying to interject on behalf of a young boy being attacked by police, he was violently shaken by a police constable, knocking his glasses off.

At Sackville Street, the crowd of nationalists encircled a lone constable, harassing and beating him. One man outside of the group shouted abuse at the crowd, calling them cowards and iniquitous. The crowd now turned on him, forcing him to run to Abbey Street, where he fired a gun in the air to discourage them. Hurriedly making his way across O'Connell Bridge, he sought refuge in the *Irish Times* office. This now came under siege from a heavy nationalist crowd, shouting 'send him out', and throwing stones at the building. The crowd later dispersed and the police arrived,[59] as Dublin increasingly fell into a state of anarchy.

At the time of Parnell's arrest in early October, he forecast that with his imprisonment, Captain Moonlight, a reference to agrarian banditry, would take his place throughout the social revolution engulfing Ireland. From his cell in Kilmainham, Parnell, despite his awareness that the Land League was breaking up, gave its members mixed messages regarding the place of Captain Moonlight.

While officially the Irish leader was opposed to organised violence and rural banditry, he was willing to stoke the flames by issuing ambiguous statements. Thus, in a letter smuggled from Kilmainham and printed in *The Freeman's Journal*, he held, 'I shall take it as evidence that the people of the country did not do their duty if I am speedily released.'[60] While this could be read as a vague statement of his desire that the Irish people should call for his release, the voice of public opinion being damning to his imprisonment, at the height of a major social revolution it could also be seen as an incitement to violence.

Throughout the countryside, violence meanwhile intensified, with land agents being boycotted or attacked and even killed. This was met by the State with increasingly draconian measures, including the prohibition of meetings and the continued dispersal of large groups congregating in town centres. At Ballina on 24 October, it was noted that the town and district was swarming with police and military, assembling to prevent four separate Land League mass meetings from taking place. At Abbeyleix, a heavy police presence was maintained in order to prevent a proscribed meeting.

Within Kilmainham Gaol, Parnell and other leaders of the Land League now fulfilled Parnell's prophecy, issuing a joint manifesto instructing farmers to pay absolutely no rent. This No Rent Manifesto was reluctantly

Parnell, from the *Illustrated London News*.

signed up to by Parnell and Dillon, who believed that it could not work and would leave a significant body of peasantry unprotected from the law. Appearing in the Irish newspapers on 19 October 1881, the No Rent Manifesto instructed farmers thus:

Fellow citizens: The hour to try your souls and redeem your pledges has arrived. The executive of the Irish National Land League, forced to abandon its policy of testing the Land Act, feels bound to advise the tenant farmers of Ireland from this day forth to pay no rents under any circumstances to their landlords until government relinquishes the existing system of terrorism and restores the constitutional rights of the people. Do not be daunted by the removal of your leaders. Do not let yourselves be intimidated by threats of military violence. It is as lawful to refuse to pay rents as it is to receive them. Against the passive resistance of the entire population military power has no weapon. Funds will be poured out unstintedly for the support of all who may endure eviction in the course of the struggle. Our exiled brothers in America may be relied upon to contribute, if necessary as many millions as they have contributed thousands to starve out landlordism and bring English tyranny to its knees. You have only to show that you are not unworthy of their boundless sacrifices. One more crowning struggle for your land, your homes, your lives – a struggle in which you have all the memories of your race, all the hopes of your kindred and all the sacrifices of your imprisoned brothers.

One more struggle in which you have the hope of happy homes and national freedom to inspire you, one more heroic effort to destroy landlordism, and the system which was, and is, the curse of your race will have disappeared forever.

Stand together in face of the brutal cowardly enemies of your race! Pay no rent under any pretext! Stand passively, firmly, fearlessly by, while the armies of England may be engaged in their hopeless struggle against the spirit which their weapons cannot touch, and their government, with its bayonets will learn in a single winter how powerless are armed forces against the will of a united, determined and self-reliant nation.

Charles S. Parnell	*Thomas Brennan*
A.J. Kettle	*Thomas Sexton*
Michael Davitt	*Patrick Egan.*[61]
John Dillon	

Parnell, who had earlier calculated that the League was almost finished, had gambled that with this call to withhold rents, the Government would move to ban the League. If it did so, he could then blame its collapse and descent into violence on Gladstone. His gamble paid off – the Government proscribed the Land League.

As predicted by Parnell, the No Rent Manifesto was a failure. Ignored by a vast array of peasantry and moderate nationalist opinion, it also faced severe condemnation from the politically significant Catholic Church, who were united in opposition with the Anglican Church. Both churches sided with large, wealthy landowners and insisted on the morality of paying what tenants owed to their landlords. Larger farmers continued to ignore the call and avail of the Land Court, leaving the smaller and poorer tenant farmer isolated, the division between the two classes of farmer greatly weakening the potential of the Land League. In reality, the No Rent Manifesto could not possibly have worked without a leadership structure sustaining a prolonged no rent campaign, and with the Land League leadership scattered or gaoled, this was non-existent.

Membership of the Land League was now illegal. However, the social revolution was to be continued by a Ladies' Land League, led by Parnell's remarkable sisters, Anna and Fanny Parnell. Founded in America in 1880 by Fanny Parnell, the Ladies' Land League was constituted to provide material aid for those suffering in Ireland as a result of the bad harvest and the social revolution. It would be organised in Ireland by Anna Parnell, who Davitt described as a 'lady of remarkable ability and energy of character'.[62] Of greater militancy than the Land League, the Ladies' Land League would actively fight for tenants' interests and, as Davitt asserted:

> *The plans which the Ladies' Land League were to put into operation were these: Offices would be provided for their executive at the headquarters of the Land League proper, which had been removed in December from Middle Abbey Street to 39 Upper O'Connell Street, Dublin. Miss Parnell and her Lieutenants would be supplied with duplicate addresses of League branches everywhere at home and abroad, and would be put in communication with the local leaders of the organisation in every county and district in Ireland. The duty of supporting evicted tenants would fall to their work, and of encouraging resistance to land grabbing. Wooden huts were to be provided, and if possible as near as possible as near the evicted holding as ground for their erection would be found available; this for shelter, but also to enable the evicted family to keep a vigilant watch over their interests in the vacant farm. Another very important task was the support of families while members of the same would be in prison. This obligation was undertaken as the general policy of the League. Men, young or old, who might be singled out by Mr Forster for punishment were assured in advance that their families would be provided for during their incarceration and that no material loss shall be incurred by them in fighting coercion.[63]*

2

THE GENESIS OF THE INVINCIBLES

In the autumn of 1881, a three-man directory of leading Irish Fenians was set up in London. These included Frank Byrne, Secretary of the Land League of Great Britain, well known to the Irish Party and having an office at Westminster. Through the London directory, Middlesborough Fenian John Walsh was sent to Dublin to make contact with leading Dublin Fenians, in order to establish an assassination society within the Fenian ranks. Born in Tipperary in 1826, Walsh was a veteran of the Fenian movement. He was involved in attempts to infiltrate the British Army, establishing Fenian circles within Crown forces, for a predicted Fenian rising. Walsh had seen active service for the IRB when he was dispatched to Australia to rescue Fenians imprisoned at Freemantle, and had been involved with the famed Catalpa rescue of 1876, when John Devoy and Clan na Gael masterminded the rescue of six Fenian convicts. Walsh was so trusted within the IRB for his past service that he was the Northern England representative to the IRB Supreme Council.

Supplied with a letter of introduction from Byrne, Walsh was instructed to make contact with leading Fenians in Dublin. He made his way to Peter Street in Dublin, and met an acquaintance, Edward McCaffrey, a working-class van driver. McCaffrey was another veteran of the Fenian cause, and active in the service of Dublin Fenianism, enjoying extensive connections to leading Dublin-based Fenian chiefs. Through McCaffrey, Walsh communicated with a well-known nationalist and leading Fenian, the builder James Carey.

James Carey had come from humble beginnings, and was now a respectable landlord, letting twelve houses in Dublin. He was well known in working-class politics as a champion of the underprivileged classes. A committed Catholic who attended masses and sodalities, he was also an energetic political man, and decidedly republican. He had successfully illustrated that the national and social causes were two sides of the same coin, having campaigned for improvements to workers' rights in Dublin and actively worked within the Home Manufacture Association. He had famously led a campaign against a Scottish contractor in Dublin who had been employed to build sewers in the capital city. Holding that the contract should have been given to an Irishman, and on the back of bad workmanship, he was successfully elected to the Dublin Trades Council on a platform of workers' rights.

Carey's involvement with Fenianism can be traced to 1861, when he enrolled in the Irish Republican Brotherhood, holding membership of the IRB's Dublin directory from 1869 to 1878. The Brotherhood employed him as a treasurer, and he was involved in a Fenian vigilance committee, tasked with exposing and removing Crown intelligence assets from the IRB.[64] Given Walsh's credentials and Carey's outspoken nationalism, the Dublin Fenian welcomed Walsh to his home at Denzille Street, sometime in November 1881.

According to Carey's later testimony, Walsh told him of his instructions to establish a society in Dublin, the purpose of which was 'to make history'.[65]

Trades Councillor and prosperous Dublin businessman James Carey.

This society, an assassination squad tasked 'to remove all tyrants from the country', would be built within the Fenian organisational network. Walsh asked Carey to assist in the building of this new strategy. Carey agreed and, at his home in Denzille Street, John Walsh swore James Carey into the Invincibles conspiracy:

I _____ of my own volition
do solemnly swear hereon and hereby that I will do my utmost to establish the
national independence of Ireland, and bear true allegiance to the organisation
of the Irish Invincibles and implicitly obey my superior officers. That I
will never unnecessarily divulge either in part or whole the secrets of this
organisation to any living being under the canopy of Heaven. That without
any hesitation or mental reservation whatsoever, I shall truly answer all
questions put me by a properly constituted authority and give whatever
other knowledge I possess in the interest of the movement. That I will never
injure by word or act a brother Invincible. … I will do my utmost to establish
fraternity and brotherly love amongst Irishmen everywhere … I do now
swear eternal allegiance. So help me God.[66]

Walsh next visited the hard-line Fenian James Mullet, who was well known to Patrick Egan, Treasurer of the Land League. Mullet owned a public house, much frequented by Dublin Fenians, in Lower Bridge Street.

Staunchly opposed to Fenian involvement in the Land League, Mullet saw it as an unnecessary diversion from the real aim of Fenianism – preparation for the conditions for Irish rebellion. Walsh seems to have persuaded Mullet to take an active part in the assassination squad, with the publican agreeing to support Walsh's organisation.

From Mullet, Walsh next visited Daniel Curley, at Love Lane near Dublin's Mount Street. Curley was of working-class origins, like much of the Dublin Fenian grassroots, and was a carpenter by trade. Like Mullet, he was well-respected within Fenian circles and a known advocate of republican politics. These two, along with Carey and McCaffrey, were to form the Dublin directory of the Irish National Invincibles, and would be sworn into the Invincibles conspiracy at Carey's home in Denzille Street.

This committee of four was to direct operations within Dublin, and plan potential targets for political assassination, drawn from the upper echelons of the British administration in Ireland. According to Patrick Tynan, their aim was to make life unbearable for the British administration in Ireland, regularly assassinating British officials. A high priority would be placed by the directory on the Viceroy, as the British Queen's Irish representative; the Chief Secretary, as the Government's most prominent Irish minister; judges, as key pillars of the political establishment; and police, as active collaborators in the administration of British rule in Ireland:

> There was no alternative but to meet the assassin rule of Britain by force. The enemy had trampled on his own constitution, and torn into shreds the last strip of mock legality under which Ireland was supposed to be governed. A species of guerrilla warfare was determined on to meet the relentless attacks of the invader. Britain's position in Ireland, they held, was that of the burglar who had broken into the nation's home, to rob and waylay the residents. Assassination and misery followed in his train. The chiefs of Ireland's ravagers, the men from whose bureaux sped the orders of bloodshed and destruction so

Leading Fenian James Mullet.

ruthlessly carried out by their armed hirelings, were termed by the enemy, 'the Chief Secretary' and 'Undersecretary of state.' It was resolved by the earliest council held by the executive of the INVINCIBLES, that these ferocious offices should be kept vacant by the continued 'suppression' of their holders. This order was not levelled at any particular or special occupant of these bloodstained posts of the foe, but against all and every succeeding foreign invader who came to occupy these 'suppressed' bureaux; and it was decided that as soon as a new comer planted his foot on Irish soil, invested by the illegal and alien administration with the authority of either of these offices to perpetuate Britain's rule of spoliation, he should be at once 'suppressed' in mercy of the Irish nation; and further that every satrap of Britain, carrying on and conducting her war of extermination in any part of the Island, should be summarily 'removed' from the scene of devastation. For 'Britain in Ireland is a beast exceeding terrible; his feet and claws are of iron, and the rest he stamps upon with his feet'.[67]

Drawing from the ranks of Dublin Fenianism, a working-class membership would be favoured. This recognised that in the struggle for Irish Independence, the labouring classes were the most dedicated and faithful adherents to the cause of the Irish republic, having a clear adherence to the cause of republicanism and a defined, militant class identity, 'more or less sincerely devoted to the national cause'.[68] Any blow to the British administration in Ireland was to be seen as a success and a means to an end.

With the establishment of the Dublin directory, Walsh unveiled a list of British administrators earmarked for assassination, including the Earl Cowper and William Forster. While an attack on Cowper, as the British Queen's Irish representative, was seen as potentially highly symbolic, it was decided that Forster – as Chief Secretary the most senior Government minister in Ireland, and responsible for coercion – would be the first target of the plot. When Forster and Cowper were assassinated, Walsh instructed the Dublin directory that other targets were to be left to their own discretion.[69] To this list it was agreed to add the permanent Undersecretary at Dublin Castle, responsible for the administration of coercion and British rule in Ireland, the Irishman Thomas Henry Burke:

> [Burke] *was generally recognised as being a capable and painstaking official, but one who was up to his neck in the tradition of Castle misgovernment and during the Forster regime had advocated and taken a leading part in enforcing the arbitrary proceedings then in daily operation.*[70]

Undertaking surveillance of Cowper, Forster and Burke in preparation for their assassination, Curley, Carey, Mullet and McCaffrey regularly visited Phoenix Park to observe their targets. In the park they watched the Chief Secretary's Lodge,[71] in order to familiarise themselves with Forster's identity and daily habits. From this surveillance, Burke was seen and examined, although there was a debate as to who he was, the Invincibles seemingly confused by the presence of Burke's brother alongside Forster. As part of the scheme to assassinate Cowper, a house was rented by Carey at Cork Hill, outside Dublin Castle, the directory planning to shoot him as he left or entered the Castle.

To undertake a series of political assassinations, the directory needed a series of recruits. Under instruction from London, the Dublin Invincibles were to number no more than fifty. As a secret society within the Fenian movement, it was to be underpinned by an oath of secrecy. The society was well funded, Walsh having donated £50 in gold and promising £10,000 from Land League funds if necessary.

The Dublin directory had little trouble recruiting members from the Fenian ranks. Daniel Curley in particular was a heavy recruiter, bringing in some twenty recruits. These included the young secretary of his Fenian circle, Joe Brady, who brought with him one of his closest friends, teenage apprentice coach builder Timothy Kelly. According to Carey, Mullet recruited several men into the conspiracy, while Carey brought his brother Peter,[72] dockworker Thomas Caffrey and several workmen, including Larry Rinkle, all of whom had been members of the Irish Republican Brotherhood. As the Invincibles continued to grow, Laurence and Joseph Hanlon; well-known Dublin cab driver James Fitzharris, known colloquially as 'Skin the Goat'; Myles Kavanagh, another cab driver; and Patrick and Daniel Delaney would be enrolled as members, although the last was well-known for criminal activity and perpetual drunkenness, evidence existing that he was in Fenianism for personal rather than national benefit.

In London, Frank Byrne was working to establish the Invincibles within the Fenian network. This was illustrated by the arrival of Patrick James Sheridan of Tubbercurry, County Sligo, a key Land League organiser and Fenian, disguised as 'Father Murphy', a Catholic priest. PJ Sheridan was well-known to Crown authorities and the Irish Party, and was tried alongside Parnell as one of the Traversers in 1881. He met with the Dublin directory at the Angel Hotel in Dublin, and they apprised him of their surveillance of Forster and Burke in Phoenix Park. Sheridan's mission was to look into the possibility of recruiting Fenians to the Invincibles conspiracy in the countryside. He was clearly in communication with London.

Meeting Sheridan at a later date at the Midlands Hotel, Carey would stress the importance of the procurement of arms.

Another veteran Fenian received by the Dublin directory was the Irish-American Captain John McCafferty. McCafferty had seen active service in the American Civil War, fighting for the Confederacy. Having been released from military service, McCafferty found himself within an Irish-America clamouring for violent retribution against British rule in Ireland. This was manifested in the establishment of the Fenian Brotherhood in 1858, on whose behalf McCafferty had tried to organise a militia in County Tipperary. Arrested at Youghal, County Cork, McCafferty was tried and acquitted at Cork. McCafferty had then returned to America, but came back to Britain on Fenian business, attending a Fenian council at Liverpool. His activities ultimately culminated in the attempted Fenian raid on Chester Castle in 1867. Returning to Ireland, McCafferty was arrested and interned in Kilmainham Gaol. Subsequently sentenced to penal servitude for life, he had received an amnesty in 1871 on the understanding that he would remain outside of Ireland.

McCafferty would act as a go-between, shuffling money and orders from Byrne, his role in the conspiracy underlined by regular trips to Britain, Ireland and France. McCafferty met with Carey on several occasions, supplying him with money and advising on how the Dublin directory was to act in terms of the stategy and recruitment.[73]

To assassinate leading figures of the political elite, the Invincibles required weaponry. Carey had stressed this to Sheridan at the Angel Hotel, and had suggested the employment of knives or daggers. This was further impressed upon McCafferty, who also favoured their use, recommending the tying of cord around their handles for a greater grip. Surgical knives, with blades of some eleven inches in length, were purchased from Weiss's, a well-known instrument maker of London's Bond Street, by a Dr Hamilton Williams on behalf of Frank Byrne. From

Hamilton Williams, the knives were passed on to Maurice Collins, a cobbler and activist of the IRB, at Bethnal Green.

Eventually finding their way to the Palace of Westminster, the knives were stored in the Land League office, in Frank Byrne's room. Byrne would give the knives to his heavily pregnant wife, who would smuggle them into Ireland concealed in her skirt. Byrne calculated that the authorities would not search a heavily pregnant woman. By early 1882, she contacted several leading Invincibles, and supplied them with weaponry:

> She brought with her a rifle, two revolvers and six knives. I am not sure if it was a Winchester rifle. She had a rifle with a string around her neck. She had a cloak on ... She brought 4,000 rounds of ammunition for the revolvers and rifle in a parcel ... In the course of a week or ten days she came again ... she brought a similar consignment, except that there was only four knives ... The knives were all the same except being different in colour in the handles ... The rifles were to be used from Cork Hill, or any other place where it would be long range.[74]

Carey had the task of doling out the weaponry. He gave heavy supplies of ammunition to James Mullet, most of which would be hidden in various safe houses in Dublin.

Frank Byrne next dispatched Patrick Joseph Tynan to Dublin, to coordinate messages between the London directory and the Dublin Invincibles. Tynan was a neighbour of Byrne's in London, living at Peckham Rye. An Irishman, he had owned a bookshop at Dún Laoghaire (Kingstown), often acting as a commercial traveller, facilitating continual trips to Ireland on apparently legitimate business. Furthermore, Tynan was a member of the 13th Middlesex Volunteer regiment, known as the Queen's Own Westminster Volunteers. Such a position within British society made him an unlikely Fenian, but Tynan seems to have shared Fenian sympathies.

When Tynan arrived, James Mullet, the Chairman of the Dublin Invincibles, had been arrested by the Dublin Metropolitan Police. He was a suspect in the assassination of an IRB informer named Bernard Bailey at Skippers Alley, Dublin, in February 1882. Bailey had informed on two brothers named Whelan, leading to the discovery of a Fenian arms depot, a sizable quantity of ammunition and explosives, in Brabazon Street, Dublin. Bailey had been shot in the head around Cook Street in Dublin, on the orders of a Fenian vigilance committee, and died at Jervis Street Hospital that evening.

Mullet had been exceptionally unlucky, and had been arrested by chance. In the police investigation of the Whelan brothers, papers were discovered implicating Mullet in the conspiracy at the Brabazon Street arms depot. Mullet was arrested and taken to Kilmainham Gaol, as a reward of £400 was issued for information leading to the arrest of the assassins. The arrest of Mullet created a vacancy in the Dublin directory, and Edward Caffrey was elected Chairman, soon to be replaced by Daniel Curley. The young secretary of Curley's Fenian circle, Joe Brady, was now co-opted onto the directory in place of Mullet.[75]

The Invincibles now actively sought retribution by assassinating Forster. In this they would be aided by Joseph Smith, who worked for the Office of Public Works in Dublin Castle. Smith knew Forster's movements, and would keep the group aware of when the Chief Secretary was scheduled to leave the Castle, either to go to his home in Phoenix Park, or to Westland Row train station en route to England.

Smith had made the acquaintance of Skin the Goat, who regularly drove to the Castle for Inspector Mallon, and drank at Wrenn's public house in Dame Street, opposite the Castle Street gate. Fitzharris sought to use Smith for reconnaissance, noting Forster's daily movements and familiarising himself with his appearance in preparation for an attack. Despite later protestations that Smith knew little of the aims of the Invincibles, Skin had informed him that Forster was to be assassinated for his actions as Chief Secretary, so it seems that Smith was not so unaware of who he was associating with. Familiarising himself with Forster and Burke, he would brief Skin at Wrenn's, recalling:

> He asked me was Mr Forster at home. He said he wanted to see him. He asked me was Mr Forster in the Castle. I said I don't know whether he was in or out, I said I did not know the man to my knowledge. Fitzharris said he was to meet a couple of friends there and that he would see me again. He didn't tell me what he wanted to see Mr Forster for. Fitzharris asked me was Mr Forster in the Castle, and to find out whether Mr Forster was at home or not. He asked me to find out what time Mr Forster came in in the morning and left in the evening. I told him he came and left at different hours.[76]

In Skin's company, Smith had met and become familiar with James Carey. Carey asked him of Burke's appearance and daily habits, cryptically commenting that he and his friends wanted to know him well. Carey would swear Smith into the conspiracy, and the Castle worker would have no contact with any other member except James Carey, although he did recollect meeting Curley and Brady, their names unknown to him:

> After I had been sworn in by Carey ... I saw Brady and Curley in Wrenn's. Curley and Brady and Carey were generally always together. I had no conversation with either Curley or Brady. Any conversation I had was with Carey himself. I had a conversation with Curley on one occasion in Wrenn's. Himself, and Brady and Carey were there. He kept looking at me, and when he got Carey away, he took out a knife and said 'do you see anything wrong with that?' I understood this as the sign. I said I did not see anything wrong with it.

Joseph Smith, of the Office of Public Works at Dublin Castle, who was to identify Forster to the assassins.

The Invincibles planned to ambush Forster as he travelled between Dublin Castle in the city centre and Phoenix Park. They had previously tried several times to assassinate the Chief Secretary, but on each occasion were dogged by bad luck. Using hand signals and reconnaissance, the Invincibles had planned to stop Forster's carriage as it passed through the Dublin streets, shooting the Chief Secretary in his compartment. On one occasion, the Invincibles had lain in wait near present-day Heuston Station, but the signalman, Henry Rowles, had failed to give notice that Forster was passing by in his carriage, and the Chief Secretary unknowingly escaped death. Later that evening, the Invincibles waited at John Street, further down the road, but the Chief Secretary never came.

With these previous failures in mind, the Dublin directory arranged for James Fitzharris to have a cab waiting for Forster at Parliament Street, opposite Dublin Castle, for when he would emerge from the Castle gates. Desperately trying to find Forster, the Invincibles continuously moved between Westland Row, Brunswick (now Pearse) Street and Phoenix Park. For four successive nights, they waited for him at St Mark's Church on Great Brunswick Street. On each occasion, they were foiled. According to Carey, he actually met Forster on Dame Street, accompanied by another man. The Invincibles had expected Forster at St Mark's Church that same evening, and were waiting for him there. Bizarrely, Carey followed Forster to a post office in College Green, but then left him, making his way to St Mark's. The Chief Secretary never showed up. On another occasion, the Invincibles had actually located Forster, and would have killed him but for the presence of his wife and daughter.

Their final attempt on Forster was marred by further misfortune. On 19 April 1882, it was learned that Forster was returning to England. The Chief Secretary's regular pattern was to travel to Westland Row train station, where he would board the boat train for Kingstown (Dún Laoghaire). This was well known to the Invincibles from their active reconnaissance and through information from Smith. By chance, Forster had been persuaded to take lunch at the Royal Yacht Club in Kingstown, necessitating that he take the earlier train out of Dublin from Westland Row. When the Invincibles arrived at the train station, the Chief Secretary had already left. An anxious Joe Brady, alongside other Invincibles, checked the train for his presence, but all to no avail.

Forster would never return to Ireland. He resigned his commission in protest at secret negotiations between the Irish Party and the British Government, which ultimately resulted in what has wrongly been termed the Kilmainham Treaty.

One of Gladstone's ministers, Birmingham MP Joseph Chamberlain, had entered into negotiations with Captain William O'Shea of the Irish Parliamentary Party, the husband of Parnell's lover, in order to work for a settlement. For his part, Parnell was anxious to leave Kilmainham. While he was happy to be portrayed as a martyr, overall he was a politician and he feared the people would forget him if he spent too long in confinement. Furthermore, Katherine had just given birth to his child, a girl called Claude Sophie, in March 1882. The child died soon after, and the devastated Parnell wanted to be with Katherine. It troubled his mind, he wrote to her from his cell on 25 April 1882, that she was alone in her time of grief: 'It is too terrible to

Ellis's Quay at John Street, the scene of Forster's planned assassination.

think that on this the saddest day of all others – and let us hope, the saddest that we both shall ever see again – my wifie should have nobody with her.'

As neither side in the discussions between Parnell and Gladstone wanted to be seen talking to the other, intermediaries of O'Shea and Chamberlain held secret discussions in order to work out a compromise. Chamberlain, however, had been instructed by the Cabinet that under no circumstances was he to negotiate with O'Shea – all communications were on his own person and were officially not Government policy. O'Shea had greatly inflated his position in the Irish Party, holding that the crux of the argument between the Land League, Parnell and the Government was the question of tenants in arrears and leaseholders in the Gladstonian Land Act. Parnell informed O'Shea, from his cell in Kilmainham:

I should strongly hope that some compromise might be arrived at this season with regard to the amendment of the tenure clauses. It is unnecessary for me to dwell upon the enormous advantages to be derived from the full extension of the purchase clauses, which now seem practically to have been adopted by all parties.

The accomplishment of the programme I have sketched would in my judgement,

be regarded by the country as a practical settlement of the land question, and

would I feel sure, enable us to co-operate cordially for the future with the Liberal

Party in forwarding Liberal principles; so that the Government, at the end

of the session, would, from the state of the country, feel themselves thoroughly

justified in dispensing with further coercive measures.[77]

Writing indirectly to the Prime Minister, he held, as FSL Lyons noted, that 'if he amended the land act to include tenants in arrears, if he set up a commission to look into the wretched condition of the agricultural labourers, then outrage would decline, the act would work its expected magic.' On 22 April, Chamberlain and O'Shea met at the Birmingham MP's London residence and, as recorded by Chamberlain, O'Shea informed him:

If the Government announce a satisfactory plan of dealing with arrears,
Mr Parnell will advise all tenants to pay rents and will denounce outrages,
resistance to the law and all processes of intimidation whether boycotting or in
any other way.

It seemed that the land question could easily be solved, and Ireland easily pacified. Given that Parnell's lover was O'Shea's wife, it was obvious that the two men didn't trust each other. Parnell had also authorised Justin McCarthy to act as his agent with Chamberlain, and for Lyons this was proof that Parnell was intent on allowing future negotiations 'to go on independently of whether O'Shea participated in them'. Knowing that O'Shea was not Parnell's only intermediary, Chamberlain also held discussions with McCarthy and with Tim Healy, and kept Gladstone informed of what he was learning. On the floor of the House of Commons, Gladstone pledged to deal swiftly with the arrears question. Agreement was in the air, and Parnell wrote to his mistress:

I think it is likely that something will be done by the Government shortly on the arrears question. If this be so, things will undoubtedly quieten down a great deal, and it will give us an opportunity of coming to some arrangements.

The arrangement was what falsely became known as the Kilmainham Treaty between Parnell and Gladstone. No treaty exists; no document was ever signed, but the terms were quite clear. Parnell would declare his opposition to the ongoing violence in the country, calling upon his supporters not to engage in it. Boycotting and agrarian violence would begin to decline and fizzle out. In return, Parnell would be released, and Gladstone would settle the arrears question, extending the Land Court to tenants in arrears and lease holders, while also helping tenants in arrears to pay off their rents. Coercion as a policy was also to be shelved. Parnell would be released on 2 May 1882, with John Dillon and James J O'Kelly. Officially, he denied any understanding between the British Government and himself. He would furthermore state that no secret meetings had taken place. Upon release from Kilmainham Gaol, Parnell was interviewed by the American journalist Henry George:

Parnell: *No only yesterday we were discussing the probability of staying in Kilmainham for another six months. We came to the conclusion that we might be as useful there as outside. Forster's resignation was a complete surprise. I was perfectly thunderstruck when I heard it. I can't imagine how it was brought about.*

George: *There is no truth, then, in the reports about negotiations between you and the Government?*

Parnell:	*Not the slightest. I had no communication whatever with the Government and no understanding with them.*
George:	*Had you any conference with any member or agent of the Government while on parole, as has been intimated?*
Parnell:	*None whatever.*
George:	*Have any of the Land League Party had any understanding with the Government?*
Parnell:	*None to my knowledge, I am satisfied there has been none.*[78]

While Parnell denied the existence of discussions between the Irish Party and the British Government, the Kilmainham understanding was a bitter blow to the hopes of many in the Land League, particularly among its left wing. Many within the League, including Parnell's incredible sisters Anna and Fanny, Michael Davitt, John Dillon and Patrick Egan, believed that more could have been gotten from the Government. They saw the so-called Kilmainham Treaty as a compromise that fell short of the Land League's most basic principles, just when victory was in sight. Parnell evidently now considered the objectives of the social revolution complete, and looked forward to an era of Irish–Liberal cooperation. He informed a disillusioned Michael Davitt, upon his release from Portland Prison:

> *We are on the eve of something like Home Rule. Mr Gladstone has thrown over coercion and Mr Forster and the Government will legislate further on the land question. The Tory party are going to advocate land purchase, almost on the lines of the Land League programme, and I see no reason why we should not soon obtain all we are looking for in the league movement. The No Rent Manifesto had failed and was withdrawn. A frightful condition of things prevailed in Ireland during the last six months culminating in several brutal murders, moonlighting outrages and alarming violence generally.*[79]

While the so-called Kilmainham Treaty was disillusioning to a good many land activists and republicans, it was equally disheartening to elements within the British Government, who viewed the understanding as surrender to the demands of Parnell. This view was certainly held by William Forster, who could not accept the understanding between his Government and the Irish Party and a new age of Parnellite–Liberal co-operation. In Forster's opinion, the Government, through its Kilmainham understanding with the Irish Party, had conferred a legitimacy upon the land activists and Parnellites. Government action was effectively recognising them as the representatives of the Irish People, which Forster incorrectly concluded they were not. Furthermore, such a policy of conciliation, the Chief Secretary argued, could not pacify Ireland. The course that he had followed needed to be continued, and the release of the suspects needed to be followed by a further round of coercion. Unable to get behind Government policy, Forster now set his mind to resignation, leaving Ireland forever in May 1882.

The departure of Forster from Ireland did not discourage the Invincibles from their objective of political assassination, however. Disheartened but not disillusioned at Forster's escape, they next turned their attention to Thomas Henry Burke, the Castle Undersecretary. The most senior civil servant in the Dublin Castle administration, Burke was responsible for the maintenance and functioning of the British administration in Ireland, 'the embodiment of English dominance and oppression. He had, they believed, been Mr Forster's evil advisor, and he had imprisoned men and women of his own race and creed.'[80]

On 5 May, within three days of Parnell's release from Kilmainham Gaol, Ballina in County Mayo was the scene of a tremendous tragedy. Turning out to celebrate the release of prisoners arrested under coercion, a boys' brass band was fired upon by police. The band, accompanied by a large crowd, had played songs and entertained local people as it marched through the town, some participants holding burning tar barrels, as was a local tradition. Reaching Bridge Street, however, it was disrupted by the RIC, who attempted to seize the drums and whistles of the boys. When the police refused to return the instruments to the boys' band, a number of people in the crowd threw stones at them. The police responded by charging the crowd and opening fire, wounding eight members of the brass band, all below the age of sixteen, and killing two boys.

3

THE PHOENIX PARK ASSASSINATIONS

O n 6 May 1882, the new Irish Viceroy, John Poyntz Spencer, arrived in Dublin, accompanied by his Chief Secretary, Frederick Cavendish:

> *The country and the capital were bathed in the glories of the early summer sun, when shortly after seven o'clock in the morning, Earl Spencer arrived at Kingstown by the mail steamer accompanied by his brother the Hon. Robert Spencer MP, Lord Frederick Cavendish, and Mr Courtney Boyle, his private secretary. The city was en fete. Those decorations in the form of flags, bunting and triumphal arches ... were to be seen everywhere.*[81]

The streets along the route of the Viceregal procession were lined with troops and intermittent bands, regularly playing the national anthem as the cortege passed. To the Invincibles, such a scene was maddening, particularly following the Ballina shootings. Spencer had served before in

Ireland as Viceroy, under a previous Liberal administration, and now it appeared he had returned as a triumphal prince:

> *Britain's red-coated defenders were burnishing up their arms and accoutrements. Bit and Snaffle were brightened in the cavalry barracks by the foreign soldiery occupying the city. Those quartered in Ireland's capital were to make a brilliant display that day to honour the incoming vice-King, and to overawe the natives of the invaded island by the martial valour of their appearance, the bravery and dash of their clanking accoutrements and clamping steeds ... The guard ships were all ready to fire the Viceregal salute, that boom of British artillery which heralds to as yet unconquered Ireland the news that another master has come to try to rule her ... The Queen of Great Britain and Ireland, and Empress of India had graciously consented to send Earl Spencer as her Majesty's Lord Deputy to reign over and represent his most puissant sovereign in that portion of her Majesties realm called Ireland; to lighten up the darkness of the lives of its people by the brilliancy of his presence ...*[82]

Frederick Cavendish, at forty-four, was somewhat of a novice, who had 'not hitherto displayed any great political talent ... Cavendish was no orator, a poor speaker prevented by a speech impediment.'[83] The new Chief Secretary was well connected, however, being married to Gladstone's niece. While he was little known in Ireland, 'his father the Duke of Devonshire, and his brother Lord Hartington, were disliked in Ireland, the one for making clearances, the other for enforcing coercion'.[84]

Arriving in Dublin Castle, the seat of the British Government in Ireland, there would be a ceremony in the Throne Room marking the swearing in of Spencer as the Queen's representative. Cavendish would have to attend, as the most senior Government Minister on the island, the *Irish Times* lamenting, 'little did anyone anticipate the Chief Secretary would be only alive for six hours longer, and that the Undersecretary would be a mangled corpse before dinner time'.[85]

That evening, there was to be a meal in the Viceregal Lodge in Dublin's Phoenix Park. Cavendish had decided to walk home alone to his residence near to Spencer's new home in the park. Walking through the streets unaccompanied was not an unusual thing for a serving politician in late Victorian Britain to do. Leaving the Castle through the Cook Street gate, past the Bedford Tower, Cavendish followed the quays towards Phoenix Park on this mild May evening.

Also leaving the Castle on foot was Inspector John Mallon of the Dublin Metropolitan Police. Like Cavendish, Mallon was making his way to Phoenix Park, to meet an informer embedded in the Fenian conspiracy – John Kenny, a thirty-three-year-old labourer – behind the Viceregal Lodge. If Mallon is to be believed, he was met at Phoenix Park by an agitated policeman, Detective Constable Thomas Simmons, who implored him to go home, as the constable had identified several of the Invincibles in the park, including James Carey and Joe Brady. Simmons gave Mallon a gun, in order to defend himself from a possible assassination attempt. The Inspector made his way home, rather than to the meeting behind the Viceregal Lodge as planned. Mallon was wearing new shoes, which he found to be pinching his feet, and he welcomed the opportunity to head for home on Dublin's North Circular Road. This story, however, is very unreliable. It has been suggested by a contemporary of Mallon, William Henry Joyce, that the story was made up to cover up Mallon's incompetence in two ways: 'to sustain his reputation

The Chief Secretary for Ireland, Lord Frederick Charles Cavendish.

Lord Cavendish's residence in the park, now the residence of the US Ambassador.

of having a number of important informers always at his disposal, and as a cloak to conceal his failure to keep under observation the suspects who were assembling in the park'.[86]

Following in the footsteps of Cavendish and Mallon, Thomas Henry Burke later left the Castle, endeavouring to meet Cavendish and initially travelling by foot. Upon reaching Parkgate Street, Burke ordered a carriage.[87] Turning into Phoenix Park, he was driven up Chesterfield Avenue, passing Cavendish as the Chief Secretary briskly walked along the footpath. Recognising Cavendish, Burke ordered his driver to stop and joined him walking, directing his carriage to drive on.

As they walked past the playing grounds, a cricket match was taking place. Approaching them in the distance was a body of men, divided into columns, two in front, two behind, followed by a further three, all working-class in appearance. Along the roadside in the distance were two carriages.

The Invincibles had been waiting all day for Burke to arrive in the park. The previous day, groups of Invincibles had sat outside Burke's gate, waiting for him to leave his home. Daniel Curley learned he had gone into town, having used another entrance, while Joe Brady actually entered the grounds of Burke's house and asked for him.

That Saturday, the Invincibles had gathered at Wrenn's public house, where James Carey collected Joseph Smith, of the Office of Public Works, in order to help identify their target. Sometime near five o'clock, the gathering left Wrenn's. James Carey, Joseph Hanlon and Joseph Smith would travel to the park by cab, driven by Skin the Goat, passing the polo ground and stopping at the Gough statue.[88]

This was the advance party; the actual assassins were driven by cab to the park by Myles Kavanagh – these included Joe Brady, Tim Kelly, Patrick Delaney and Thomas Caffrey. On their way, they stopped at taverns in Thomas Street and Parkgate Street, eventually stopping off near the Phoenix monument. Other members of the group were also in the park, watching for Burke's arrival, including Daniel Curley, Michael Fagan and Edward McCaffrey, among others. Entering the park, Skin left his passengers near the polo ground and drove to the advance party deposited by Kavanagh near the Phoenix monument. Kavanagh then headed back to where Carey and Smith were.

In the park, Carey was instructed to stay with Smith, who was to identify Burke as he came into view. Waiting

The most senior civil servant in the Dublin Castle administration, Undersecretary Thomas Henry Burke.

Ashtown Lodge, the Undersecretary's residence in Phoenix Park.

for the arrival of the Undersecretary, Carey took in an ongoing game of Polo and enjoyed a cigar. Smith sat on a bench waiting for Burke, while Kavanagh stood by his horse, feeding it from a nosebag. When Smith identified Burke, Carey was to signal the men waiting to assassinate the Undersecretary. At 7.10 that evening, Smith saw Burke and Cavendish, Smith recalling:

> *Mr Burke came driving up ... I got up on the seat and went a couple of yards away from Carey. Carey said who is this coming? I said it was very like Mr Burke, 'it is Mr Burke,' says I! Get up on the car said Carey at once. At this time Mr Burke was only about twenty yards from me.*[89]

Driving past Skin the Goat, Carey waved a white handkerchief toward the assassins, alerting them to Burke's presence. Getting out of the cab, he passed on what Smith had told him to Daniel Curley, including that Burke was wearing a grey suit. Brady now dismissed Smith, who made his way out of the Park toward Islandbridge.

Despite the failure of earlier assassination attempts on Forster, the Invincibles were certain that this time they could not fail. They arranged themselves into columns, walking down the footpath along Chesterfield Avenue toward the approaching Cavendish and Burke. Joe Brady and Tim Kelly would carry out the assassination; if they failed, the two behind them, Thomas Caffrey and Patrick Delaney, would make the attempt.

Curley, Fagan and Hanlon, fully armed, were at the front of the party. Burke and Cavendish walked past them, straight toward Brady and Kelly. By 7.17pm, they had met the two assassins. Brady bent down as if to tie his shoe, waiting to grab Burke, but a car was passing by, and Brady and Kelly chose not to attack the two straight away. When Burke and Cavendish had passed Brady and Kelly, and the car was gone, Brady turned half-circle, wielding his eleven-inch surgical knife. Crying out, 'You villain,' he stabbed Burke repeatedly in the chest and neck, piercing through to the left ventricle of his heart. Burke would receive eleven stab wounds:

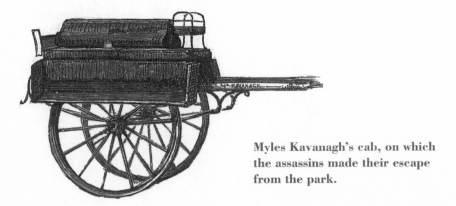

Myles Kavanagh's cab, on which the assassins made their escape from the park.

He was stabbed in the heart and his throat cut right across, severing the windpipe. He received a stab at the base of his neck, and there were several small wounds on his hands, both of which were gloved. These latter wounds would indicate that a struggle took place between him and his assailants.[90]

While Brady was assaulting Burke, Kelly used a similar knife to attack the Chief Secretary, stabbing him in the right shoulder. The two men scuffled, and Cavendish made his way to the roadway. Falling and raising his arm to protect himself, his arm was fiercely cut, almost severed by the force of the blow:

He received one terrible wound in the upper part of the chest and another which penetrated far into the neck. The bone of one of his arms was broken by a wound which he received in the fore part of the limb ... his clothes were perforated in all directions as if he was confronted by a number of foes.[91]

To make sure Cavendish was dead, Brady now cut his throat, severing the jugular vein. Thomas Henry Burke was by now dead, and Cavendish would die by haemorrhage, both bodies lying in pools of blood:[92]

The place where the tragedy occurred was an open highway. It is the leading road to the Viceregal lodge, the Chief Secretary's residence and the residence of the Undersecretary and continues outwards to the country generally. In summer it is an extremely popular walk, and at the time this crime was perpetuated there must have been hundreds of people within a short distance of the spot. Possibly this was the reason the knife or dagger was resorted to instead of the revolver. The report of firearms would necessarily have attracted attention, and this from both quarters of the park, so that detection might easily have followed. This method adopted had the advantage of being silent and sure, no matter how savage; and as the result proved, the assassins got away without the faintest shadow.[93]

THE INVINCIBLES

In Irish historiography, there has been debate as to the extent to which the Invincibles set out to assassinate Cavendish. In the subsequent trials and in media speculation, an idea was established that Cavendish died trying to save Burke, and was simply unlucky to have been with him at the time of the attack. Having carried out extensive surveillance of Burke for the purpose of his assassination, the Invincibles knew that Burke regularly travelled by car, and yet they were waiting for him to walk into the park. Furthermore, Tynan hints in his book chronicling the history of the Invincibles, which is by no means a reliable account, that the Invincibles understood that the Chief Secretary was to meet Burke, and that they had planned to assassinate him also. Tynan asserts in his book that:

> ... the chiefs of Ireland's ravagers, the men from whose bureaux sped the orders of bloodshed and destruction so ruthlessly carried out by their armed hirelings, were termed by the enemy, 'the Chief Secretary' and 'Undersecretary of state.' It was resolved by the earliest council held by the executive of the INVINCIBLES, that these ferocious offices should be kept vacant by the continued 'suppression' of their holders. This order was not levelled at any particular or special occupant of these bloodstained posts of the foe, but against all and every succeeding foreign invader who came to occupy these 'suppressed' bureaux; and it was decided that as soon as a new comer planted his foot on Irish soil, invested by the illegal and alien administration with the authority of either of these offices to perpetuate Britain's rule of spoliation, he should be at once 'suppressed' in mercy of the Irish nation.[94]

Tynan further notes that Burke had met Cavendish by appointment, tending to indicate that the Invincibles knew the Undersecretary was to meet the Englishman and that Cavendish was certainly a target of the assassins:

The new Chief Secretary – who had that morning invaded the island with all the emblems of force, surrounded by the naked steel of Britain's soldiery emblematical of the wounds and death this usurping Government was inflicting on the natives of this country – true to the instincts implanted in all of those men who came to Ireland on the same bloody mission of destruction, sought private conference as soon as he could with the Permanent Undersecretary Burke, whose hands were imbrued with Irish blood; as everyone of his predecessors, without one single exception, have also been.[95]

Having successfully assassinated the two, Brady, Kelly, Caffrey and Delaney joined Kavanagh aboard the cab, Brady dropping a revolver as he boarded. Stepping down, he picked up his fallen revolver and quickly regained himself onboard, the cabman whipping up his horse to get away at a fast pace. According to the chronicler Tighe Hopkins:

Kavanagh let out the reins and the mare went away at the gallop ... Kavanagh took the first turn to the left – the well-known road that leads across the fifteen acres. At the Hill just beyond the Hibernian School there are two sharp curves forming together a letter S ... Out at the Chapelizod gate, and round to the right, and Kavanagh swept through the village of Chapelizod nearly killing a child on the bridge crossing the Liffey. Another turn on the left brought the car on a road parallel to the one just traversed, and in a few moments glancing across the Chapelizod gate.[96]

Rushing down Inchicore Road, Kavanagh brought the Invincibles past the imposing facade of Kilmainham Gaol, as the evening faded toward darkness. A Mr Edward Holohan, at his front gate at 7.50pm, noted the appearance of four men moving at a rapid pace, the horse appearing very much exhausted.[97] Driving through Inchicore village, Kavanagh rapidly made his way towards the Naas Road, moving further and further out of Dublin and into the countryside, along the Tallaght Road. Stopping at a milestone, Brady and Kelly urinated, and cleaned their hands and the knives along the grass.

Again boarding Kavanagh's cab, they drove away at speed, passing through the village of Crumlin and towards the Dublin suburb of Terenure:

> *It was death to anything that met the brown mare's hoofs that night, and a dog which sprang barking at her at Crumlin had its brains kicked out. In then to Terenure, where at length town life began again, for the car was spanking over the stones of a Dublin suburb. It is at Terenure that the tramway service ends, and at the terminus of the Palmerston Park tramway Kelly was sent down and went home by tram to his mother's house, the car now at a sober jog, continued along the tram line through Palmerston Park and Ranelagh, where Kavanagh made a final bend to the right to fetch Leeson Park.*[98]

At Leeson Park, the escape was over. The Invincibles had travelled across the city unfollowed, their presence at a location far away from Phoenix Park intended to give them a valuable alibi in any subsequent investigation of the assassinations. They now went into Davy's pub at Leeson Street, and ordered drinks. They parted ways later, Kavanagh returning to his home in Townsend Street, having been paid £1 by Brady, and the other three making for Westland Row Church, where they would meet Carey by appointment.

Myles Kavanagh, who drove the getaway cab.

A FEW YARDS FROM HERE IS WHERE
THE MURDERS WERE COMMITTED

The road leading to Chapelizod, near the spot where the assassinations occured.

Running parallel to Kavanagh's escape, Skin the Goat had taken Daniel Curley, Michael Fagan and Joseph Hanlon toward Phibsborough. Driving at speed, they noticed two cyclists apparently following them, and had revolvers at the ready should they try to stop them or bring attention to them. Turning onto the North Circular Road, Skin the Goat actually passed Inspector John Mallon's home. Arriving in the city, the three made their separate ways. Curley dropped in to *The Express* newspaper office, leaving a card reading 'executed by order of the Irish Invincibles'. The following day, he would leave cards in the letter boxes of *The Freeman's Journal*, *The Irish Times* and *The Irishman*.[99]

4

THE INVESTIGATION

Shortly after the assassinations, the bodies of Cavendish and Burke were discovered by two young men, William Patrick Maguire and Thomas A Foley. The two work colleagues, riding tricycles, had been the men behind Skin the Goat's cab. Cycling down to the Viceregal Lodge, they saw Cavendish, whom they did not recognise as the Chief Secretary, lying on the road. Parallel to Cavendish, they found Burke on the pathway about six or eight yards away, dead.

Maguire left Foley with the bodies, and cycled away to get help, shouting, 'Murder!' He eventually met two RIC policemen, but the police took no notice of him and dismissed him, as they were off duty. Cycling to the Parkgate entrance, Maguire found a DMP constable, who listened to his story and agreed to make for the bodies with assistance. Leaping into a cab, they rode up to the scene, discovering Foley beside the bodies, alongside two other men, Alfred Walters and John Power, and a boy named Samuel Watson Jacob, who had been bird nesting in the park.

Walters and Power had been sitting under trees in the park when,

The three-mile stone
on the Naas road.

… their attention was first attracted by Maguire riding down the road on
his tricycle shouting 'Murder.'[100] *They then rushed to the spot it was 7.28 by*
Power's watch. Power remained with the bodies, and Walters rushed over the
fence to the Vice Regal lodge and alarmed the people there.[101]

Watson Jacob, the boy, had seen the assassination, but had not realised what was
happening, believing he was witnessing a brawl. He could not identify anyone,
but recalled after Cavendish fell that the assassins boarded a cab, making their
way at speed toward the Phoenix column. After the deed was done:

Three or four of the group ran towards the car, and one of them ran from the
man on the ground to the other man on the ground, and hit him, and then ran
after the car which was in rapid motion. He had some difficulty getting up. I
think there were four men besides the driver. The driver whipped up the horse
and went towards Chapelizod … When I came up to the place I saw one body
on the road and the other on the footway. The one on the road fell first. It was
from this body the man went to the one on the footway and struck it … The car
was in motion, walking all the time towards the Phoenix.[102]

Davy's public house in Leeson Street, now the Leeson Lounge, where the Invincibles went for a drink after the assassinations.

William Dawson, of Mountjoy Barracks, Dublin, had been walking down Chesterfield Avenue toward Dublin, when he was approached by a woman, who warned him he would not go any further. Thinking the woman drunk, he dismissed her, but as he walked along, the bodies of Burke and Cavendish came into view. Dawson, shocked, ran towards Burke:

> *I observed two men lying on and near footpath a few yard in front of me, and at same time I observed two Constabulary men running towards where the bodies were. I also then ran to the bodies same time as Constabulary. I put my hand on Mr Burke's forehead, whom I at once recognised, his eyes were open and glaring. I believed him to be dead.*[103]

Dawson, however, saw no car and no suspects relative to the assassination. He left the scene after a brief interview with a police constable.

Inspector Mallon, at his home near the park, had been informed of the assassinations by Inspector John Bride of the Dublin Metropolitan Police

The aftermath of the assassinations: Thomas Foley stayed with the bodies while his work colleague William McGuire went for help.

at 8pm. The inspector was under the impression that Burke and his brother had been killed.[104] He made his way to Phoenix Park,[105] after telegraphing all the seaports in Ireland and Britain, effectively learning that the last ferry had departed from Kingstown and North Wall before the assassinations, omitting the possibility that the assassins had left the country. He also arranged to have telegraph offices opened on the Sunday for police business. Mallon telegraphed word that detective cars were to make for RIC stations outside County Dublin and coordinate operations, while special constables were communicated with.

Mallon now set about interviewing witnesses. One witness he found of interest was Samuel Watson Jacob, who recalled seeing four men, 'dressed alike with slouched hats, the car looked a red panelled one and the horse a good goer'.[106] After Watson Jacob, Mallon interviewed Lieutenant Ferdinand William Greatrux of the Royal Dragoons. Greatrux had been out walking his dogs, and confirmed what the teenager had seen, noting what he also perceived to be a drunken scuffle in the far distance: 'what he considered a drunken row, one man followed another onto the roadway, one fell, four men jumped onto the car, galloped off rapidly, taking the first turn to the fifteen acres ...'[107] Importantly, Greatrux could possibly identify the men, recalling, 'The driver looked of the middle age, with a bloated and red face, with about three days beard on, wore a black soft hat down his face and neck. One of the men on the car was very sallow complexion, pale sandy moustache and chin beard, full fronted shirt, and long black tie, dark colour overcoat and soft hat. He thought he could identify this man. The whole four appeared to be slight rather respectable looking well to do tradesmen.'[108]

Alongside Greatrux's evidence, Mallon met George Godden, a former park ranger, who Mallon described as a 'sensible, steady old man'.[109] Godden had been near the Chapelizod gate of the park as Myles Kavanagh had hurriedly driven out. According to Godden,

> ... about 25 to 8 the previous evening, he was near the Chapelizod gate, and the Hibernian military school, when a pickled green coloured car with four passengers and driver dashed along from the 15 acres at a rapid pace. The driver had the appearance of a hack car man, and must have had his horse well in hand; otherwise he would have come down. The horse he said was chestnut of splendid action, and in thin, but good working condition. The car was olive green picked out with white, and he did not think it was a hack car, although it first struck him as one before it first came up to him. At all events it had no number on it.[110]

This was certainly useful evidence for John Mallon. Godden had actually seen the assassins, and could describe them:

1st about 35 years old, stout build, dark complexion, hair whiskers and
moustache recently cut as if with a hand scissors giving it a bristling appearance,
narrow forehead, and a natural hollow or dinge over the nose. He wore a soft
black jerry hat and dark clothes.
2nd About 30 years old, sandy hair whiskers and moustache, no beard, soft black
jerry hat and brown faded colour overcoat.
3rd About 20 years, small dark moustache, no beard, soft black jerry hat and
dark clothes.
4th About 30 years old, small dark moustache and beard on chin, wore a soft
jerry hat, and dark clothes.[111]

In a more detailed interview, Godden would vividly describe the assassins and their getaway, stating that he was on the left of the horse and its driver as it passed. He described Brady as a 'broad shouldered man', wearing a blue cloth jacket and a soft jerry hat.[112]

A Laurence Edmund Kavanagh, who had worked at Mountjoy Barracks, Dublin, recalled passing six or seven men standing under trees near the Viceregal Lodge. According to Kavanagh, the men were 'roughs', and of the working class, and associated with three gentlemanly-looking men. Kavanagh looked on, as he found it strange that these three men were fraternising with tradesmen. Near the men was a cab, which he described as shabby, standing about seven yards from them on the Dublin side of the road.

This story was corroborated by a Mr Powell, who similarly had seen four men standing near a clump of trees, all ordinarily dressed and obviously tradesmen. Near the men was a cab, the driver of which was described as stout and about five feet eight inches tall (Skin the Goat). A third witness,

The Chapelizod Gate, near to which George Godden saw the assassins leaving the park.

a Mrs Harris, also saw these men while walking with her husband towards Dublin. She described them as lying on the grass with their heads visible, and rather 'rough looking'.

In further evidence, Mary Sharpe, a gatekeeper's wife, had been walking through the park with her dog to meet her mother that evening. She was passing the Hibernian School when, like Godden, she met a car with three or four men, driving at a rapid pace out of the park toward Chapelizod. While she saw the men, she said she would not recognise them in the future, but remembered they were very much excited and looked soberly at her and her dog as they drove past.[113]

The description of a cab speedily driving past the Hibernian School was echoed by a third independent witness, one Ellen Brewster, who, like Godden, could identify the assassins. In Brewster's narrative, as Godden had suggested, there were four men, but contradictory to Godden's description, the cab seen by Brewster was red. The driver, she said, had a round, red face (Kavanagh). Each of the assassins was wearing, as Godden had independently suggested, a Jerry hat and either dark or blue clothes, and they were much excited. The similarities between Godden's and Brewster's descriptions led to the conclusion that both had seen the actual assassins, the investigation concluding the importance of finding the red cab:

> *The Inspector General directs that the Sub-Inspector will relieve from all duty, and sit apart for making inquiries related to the Phoenix Park Assassinations, two of the most intelligent men at each of the stations in his district which adjourn the D.M. Police district. These men should devote all their time and energies to this important case in endeavouring to trace the car and the four persons who left the Park by the Chapelizod gate.*[114]

In the park, a large crowd gathered at the scene, held back by a cordon of police officers. Doctors were called for at Dr Steeven's Hospital, with a Dr Thomas Myles, resident surgeon, arriving to examine the bodies. Myles concluded that Burke had died instantly. He found that Cavendish's last breath had been taken, but he recorded a pulse. The body of Burke was placed on a back car, while Cavendish was laid to rest on a stretcher. The bodies were now taken to Dr Steeven's Hospital, and locked in a room under police guard until the city coroner arrived:

> *When the bodies were removed to the hospital they were placed in a small ward at the end of the corridor on two ordinary beds, and were left just as they had been found. They were not touched until the coroner arrived. The bodies lay each in a corner of the room and tables draped in white in which wax candles were placed beside the corpses.*[115]

On arrival in the hospital, Cavendish was noted to be saturated with blood, while Burke's face was in agony. An inquest was held at the hospital, headed by Dr Nicholas C Whyte, coroner for the City of Dublin, and assisted by Dr George Porter, the consulting surgeon of Dr Steeven's hospital and surgeon to Queen Victoria in Ireland. He would undertake the rather unpleasant task of conducting a post mortem, recording:

> *I first examined the body of Mr Burke. I found his clothing cut in several places. On removing the clothing I found several wounds. There was a deep and long wound on the front and side of the neck. There was a wound of the left breast about an inch above the nipple. There was a wound over the cartilage of the second rib left side. There was a wound over the breast bone. There were two slight wounds on the finger (the index finger of the left hand), and also a wound of the second finger of the same hand, splitting the nail and finger for about an inch. There was a deep wound of the back over the inferior angle of the shoulder blade – a deep wound on the side and back of the neck which penetrated to the spine. I opened the chest and found that the wound in front of the neck, though deep, did not sever any large vessels. The wound over the cartilage of the second rib penetrated the apex of the left lung and wounded the lung. There was copious haemorrhage into the mouth from this wound.*
>
> *I now come to the fatal wound. The wound on the back over the inferior angle of the scapula penetrated the pericardium and the heart. The pericardium was filled with blood. I think death as a consequence of that wound was immediate.*[116]

Moving on to examine Cavendish, Porter noted similarities in the tears of their clothing, judging that by the scale of their wounds they were set upon quite roughly. Of Cavendish's injuries, the surgeon noted:

> *I found a deep transverse cut on the middle of the left forearm, which cut through some of the muscles and fractured the ulna, one of the bones of the forearm. A small portion of the bone was sliced off by a very sharp weapon. I found a deep wound of the right arm pit, which passed up to articulation*

The bodies of Cavendish and Burke are conveyed to Steeven's Hospital (*Illustrated London News*, 13 May 1882).

of the shoulder joint. I found a slight abrasion over the right malar bone. There was a wound on the root of the neck just above the right clavicle. There was a wound over the cartilage of the second rib of the right side. On the back I found a deep angular wound over the right shoulder that penetrated to the scapula. I found also a deep wound at the outer edge of the inferior angle of the right of the scapula involving that bone. I found a wound over the centre of the back of the neck injuring the sixth cervical vertebrae. On opening the chest I could not find the cause of death there. I then found the wound of the shoulder severed the main artery and vein going to the arm – the auxiliary vessels. This wound caused death by haemorrhage. Death was very rapid.[117]

On this evidence, Dr Whyte confirmed that the men had been assassinated by exceedingly keen and well-tempered knives.[118]

Cavendish and Burke's bodies were removed from Steeven's Hospital, placed into temporary coffins, and then secured in covered biers. Leaving the hospital, they were accompanied by an escort of mounted police. It was desired that their bodies would temporarily lie in state at the Chief Secretary's lodge before burial. However, given the public interest in the assassinations, it was recommended that the procession should enter the park by a different route, to avoid the crowds, gathering to see the spot where the assassinations had taken place. So, avoiding the Parkgate entrance to Phoenix Park, the most convenient route toward the Chief Secretary's lodge, it was decided to enter the park by the Islandbridge gate, and then by the Phoenix monument.

Given the pomp of the procession, however, groups of spectators were gathering to witness the final pageant of the assassinated Government officials. When the procession arrived at Islandbridge gate, further lines of police were stationed to ensure public order, while a guard of Dublin Metropolitan Police detectives cordoned off the Chief Secretary's lodge, meeting the procession as it entered the walled grounds. Just as the cortège entered the grounds, a tremendous shower of rain was recorded, a heavy thunderstorm beating overhead. The bodies were taken to the lodge's deer room, where the curtains were drawn and the bodies could be viewed.

Thomas Henry Burke was removed to Glasnevin Cemetery on the following Tuesday, 9 May. By 9.15 that morning, Burke's procession had left the Chief Secretary's lodge. The funeral cortège passed through the phoenix Park, turning at the Phoenix monument and making its way out onto the North Circular Road, surrounded by a heavy police guard. Receiving the coffin at Glasnevin, a funeral mass for the assassinated Undersecretary was said in the Mortuary Chapel.

Frederick Cavendish would lie in State in Dublin until he made his final journey to England. He was buried at Edensor churchyard, near Chatsworth in Derbyshire, on 11 May:

About five o'clock a troop of Royal Dragoon Guards, a gun carriage, driven and escorted by a party of Royal Horse Artillery, and a number of mounted policemen took up a position outside the Viceregal Lodge, and soon afterwards the remains of the late Chief Secretary, which were enclosed in a leaden coffin, placed in a mahogany shell with embonised moldings and rich gilt handles were carried out of the lodge on the shoulders of six of the Royal Horse Artillery, and placed on the gun carriage, a Union Jack being thrown over the coffin. Upon the breast plate, which was of brass, was of the following inscription:

'Lord Frederick Charles Cavendish,

Second son of the Duke of Devonshire,

Born November 30 1836

Died May 6 1882.'[119]

Cavendish's procession passed slowly through Phoenix Park, past the spot where he had been assassinated and out the Parkgate entrance. Large crowds looked on, controlled by a police guard. At the top of the procession were six mounted policemen, each carrying a sword, followed by two officers of the Royal Dragoon Guards with their carbines. Behind these two officers followed a Royal Dragoon sergeant with a drawn sabre. Next came the gun carriage carrying Cavendish, surrounded by Royal Dragoon Guards and Royal Horse Artillery. Many senior British officials in Ireland followed behind in cars.

Arriving at the North Wall, the procession was met by the Coldstream Guards. Six officers of the Royal Horse Artillery dismounted and carried Cavendish's body aboard a steamer waiting to transport the former Chief Secretary to England. Arriving at Holyhead, Cavendish was placed aboard a train specially detailed to take the body of the assassinated Chief Secretary to Rowsley in Derbyshire. From Rowsley, he was taken to his home at Chatsworth, where he was laid out at the home of his father, the Duke of Devonshire, on 9 May.

The funeral of Thomas Henry Burke at Glasnevin Cemetery, 9 May 1882.

In his father's home, Cavendish's body was displayed in an open coffin, and his wife, Lucy, was permitted to place a cross of hothouse flowers on his body. Remaining in his father's home for three days, Cavendish was interred in the family plot at Edensor, Derbyshire, on Thursday, 11 May. The funeral was largely a private affair, but was watched with much interest. Such was the size of the public gathering to watch the affair that the funeral was compared to that of the former prime minister Benjamin Disraeli, who had died in April of the previous year.

While this gathering was undoubtedly motivated by much sympathy for the grieving family, it was also curious. The funeral of a senior Government official was bound to bring the great and the good to the small, rural town. A special train was hired by the Government in anticipation of the funeral, conveying ministers and members of Parliament to Chatsworth, including Prime Minister William Gladstone, with his wife and family.

Beginning at half past two, the funeral procession left for Edensor Church.

Supported by his other sons Edward and Spencer Crompton Cavendish, the Duke of Devonshire walked behind the hearse carrying the former Irish Chief Secretary. Following the Duke and his sons were the Prime Minister, the Foreign Secretary, Earl Grenville, and the Speaker of the House of Commons. Arriving at the church, Lucy Cavendish, widow of the former Chief Secretary, waited at the porch, from where she was taken to the Duke by Gladstone, who had temporarily left the procession. Inside Edensor Church, Frederick Cavendish was laid to rest in the Chancel. On top of his coffin rested a wreath of crimson roses sent that morning by Queen Victoria.

The Irish Chief Secretary and the Undersecretary for Ireland would be replaced by George Otto Trevelyan and Robert Hamilton respectively. The hunt for the Invincibles would continue, however, and on 13 May, the Irish Viceroy John Poyntz Spencer issued a proclamation from Dublin Castle:

A Proclamation

By the Lord Lieutenant General and Governor General of Ireland – Spencer. Lord Frederick Charles Cavendish, the Chief Secretary, and Thomas Henry Burke, Esq., the undersecretary to the Lord Lieutenant of Ireland were brutally murdered in the Phoenix Park in the County of Dublin, on the evening of Saturday 6 May, 1882, and whereas a reward of ten thousand pounds has been offered by us to any person or persons who shall within the time specified in the proclamation offering the same give such information as shall lead to the conviction of the murderers; and whereas any person who shall knowingly receive, into his or her house, or otherwise harbour or maintain any of the persons who committed the said murders, or shall conceal or aid any of them in escaping or endeavouring to escape from justice, becomes libel to penal servitude for life; now we, John Poyntz, Earl Spencer, Lord Lieutenant General and Governor General of Ireland, are pleased hereby to offer a reward of five hundred pounds to any person or persons who shall within three months

from the date hereof give such information as shall lead to the arrest of any
person who has so received, harboured, maintained, or concealed, or assisted in
endeavouring to escape from justice, or who shall receive, harbour, maintain,
or conceal, or assist in endeavouring to escape from justice, any persons who
committed the said murders.

Dublin Castle, 13 May 1882.[120]

Never before had two senior Government ministers been assassinated in such fashion. As the news reverberated through the British political elite, it seemed highly likely that a new round of coercion was inevitable. The British Home Secretary, Sir William Vernon Harcourt, who had shared Forster's dislike of the so-called Kilmainham Treaty, increasingly insisted that the Government policy of conciliation had led to the Dublin assassinations. Harcourt argued that only firm measures could calm Ireland, and this view had royal backing and the support of public opinion:

The shaken British establishment gather for the funeral of Lord Cavendish at Edensor, Derbyshire, 11 May 1882.

There is a frightful plague set upon [Ireland], *and I firmly believe that the Irish no less than the English nation desires that the plague spot should be removed. There is a cancerous sore in Ireland, and the House will anticipate that the great malady which corrodes and cripples its healthy frame comes from the baneful demons of secret societies and unlawful combinations. That being so, it is necessary that the surgeon's hand should cauterize and extirpate the disease.*[121]

Privately, Gladstone was horrified of all the talk of a new Irish coercion bill,[122] but was too shaken by Cavendish's death to stage a fight. Harcourt was well aware of this, and wrote, 'in his heart Gladstone hates the bill and will with great difficulty be kept up to the mark. I can see that he secretly – perhaps unconsciously – favours every proposal to weaken it and whittle it away.'[123] Harcourt could take solace, however, from the fact that the so-called Kilmainham Treaty had immensely weakened his opponents within the Cabinet, most of whom were haunted by the idea that it directly correlated with the assassinations.

Gladstone privately believed that 'Parnell, Davitt and Dillon will denounce the late murders openly ... and that their action will so tranquilise the country that very stringent powers may not be necessary',[124] but he eventually bowed to pressure. He watched on as a new coercion bill arrived, allowing the Viceroyalty to establish special courts of three Supreme Court judges to try cases of treason and murder without juries. Extensive powers were given to Dublin Castle to suppress newspapers, to search homes for arms and suspects, and to extend curfew, arresting people on the streets who were unable to account for themselves.

Alongside the Coercion Act, Spencer had grave concerns as to the ability of the Irish police to crack the Fenian–Invincible conspiracy. He lamented, 'We know little more than they exist.'[125] Underlined by an understanding that information was key to breaking the Fenian conspiracy, Spencer made it clear that he was very keen on 'police rearrangements. The whole thing is rotten. I want to decentralise a bit in one way with the resident magistrates, and centralise in on one point only ... In the directive department which must be in one hand for the whole country.'[127] Spencer's concerns were not new to the Castle administration; Thomas Henry Burke had previously sought the establishment of a permanent Police and Crime Department in Dublin for dealing with Fenianism.[128] The park assassinations had convinced Spencer of the necessity of a centralised and co-ordinated response at a national level.

As part of this reorganisation, Spencer insisted on the resignation of the head of the RIC.[129] He sought to replace him with career soldier Colonel Henry Brackenbury, a former Private Secretary to Lord Lytton, the Indian Viceroy, a former Chief Commandant of the police in Nicosia, and now Parisian military attaché. On 9 May, Brackenbury learned from the Secretary of State for the War Office, Hugh Childers, that he was being sent to Ireland to take charge of the police. Brackenbury was reluctant, registering his opposition to the proposal. He told the War Secretary he was a soldier, and had a keen eye on Imperial affairs. He wished to fight for Empire in Egypt, expecting war imminently between the Crown and Egyptian nationalists under Arabi Pasha. Childers ignored his pleas bluntly, telling him, 'It is war in Ireland, the Government have selected you and I do not think you can refuse.'[130]

Brackenbury was therefore told he was going to Dublin, for a job he did not want; he would become the first Assistant Undersecretary for Police and Crime, a role Brackenbury later recalled as an 'unfortunate episode in my career'.[131] Brackenbury would now head a permanent secret service department based in Dublin Castle coordinating action between the Irish police forces, the Army and the Cabinet. Under Brackenbury, and upon his dismissal later that year under Edward George Jenkinson, a system of intelligence assets for penetration of the Fenian conspiracy would be developed, working in absolute secrecy.

In Kilmainham Gaol, James Mullet was left inside his cell as news filtered through the prison of the park assassinations. Mullet knew exactly who was behind the action. He sat on this information for a number of weeks, yet he had pressing concerns – he had had enough of Kilmainham, and he worried for the stability of his financial interests outside of gaol. He eventually requested to see Inspector Mallon to make a deal. Mallon obliged the publican, arriving at the gaol to interview him out of sight from other concerned prisoners. Mallon listened attentively as Mullet spoke of the Invincibles conspiracy and named James Carey, Joe Brady, Daniel Curley and Skin the Goat Fitzharris, among others, as being involved.[132] In return, Mullet would be released from Kilmainham, his one condition being that he would give no evidence in Court. Mallon obliged, the irony being that no evidence existed of Mullet's involvement in the Bailey assassination, and so he would have been released from prison anyway, sooner rather than later.

Meanwhile, Michael Davitt had also been released from Portland Prison. Parnell and Dillon escorted him to London, where they stayed at the Westminster Palace hotel. Parnell left to meet Katherine O'Shea, leaving Davitt and Dillon alone, sitting down to dinner. The two discussed the so-called Kilmainham Treaty and the possibilities for the future. They had sat down no longer than a few minutes before they were informed of the Dublin assassinations. They didn't entirely believe the reports, but the following morning at 5am, Davitt received word from a trusted Dublin source confirming the news, and 'a short time afterwards Mr Parnell entered the room, his face was deadly pale, with a look of alarm in his eyes, which I had never seen in any expression of his before or after'.[133]

According to Davitt, Parnell expressed a desire to retire from politics forever. Davitt recalled urging Parnell not to follow such a course, though evidence exists that the Irish leader chose not to follow Davitt's advice, but was later dissuaded from resigning by Joseph Chamberlain MP.

Parnell was certainly shaken by the Dublin assassinations. Katherine O'Shea would recall, as he left her to see Davitt and Dillon on the morning the news broke:

> I drove with him to Blackheath Station, as he had to go to London to see Davitt and others. At the station I asked him to get me a newspaper before he left and waited for him in the carriage. From where I sat in the carriage I could see Parnell's back as he stood just inside the station door. I was watching him and then he half turned and smiled at me as he opened the paper – The Sunday Observer – to glance at the news before he brought it to me ... He had now come to the top of the steps and, as he suddenly stopped, I noticed a curious rigidity about his arms – raised in holding the newspaper open. He stood so absolutely still that I was suddenly frightened, horribly, sickeningly afraid – of I knew not what and leaning forward called out ... 'what is it?' Then he came down the steps to me and, pointing to the headline, said, 'Look!' And I read, 'Murder of Lord Frederick Cavendish and Mr Burke ...' the awful significance of the horrible thing to my lover, just released from Kilmainham on the treaty, came home to me with a rush of pain. His face was ashen and he stared, frowning heavily, before him, unconsciously crushing the hand I had slipped into his until the rings I wore cut and bruised my fingers.[134]

According to Davitt, the trio, now housed in the Westminster Palace hotel, wondered,

> ... what was to be done to mitigate the horror of the situation? There might be a spirit of murderous retaliation ... appealed to in the British press against our people in England. Could any measures of any kind be taken which might isolate the terrible deed as far as possible in the public mind from any connection with the league movement?[135]

It was resolved to publicly denounce the assassinations, issuing a manifesto to the Irish people, designed for public opinion in Britain:

The Manifesto of the Chiefs to the people of Ireland,

On the eve of what seemed a bright future for our country, that evil destiny which has apparently pursued us for centuries has struck another blow at our hopes which cannot be exaggerated in its disastrous consequences. In this hour of sorrowful gloom we venture to give an expression of our profound sympathy with the people of Ireland in the calamity which has befallen our cause through a horrible deed, and with those who have determined at the last hour that a policy of conciliation should supplant that of terrorism and national distrust.

We earnestly hope that the attitude and action of the whole Irish people will assure the world that assassination such as that which has startled us almost to the abandonment of hope for our country's cause is deeply and religiously abhorrent to their every feeling and instinct. We appeal to you to show by every manner of expression possible, that amidst the universal feeling of horror which the assassination has excited, no people are so intense in their detestation of its atrocity, or entertain so deep a sympathy for those whose hearts might be scared by it, as the nation upon whose prospects and reviving hopes it may entail more ruinous effects than have fallen on the lot of unhappy Ireland during the present generation.

We feel that no act has ever been perpetuated in our country during the struggles for social and political rights of the past fifty years that has so stained the name of hospitable Ireland than this cowardly and unprovoked assassination of a friendly stranger, and that until the murderers of Lord Frederick Cavendish and Mr Burke are brought to justice that stain will sully our country's name.

Chas. S. Parnell

John Dillon

Michael Davitt

Parallel to the manifesto issued by Parnell, Dillon and Davitt, John Redmond made a powerful speech at Manchester, condemning the assassinations. Parnell also communicated with the lord mayors of Cork, Waterford, Dublin and Limerick, calling for them to assemble immediate meetings to denounce the killings.

While the leadership of the Irish Party, with Davitt, had denounced the assassinations, in Ireland there were certainly elements supportive of the Irish National Invincibles. Among the most vocal supporters of the assassination were many of the Dublin working class, and significant elements in mainstream nationalism. When the excitement of the assassinations had died down, few nationalists could be found who deplored the assassination of Burke, who was one of the most hated men among Fenian circles. This was not merely for his role as Undersecretary at Dublin Castle – because of his Irishness and his work in administration of British policy in Ireland, as far as Fenianism was concerned Burke was a collaborator with the Irish occupation. Elements within the IRB contrasted denunciation with support along these lines, and released a statement to this effect:

> Dublin, May 8, 1882.
>
> To the Irish people and all lovers of liberty, and particularly our brothers of the IRB and kindred organisations.
>
> As there seems to be a grave misunderstanding as to the aim and scope of the late executions at Dublin, we the executive of the IRB wish to withhold their opinion of this matter at the present, and to refrain from expression of sympathy at public meetings which tend to humiliate Ireland and to give aid and comfort to England.
>
> As to the monster Burke, he has preyed upon the lives and liberties of his own countrymen for many years, and has deserved death a thousand times at our hands; and as to lord Frederick Cavendish, the lineal descendent of the infamous Lord Broghill, who hanged the gallant and patriotic MacEgan Bishop of Ross,

at Carrigadrohid, because he would not betray his country – his very name stinks in the nostrils of the Irish people by the iniquities of his brother, Lord Hartington, and the wholesale evictions of his father, the Duke of Devonshire, thereby driving thousands of the rightful owners of the soil to the poorhouse, exile and death.

This organisation has tolerated the vagaries of Mr Parnell and his late treason-mongers who have filled the bastilles in our country with the victims of a useless Parliamentary agitation, which left 20,000 persons homeless last year, and drove millions of the flower of our people to exile. This ceases to be harmless when a truce is made by which he himself and his friends are allowed go free, and eighty of Ireland's bravest patriots are left to languish in prison to be exiled or assassinated, and these the men who by so-called 'outrages,' opened the prison doors to Mr Parnell and his friends.

If England really wished to do fairly by Ireland why did she not issue a general amnesty by which the prison doors would be opened and thousands of our exiled brethren who now pine in foreign lands could return home in safety and honour? Instead of this Mr Gladstone sent emissaries to the venerated head of the Catholic Church, who by lies and false representations have deprived thousands of our poor, persecuted people of the comforts of religion by turning our altars into political platforms. Let us ask the people of Ireland, are there no classes of the people to be considered except the farmers, and of what avail will it be to Ireland if a selfish class is firmly rooted in the soil and becomes thoroughly loyal to England?

We ask our friends in America to ponder on our desperate circumstances, to think of a brave and honourable people driven to despair by witnessing the white bosoms of our women torn open by the bayonets of English mercenaries, and our children of tender age shot down in the highways, while our wails of anguish are stifled in blood.

We are convinced that no true prosperity can exist in Ireland so long as England possesses her custom houses, these allowing her manufactures to pass into Ireland duty free, thereby leaving our Irish mechanics unemployed, and the enormous war tribute enacted by England taking away the produce of the land, thereby forcing the Irish people to starve.

Now, furthermore, we call upon our brothers in America, particularly the advanced nationalists, to aid by every means in their power the men who have carried out this execution, and we hereby declare that they deserve well of their country.

By order of the Executive of the IRB.[136]

Mallon wasted little time. From Mullet's information secured in Kilmainham Gaol, and further private information, the detective could claim he knew the identities of the assassins within one week.[137] Having gone through the witness statements regarding the car that had been driven through the Chapelizod gate of Phoenix Park, Mallon noted that at Cork Street in the city, the car seemingly disappeared or stopped. He wondered about this, and increasingly investigated possibilities regarding Fenianism within the Dublin Liberties. Within two weeks, he had evaluated a number of theories as to the assassinations:

I have to report that in the course of my enquiries about the Phoenix Park Murders I came across almost all classes of persons and it may not be considered out of place to state the different views current with regard to the subject.

The murders are attributed to the low reckless Fenians in Dublin who recently murdered Bailey ... Mr Burke is stated to have been their intended victim because it was generally believed that he was so long a permanent official at the Castle that he had a thorough knowledge of the state of affairs in the city and was in great measure responsible for the recent arrests ...

... It is said Mr Egan and his Paris friends were the assassins as they did not approve of what is now known as the Kilmainham Treaty ... With regard to the first theory there can be no doubt that we have men in Dublin desperate

enough to commit the murders, and the way in which they are perpetrated justifies the opinion that the assassins were not strangers; assuming that Mr Burke was aimed at and that Lord Cavendish who by accident happened to be in his company was murdered on the principle that dead men tell no tales. Of late Mr Burke drove home a good deal, and it is quite possible that the assassins would have dragged him off a car had he continued to drive on the evening of the murders. It was about his usual hour to return home ... It is quite certain that Egan and his party were the assassins. Egan was aware of the new departure early in the week, he has lots of money at his back, knows the low desperados in Dublin, and is trusted by them ...[138]

Mallon was certain of one thing: he had concluded that the Invincibles were an organisation dedicated to the assassination of any obnoxious governmental official, and were prepared to lose their lives in doing so.[139] One figure whose name kept coming up through all his investigations and interviews was James Carey, and Mallon determined to watch him intently.

Mallon was keenly interested in the mode of escape employed by the Invincibles after the assassinations. Every cab driver in Dublin was to be questioned, searched and thoroughly examined by the Dublin Metropolitan Police. A parade was made of all the cabs in Dublin city, and they were examined by police detectives. Furthermore, the police investigation dragged the river Liffey, to examine the possibility that the assassins had dumped the knives in the river. This task was undertaken by marines from the Man-of-War *Bellisle*.

Alongside this practical police work, the evidence of witnesses to the actual assassinations produced additional valuable information. Godden's description of the assassins and the cab they had used in their escape was of major importance. Four men matching the description of the assassins had been observed on the day of the attack near Kingsbridge train station. Mallon traced these four men to a pub near the Parkgate entrance to the park, and to another public house at Chapelizod. The men were eventually located at Lucan, but providing sufficient alibis, they were found to be entirely innocent.

Mallon was convinced that the assassins had entered Phoenix Park on a cab, sometime on the evening of 6 May, arriving via the Islandbridge gate, quickly passing between the Civil Service and Garrison cricket grounds and making their way to near the Phoenix monument. From the evidence of various witnesses, the inspector was strongly of the opinion that they had waited under a clump of trees until they had identified Cavendish and Burke.

Investigating the connection of the cab to Cork Street, Mallon looked into what Fenians lived in the vicinity. Increasingly, Carey's name stood out as a leading Fenian. On their convoluted escape from the park, Cork Street was the only thickly populated area that they could arrive in, and Carey was a respected figure within that locality, powerful enough to be feared, being connected to the Fenian vigilance committee. This was consolidated by Mullet's earlier information from Kilmainham as to Carey's involvement in the assassination. On researching Carey, Mallon learned that he was heavily connected to Fenianism in the Liberties. Carey had once worked in the School of Medicine at Peter Street, and had access to dispensaries in the building. Mallon mused the question of whether the knives used to assassinate Cavendish and Burke came from this source. An inventory proved they did not.

On 4 July 1882, the Fenian informer John Kenny was assassinated by a Fenian vigilance committee, his body found under a railway archway at Seville Place, Dublin. The assassination was witnessed by a Mrs Lawson, living at Seville Place, who recalled hearing and seeing gunfire:

They were fired in rapid succession. Then three men emerged from the archway. One kept on the side that the shots were fired at. Two came towards Amelia Street

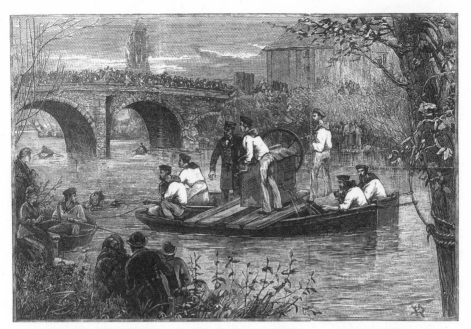

Marines dragging the River Liffey, looking for the assassins' weapons.

... They paused and then ran back to the Arch and the one on the opposite side turned at the same time ... she heard a female's voice calling after them, the Woman called out 'Police' and 'stop them.'[140]

The police were determined to treat the killing of John Kenny as a Fenian-related activity, given his employment as an informer by John Mallon. In subsequent investigations, it was revealed that Kenny had been connected to the leading Dublin Fenian and centre of a Fenian circle, Joseph Poole, who had allegedly been with Kenny on the night of his execution. Having been introduced to Kenny's family and fellow lodgers in a small tenement, Poole had left with Kenny. Kenny instructed that the door behind him was not to be closed, and walked with Poole towards the railway arch. Within minutes, Kenny was killed.

In life, Kenny's services to the Dublin Metropolitan Police were valuable, but in death they were greater, as Inspector Mallon now used his

A demonstration by the cab drivers of Dublin, gathering to condemn the killings of Cavendish and Burke.

assassination as an excuse to imprison leading Invincibles, including Daniel Curley, Thomas Caffrey and Joseph Poole.[141]

Following the arrests, Carey came to Kilmainham to visit Curley, and was arrested as he left the prison, under the Coercion Act. Carey was interred inside for questioning, the police heavily playing the prisoner's dilemma between Curley and Carey, hoping to gain enough leverage to make either one crack, giving information to the investigation.

With Carey's unexpected arrest, however, one of his tenants had grown increasingly suspicious of his earlier activities. John Fitzsimons rented a tenement house from Carey at South Cumberland Street, Dublin. He had noticed that since 6 May, Carey had made continual visits to the loft of the house, under the auspices of maintenance work. On hearing of Carey's arrest, this tenant decided to investigate what his landlord had really been up to. Entering the loft, Fitzsimons found, hidden in a dark corner, surgical knives with fine black horn handles, with 'Weiss and Son, London' engraved upon them, and a nine-shot Winchester repeating rifle. He moved the weapons away and hid them for two weeks. Meanwhile, on 29 July, Carey's wife and brother, Maggie and Peter, arrived to inspect the loft, along with Joe Brady. Maggie Carey remained at the foot of the ladder as Peter Carey and Joe Brady searched upstairs, but they left empty-handed after some two hours of searching.

Fitzsimons now decided to inform the Dublin Metropolitan Police of his discovery, believing Carey to be implicated in the conspiracy, and invited the police to his home to show detectives the find. That Carey was implicated in the park assassinations was clear to Mallon, yet the discovery of the weaponry was weak as evidence – the loft was accessible to all the tenants of the South Cumberland Street tenement. Carey had also been in gaol when the discovery was made, making Carey's links to the weapons purely circumstantial.

Within two months, Carey and Curley were released from Kilmainham Gaol. Despite extensive questioning and an identity parade, neither revealed any details of the Invincibles conspiracy.

The Invincibles would continue to plot political assassination. Carey, ever bombastic, sought election to the Dublin Trades Council. Winning strong nationalist support in the Trinity Ward, on a platform largely of cited victimisation by the Dublin Metropolitan Police, he defeated a conservative member by a large majority and secured election.

Joseph Poole, tailor and a Dublin centre of the IRB.

Buoyed by the failure of the authorities to break the Invincibles conspiracy, the Dublin directory next plotted to assassinate a leading pillar of the British administration in Ireland, Judge James Anthony Lawson. Lawson had been outspoken in his anti-nationalist views, and was the first judge to preside over a trial established under the terms of the 1882 Coercion Act. Lawson was adept at packing juries in trials. While he had the authority to conduct a trial without a jury under the Coercion Act, he favoured the presence of a jury in order to lend the trial legitimacy. The jury was almost always in favour of the State, as *The Daily Telegraph* noted: 'We must, to convict murderers, secure by hook or by crook, by law or challenge, metropolitan, Protestant and loyal juries.'[142]

Lawson had presided over the case of Francis Hynes, who was alleged to have murdered an old man, John Doloughty, in County Clare. The trial was carefully and systematically designed to secure a prosecution. From a panel of forty-nine potential jurors selected for duty, eleven Protestants were selected by the court, the remainder, all Catholics, being excused. Hynes's solicitor, John Frost, wrote to Dublin newspaper *The Freeman's Journal*, complaining that:

> *The gentleman acting as Solicitor for the Crown, as it appears he had a legal right to do, in exercise of the powers in which he is vested by the laws, as at present constituted, ordered every gentleman of the Roman Catholic persuasion or of liberal principles in politics to stand aside ... Whilst the jury were being empanelled, I felt it my duty to challenge 11 out of the 49 who were called and answered, but what was my astonishment to find that the Crown ordered not less than twenty-six of those specially summoned jurors to stand aside, as if unfit to sit in judgement as jurors in the case, and particularly when I was constrained to observe that amongst the persons so included were also those who happened to be called who professed the religious or political principles to which I have before referred.*[143]

Francis Hynes was sentenced to death by the Court on extremely weak evidence, the capability of the jury under serious question. *The Freeman's Journal* reported that 'the circumstances of the case were in every way most lamentable'.[144] William O'Brien, an Irish Party Member of Parliament for Cork, had been staying in the Imperial Hotel in Dublin's O'Connell Street alongside the jury during the case. He experienced what he described as raucous and lurid behaviour on their part. Incensed by their behaviour, and seeking to illustrate the inappropriateness of their selection as jurors, he wrote a letter to *The Freeman's Journal*:

The Jury in the Hynes Murder case
'Imperial Hotel, Dublin August 13, 1882'

Dear Sir, – I think the public ought to be made aware of the following facts: The jury in the murder case of the Queen v. Hynes were last night 'locked up,' as it is termed for the night at the Imperial Hotel, where I also was staying. I was awakened from sleep shortly after midnight by the sounds of drunken chorus, succeeded after a time by scuffling, rushing, coarse laughter, and horseplay. Along the corridor on which my bedroom opens, a number of men, it seemed to me, were falling about the passage in a maudlin state of drunkenness, playing ribald jokes. I listened with patience for a considerable time, when the door of my bedroom was burst open, and a man whom I can identify (for he carried a candle unsteadily in his hand), staggered in, plainly under the influence of drink, hiccupping, 'Halloa, old fellow, all alone?' My answer was of a character that induced him to bolt out of my room, in as disordered a manner as he had entered. Having rung the bell I ascertained that these disorderly persons were jurors in the case of The Queen v. Hynes, and that the servants of the hotel had been endeavouring in vain to bring them to a sense of their misconduct ... I leave the public to judge the loathsomeness of such a scene upon the night when these men held the issues of

life and death for a young man in the flower of youth, when they had already
heard evidence which, if unrebutted, they must have known would send him
to a felon's grave. These facts I am ready to support on oath.[145]

O'Brien's letter was followed by an intervention from Edmund Grey, editor of *The Freeman's Journal*, a former Lord Mayor of Dublin, a prominent supporter of the Irish Party and a Member of Parliament. Justice Lawson looked unfavourably upon Grey's intervention, and the editor was imprisoned for three months in Richmond Gaol, Dublin, along with a fine of £500 for contempt of court.[146] Denouncing Grey's imprisonment, Parnell said that it was clear that liberty of speech no longer existed in Ireland. Judge Lawson increasingly became a significant target of the Invincibles.

On 12 November 1882, Lawson was invited to a legal dinner near the King's Inns, Dublin. Lawson readily accepted the invitation to dine with the great and the good of the Dublin legal profession. The Invincibles, however, had done their homework, and knew of Lawson's intended departure from his home in Fitzwilliam Square. Men were stationed outside his home to identify the judge to the assassins. On seeing him, they would give word of his approach and point him out. A tramcar was to be used to aid the escape of the assassin following the shock of Lawson's death, strategists predicting that people would gather around the body, enabling the assassin to leave the scene.

The plan was put in motion, with a team of Invincibles shadowing the Judge. Lawson and his son Henry made their way towards Kildare Street, passing Leinster House, around five o'clock in the evening,[147] accompanied by a protective force of four men, two in front and two behind on the other side of the road, all in plain clothes. These men were constables of the B division of the Metropolitan Police, accompanied by two Army pensioners. This guard had been placed on Lawson since the execution of Hynes, as he was seen as a likely target of Fenian grievance.

The Invincibles had chosen Patrick Delaney to carry out the operation, and evidence exists that Delaney, a petty criminal and perpetual drunkard, was inebriated. Continuing down Kildare Street, Lawson now passed the Kildare Street Club, filled with gentlemen speaking politics, drinking alcohol and smoking cigars. As the party crossed over to the corner of Leinster Street and Nassau Street, Patrick Delaney emerged. One of Lawson's entourage, Army pensioner Captain McDonnell, noticed Delaney slowly following them. Delaney staggered up to him, touched him on the shoulder and said, 'You already know me.' Delaney, drunk and confused, seemed to think that the entourage were Invincibles. Before McDonnell could do anything, Delaney was away, running ahead of Lawson and crossing the street:

> Turning back to meet the judge who was only a few yards off when McDonnell noticed the butt of a revolver sticking out of the inner breast pocket of his coat. In an instant he rushed at the man shouting 'here is a fellow with a revolver!' knocked him down and seized the revolver which he obtained after a violent effort. The revolver proved to be a remarkably large six-chambered one, fully loaded.[148]

Within minutes, Delaney was arrested. Judge Lawson, somewhat shaken, was shuffled off to the safety of the Kildare Street Club and increased police protection. Delaney was spirited away in a police car, summoned due to the increasing crowd – onlookers eager to investigate the scuffle could have given Delaney's companions ample opportunity to mount a getaway with the prisoner. Grabbed by the collar of his shirt, Delaney was brought to the nearby College Street Police Station. Here, he refused to cooperate with the police, giving his name as Mr Corrigan. He was, however, identified quite easily by police as Patrick Delaney, being known already to police on account of his petty criminality.

It is hard to understand why Delaney acted so bizarrely during the failed attempt on Judge Lawson. As mentioned above there is a strong possibility that Delaney, drunk and confused, believed that McDonnell was an Invincible, shadowing the infamous judge. However, it is also likely that Delaney had decided he could not go through with the assassination, and, rather than risk reprisal from the Invincibles, decided to make himself known to the Judge and his entourage. Patrick Tynan recalled:

> Delaney was influenced by nervous excitement; he literally got intoxicated with recklessness; he was no more master of his own actions than a man under the influence of alcohol ... it would be difficult to tell whether Delaney or the judge's guards were the most stupid: it is evident that Judge Lawson's life was little guarded by his five armed protectors, and Delaney, if he was sane, could easily have shot him at that time. Why they did not arrest this excitable madman on his first approaching them is incomprehensible ... Delaney's arrest was the pinhole by which the British hoped to brighten their vision.[149]

Mallon could not have been happier with the arrest of Patrick Delaney. He knew the failed assassin was connected to the Invincibles, and he knew he was also present in Phoenix Park on 6 May 1882, when Burke and Cavendish were assassinated. Furthermore, Mallon could easily connect the prisoner to Carey, whom he knew to have employed him as a carpenter in Peter Street. The problem, however, was

Patrick Delaney, petty criminal and drunkard.

finding solid evidence that would stand up in court, given that any connection between Delaney and the Invincibles was only circumstantial. Mallon understood the psychology of Delaney, recognising that he was a depressive, suffering from alcohol addiction; this would be a key asset in his effort to break Delaney and wring information from him. Ultimately, at the Dublin assizes on 3 January 1883, the prisoner received ten years' imprisonment for his attempt on Lawson.

Behind the scenes, events were progressing rapidly to a climax. The police investigation had learned of a prisoner, by the name of Ryan, detained in Walton Gaol, Liverpool, who had implicated himself in the Invincibles conspiracy. Ryan had spoken to a fellow prisoner, Joseph Dickson, who recognised him as an Irishman and asked about the situation in Ireland. The pair spoke of the Phoenix Park assassinations, Ryan wondering whether anyone had been arrested by the Irish police. Dickson responded in a despondent tone, saying that the assassins would probably never be seen. Ryan revealed to Dickson his knowledge that the assassins were Irish and living in Dublin, and that two of them were publicans, and others farmers from Waterford and Tipperary. He claimed that he could easily identify them to the police. Ryan described how Cavendish and Burke had been followed into the park by one of the assassins, who had been instructed to wave a handkerchief to the conspirators as a sign, the assassins making their way on a car out of the park. It was all nonsense – Ryan knew nothing about the conspiracy – but Dickson made his way to the police upon his release from gaol, telling them of Ryan's statement.

Given the aggrieved state of Dublin, and an upsurge in Fenian activity following the Phoenix Park assassinations, police detectives were actively working up known Fenian districts, haunts and sympathisers. This was an operation of immense scale, with ordinary police officers taken off their regular beats and duties to augment it. While the police operation was not showing much success, and had failed to deliver solid arrests and arms finds, police had noticed that Fenian gangs assembled frequently at Sackville Street, where they tended to loiter and frequent public houses. On 25 November, one of these gangs under observation assembled at Abbey Street, having left Sackville Street. Arriving at Abbey Street, police noticed a number of other men standing in a laneway at Bachelor's Walk, looking toward Abbey Street. Seeing the first group pass, they left the laneway and walked toward Capel Street, walking on the other side of the street to the first gang. The police had stumbled on two rival Fenian gangs:

> Six detectives named Eastwood, Beatty, Cox, Naughton, Williams, and Strafford were on duty in Middle Abbey Street near Sackville Street shortly before 11[pm] ... Their suspicions were aroused by the movements of a number of men who were going from one public house to another. Whether the detectives were actually watching these men or what the nature of their special duty was, does not as yet appear and accounts differ as to whether they were all together originally ... Two of the men turned round and one of them displayed a revolver. Detective Eastwood ordered Constable Cox to arrest him, whereupon the man fired on Cox and shot him through the head.[150]

The Fenian gangs had gathered to assassinate Joseph Poole, a Stephensite, who had been charged with threatening Dublin Fenians associated with the Supreme Council, and making raids on their homes for weapons. The affair had been arranged by Poole's rival Christy Devine. The Dublin directory of the Invincibles could not understand the Abbey Street affray, and opposed it as counterproductive, Patrick Tynan recalling:

> A certain circle of the IRB, without any instructions from the central authority, formed itself into a vigilance committee. Their purpose was to commence against the enemy ... they had scarcely more than organised when through some fatuity ... these brave but unthinking men began to look into their own ranks for a traitor.

They had no efficient leader, and the bonds of discipline hung upon them very lightly. They decided on suspecting one of their number of treason, and their first warlike attempt was to go out and search for him, in order to shoot him. As their actions were very open and very remarkable, they were followed from the rendezvous where they met at the corner of Abbey and Sackville Streets, by some armed detectives of the enemy.[151]

Two of the Police Constables shadowing the men, Eastwood and Cox, saw a revolver protruding from the jacket of Christopher Dooley, one of the men under observation. In Eastwood's narrative, he instructed Cox to disarm the man. Cox shouted at him to surrender his weapon, whereupon Dooley stepped off the path and fired at Cox, hitting him at the base of his skull and severing the spinal column. Dooley disputed this, and stated that Eastwood had fired upon him first.

What is not disputable, however, is that Eastwood opened fire at Dooley, wounding him, while another officer, Constable Strafford, fired repeatedly at Dooley, the shooter falling with Cox. There is significant evidence that shows, however, that it was Eastwood who mistakenly killed Cox, the constable falling toward Dooley at the same time as Eastwood shot at the Fenian. Some twelve shots were discharged between the dispersing Fenian gangs and the police, in what became known as the Battle of Abbey Street. The group began to disperse, but Eastwood was grabbed from behind by Christy Devine, who knocked him to the ground with a blow to his head. Devine was now tugged to the ground by a nearby soldier who had witnessed the attack and answered Eastwood's pleas for assistance. Quickly getting up, Eastwood pinned Devine to the ground. He felt in his jacket the presence of two revolvers near his chest. Four other men would be arrested: James Dowling, William Ryan, Thomas Devine and – once again, notably – Joseph Poole. They were taken for questioning to the nearby Store Street Station.

Cox and Dooley were taken by cart to the nearby Jervis Street Hospital, where Cox was pronounced dead. Dooley was in a critical condition, having received bullet wounds to the head, neck, arm and wrist. Within two days, tremendous crowds had descended on Jervis Street Hospital in support of Dooley. Such was the size of the crowd that a telegram was sent demanding immediate extra police reinforcements, while anxious staff had locked themselves into the building to stop a stampede seeking to rescue the injured man. The crowd continued to grow, as much through curiosity as support for the injured Fenian, yet with the arrival of armed police reinforcements from Store Street Station, it dispersed quickly.

That evening, a further incident was to take place. As the crowd dispersed from around Jervis Street, there was another attempted assassination in Dublin. The Invincibles were now targetting one Denis Field for assassination, in what one newspaper would assert would transcend the interest in the Middle Abbey Street affray.[152] Denis Field was a juror in the case of Michael Walsh, who was convicted of the killing of a police constable at Letterfrack, Galway. Field, alongside the jury foreman William Barrett, was seen passing notes to the Crown solicitor. That the jury consisted entirely of loyal citizens, with those of a Catholic persuasion turned away, tended to indicate foul play. The notes, however, were innocuous.

Two groups of Invincibles had been chosen to carry out the assassinations, as a message to other packed juries. Mullet would lead the first party, waiting for William Barrett at Westland Row in Dublin, but the juror didn't show up as expected. At the other end of the city, at Frederick Street, was another Invincible party, consisting of Joseph Brady, Timothy Kelly, Daniel Curley and Laurence Hanlon, with Kavanagh again waiting on his cab, ready to speed the assassins away.

Followed from his stationer's shop at Westmoreland Street, as Field approached his home at 14 North Frederick Street in broad daylight, Laurence Hanlon gave the signal to act, placing his handkerchief over his mouth. On sight of this, four men immediately surrounded Field. Brady grabbed the juror by the shoulder, again shouting, 'You villain!' as he had done with Burke. Flinging him against nearby railings, he attacked him with a sword cane. Kelly stabbed him three times, as Field recalled:

> *I fell on the broad of my back, and when down a prod was made at my heart, which I warded off with my left arm, which was pierced right through, by whatever instrument the man had in his hand which appeared to me to be a sword cane, as I grasped it when it was withdrawn from my arm. The next stab was made at my right side, which I warded off with an umbrella. I received from that stab a slight wound on the right side, and my finger was a little cut. The next stab penetrated my under jaw, cutting the gum and tongue. The next stab went right through my left cheek.*[153]

Pretending to be dead, watched by onlookers, Field gave up struggling, 'thinking it was all up'.[154] The assassins, believing him dead, boarded Kavanagh's car. Kelly dropped his hat, which was left on the sidewalk, a bystander eventually taking it.

> *A car was standing near an Archway, with another man on it besides the driver. Mounting the car with desperate celerity the words were heard, 'drive away for Heavens sake, as fast as you can,' and the car dashed off at a furious pace.*[155]

Eyewitnesses furiously chased after Kavanagh's car, hoping to identify the men. They followed the car along Hardwicke Street, and into Dorset Street, but lost it at nearby Synnott Place.

Lying on the ground paralysed, Field had not been attended to by any passers by. He managed to rise, and stumbled to his home. He weakly knocked on the door, losing much blood, and was greeted by his horrified maidservant:

[Field's] face was covered with blood, and it streamed over his clothes from his throat and face. Reaching the hall he sank into a chair and almost lost consciousness. He was assisted to his bedroom and there the blood was washed from his face, and a messenger for medical aid was despatched.[156]

Field was attended to by Dr Henry Kennedy, assisted by Doctor Wyse and Surgeon Kelly, living at nearby Rutland Square. Dr Kennedy judged that Field was extraordinarily lucky to be alive, noting multiple wounds, including two in the back near to his spinal cord, a punctured left lung, and injuries to his lower jaw, cheek and tongue.

According to *The London Times*, the attempted assassination of Field was an act of intimidation directed against the jury system in Ireland.[157] It certainly did serve to frighten potential jurors relative to nationalist cases. The attack on Field left the legal system thoroughly shaken, with subsequent rumour generating a climate of fear among the Dublin Castle administration. Tynan noted: 'it had been arranged for moral effect, to strike down both jurymen simultaneously. The enemy was alarmed; another panic took place this time; it extended to the bench and the rebel caste from which this class of juryman was selected.'[158] Such was the shock in Dublin Castle at the audacious attack that the Privy Council met that evening, resolving:

Whereas Mr Denis Field of Westmorland Street was, in this city on the 27 November, about 6 o'clock in North Frederick Street in this city feloniously and maliciously stabbed and wounded by some person, or persons, who immediately afterwards got on an outside car which was waiting in Hardwicke Street and drove off rapidly through Hardwicke place; now we John Poyntz, Earl Spencer, Lord Lieutenant General and Governor General of Ireland, for the better apprehending and bringing to Justice the offenders and other accomplices, hereby offer a reward of £5,000 to any person or persons, who within three months of the date hereof, shall give information as will lead to the conviction of the said

offenders or their accomplices, or any of them, and a further reward of £500 for
such private information as shall within the said period lead to the same result,
and ensure that the name or names of any person or persons who may become
entitled to the said reward for private information shall not be disclosed or
made public, and that the said reward shall be paid in any manner which such
person shall desire. Any person having information to give may communicate
it to the Assistant Undersecretary for Police and Crime, Dublin Castle, the
Superintendent of the Detective Department of the Dublin Metropolitan
Police, Dublin Castle, or to any other Government official in Great Britain or
Ireland.
Given at Dublin Castle on the 28ᵗʰ Day of November 1882.

Dublin was increasingly becoming a dangerous place for the political elite and those who cooperated with them. This was now evidenced by the extension of a curfew in Dublin city, imposed by the Privy Council at Dublin Castle under the Crimes Act.[159] *The New York Times* would capture the pervading sense of fear, writing:

In a time of trouble like the present there is always observable a more or less
mysterious appearance of comfortably dressed idle men who do no work, and
yet do not seem in want of money. These men are to be seen lounging about
in an apparently purposeless manner, smoking pipes in the sun, at the public
house corner, or drinking pints of porter at the counters. What are these idle
comfortably dressed men doing? Where does the money come from which
enables them to smoke pipes in the sun all day long, and to 'stand treats' to their
acquaintances? What are they planning when they are not smoking or 'standing
treats?' Those are questions upon which the police have their own opinions.
We have this class of men among us now in great force, and we feel that their
presence is not good for the city.[160]

5

CRACKS IN THE CONSPIRACY

Having failed to break the Invincibles conspiracy by means of imprisonment, surveillance and identity parades, the State sorely required a new means of counter-attack. To this end, it increasingly looked to the powers afforded the Dublin Castle administration through the 1882 Coercion Act. Upon extensive examination of the Act, it was noted that it provided for the establishment of what would become known as the Star Chamber inquiry. Section sixteen of the Coercion Act empowered a magistrate to summon a suspected individual for interrogation under oath, without legal representation, each witness compelled to give evidence in any subsequent trial, facing imprisonment if they refused to do so.[161]

Police Magistrate John Adye Curran was selected to head up the inquiry, working alongside Mallon. Curran understood his brief as being to get detailed information that was not circumstantial and would stand up in a court of law.[162]

A room was provided for Curran within the confines of the Lower Castle Yard in Dublin Castle. Ironically, it overlooked Wrenn's public house, a favoured haunt of the Invincibles. On his first day, Curran met Joseph Smith, who had been in Phoenix Park on 6 May to identify Burke as he entered the Parkgate entrance. At the time, Curran had no suspicion of Smith's involvement in the conspiracy, but he recalled of that first meeting:

> On my first entry into the room, I found there a man from the Board of Works nailing down a carpet for my use. On his departure, Mr Boulger, whom I had brought with me from the police courts, and whom I found to be a most efficient officer, asked me if I had remarked the wicked scowl which the man laying the carpet had given me.[163]

Curran was well briefed on the particulars of the Invincibles conspiracy and, through Mallon, knew the names of the men involved. Within a couple of days, he saw Field, and made a connection with the Phoenix Park assassinations on the basis of one of the assassins referring to Field as a villain. Having come to this conclusion, Curran requested that Spencer extend his inquiry into the Phoenix Park assassinations, devoting greater resources and time, and drawing upon all the notes of the inquiry made by Mallon and the DMP into the May assassinations. Spencer agreed, lamenting that he had long lost hope of the assassins ever being captured.

Through his inquiries, Curran met a Mary Brophy, a servant girl who lived at North Frederick Street. Brophy recalled seeing the cab driver, and identified him as Kavanagh, an identification that was confirmed by a Michael Farrell of Hardwicke Place. A further lead came from Alice Carroll, who could identify Brady, Kelly and again Kavanagh, stating that Brady had stabbed Field repeatedly. The servant girl Mary Brophy told Curran:

I heard cries of murder and I ran up to the hall door to see what was the matter.
When I came to the door I saw the carman in the drivers seat of the car … there
were two young men sitting on the side of the car opposite me. I saw another
young man run round the corner and put something black under the cushion of
the car next to me, and he then sat down on the cushion. This man gave a jerk
turning round to sit on the cushion and his hat fell off. This man then called out
to the driver to drive on fast.[164]

In the course of interviewing several witnesses, the same names kept
cropping up, and each one was connected to James Carey. The Magistrate
concluded:

Gradually I formed a suspicion as to the parties responsible, if not actually
implicated; and at the same time I came to the conclusion that they were
recruited from the Fenian body. My conclusion proved to be absolutely correct;
I came afterwards to know that the Invincibles as they styled themselves, were
of necessity all Fenians who had formed themselves into an inner circle. They
became so to speak, an excrescence upon the original body, and were at the time
of which, I write altogether outside of its rules and objectives.[165]

With this in mind, Curran now called upon all of the suspects, and 'day
after day Curran and Mallon harassed the Dublin revolutionary under-
world and in particular the Invincibles, interrogating some individuals
repeatedly. Sometimes just one question was asked and the victim released,
at other times the questions lasted a whole day …'[166] Tighe Hopkins
recalled: 'The men were charged with nothing, but their brains were picked
and sifted and the catechism was severe enough to shake the hearts of the
guilty ones.'[167] With each interrogation before the Star Chamber inquiry,
Curran could boast:

I had before me nearly all the Invincibles. They of course denied everything. Nevertheless I was able to extract a little of the truth from each of them. When it came to the point of calling before me those whom I suspected of being the actual murderers and those in command of the body ... In plain words I was engaged in fixing the rope around their necks.[168]

While this was certainly the case, Curran furthermore understood that the purpose of the Invincibles was to assassinate senior figures in the British administration in Ireland. As a man charged with enquiring into their affairs, he was undoubtedly a key target for assassination, a fact illustrated by an increase in security about his person, family and home. Curran later admitted that, when interviewing suspects in Dublin Castle, he kept a gun in his pocket and a finger on the trigger.

On 14 December, Joe Brady was arrested during his working day, and questioned before Curran. The stonecutter remained defiant, denying all knowledge of the charges laid before him. An extremely difficult prisoner from Curran and Mallon's point of view, Brady answered every question with, 'I disremember.' He was eventually released from custody. Recalling Brady's inquisition to his biographer, F.M. Bussy, Mallon said:

Brady was examined. Joe was stolid and firm as a rock in his disremembrance. 'I disremember,' was the burden of his lay throughout, and the measure of his virtuous indignation at being even so much as suspected was almost convincing. Not only were his protests of innocence loud and firm, but he invested them with verisimilitude by enlarging upon the loss of reputation involved in the mere suggestion of suspicion. Indeed he vehemently demanded compensation for his loss of time.[169]

Despite his protestations, the Star Chamber inquiry unnerved Brady, who increasingly fell into the trap of believing that Mallon and Curran knew more than they actually did. It has been stated that following questioning, he made for a Dublin pub, meeting several Invincibles:

> *Mallon loved to describe the scene in the public house in Princes Street, facing the GPO ... when Joe Brady, the Invincible who had struck the first terrible blow that day in the Phoenix Park, came back from the Castle where he had had his third grilling at the hands of Mallon and Judge Adye-Curran. He was convinced that it was 'all up with him.' Mallon had the rope around his neck for certain, and the only way he saw out of the dilemma was to remove Mallon ...*[170]

Brady was dissuaded from this course by Patrick Egan, who despite his republicanism, remained a personal friend of Mallon's.

Following Brady came Daniel Curley, a known Fenian and associate of Brady's. Like Brady, Curley was deliberately difficult, and answered every question regarding his activities and whereabouts on 6 May 1882 with, 'I disremember.'[171]

Curran and Mallon found a much better prisoner in Robert Farrell. Farrell, another Invincible, although not in Phoenix Park that day, was questioned on his relationship with Fenianism and the May assassinations. Like Brady, he was recalcitrant and denied everything. Asked about his relationship with Joseph Brady, he claimed to have never heard of him, and a similar response was elicited when questioned about his relationship with Daniel Curley. Adye Curran pressed him under oath on his membership of Daniel Curley's Fenian circle:

> *Adye Curran: It is suggested by some people whom you regard as friends that there is a secret society in Dublin, that a man whose name I have mentioned to you [Curley] was the Head-Centre and you his Sub-Centre. You won't swear that you don't believe there is nothing secret going on there?*
>
> *Farrell: I swear that I have never been attached to any secret society and that the parties who told that of me are belying me, no matter who they are.*[172]

Pressing Farrell as to his knowledge of the attack on Field, and of the Battle of Abbey Street, the interviewee claimed to have been drunk on both occasions, alcohol affecting his memory. Regarding the Battle of Abbey Street, he said:

> *I was screwed that night. I must convey to you I am a Catholic myself, and unfortunately I got so tight on that night, which is very much against the character of any man, I slept on the following morning* [Sunday] *until one o'clock. The time I heard of it was something about half past one or two.*[173]

Farrell had shown Mallon and Adye Curran a fatal weakness, one that they would play upon – his Catholicism. He had inadvertently admitted that he had missed mass on Sunday, 26 November 1883, and that it weighed on his mind. Farrell regularly attended mass, and Mallon now decided to play on Farrell's Catholicism. Following him to church, he arrested him after he had received the Eucharist, bringing him to Curran on a Sunday morning. Mallon played heavily on Farrell's taking of the Eucharist before the meeting, drawing on 'the sacrament that had rested upon his tongue',[174] and how he believed Farrell had been involved with the blood drawn in Phoenix Park. Mallon and Curran were continuing their impudent strategy of allowing Invincibles, such as Farrell, to believe they knew more than they actually did, hoping to:

> *Induce an informer to come forward – to suggest by the subtlety of the questioning and the amplitude of the details at his command that he was completely advised as to the constitution and the methods and movements of the Invincibles. It was by this means that he hoped to impress upon some one of the more highly placed of the Invincibles that the game was up – that there was some body 'peaching' – that the safest course was to vomit the whole wicked business and become a Government pensioner under an assumed name rather than risk the penalties of a rope or prolonged imprisonment.*[175]

Curran, with Mallon's help, managed to trick Farrell into believing that he knew the in-depth details of the Invincible conspiracy, leading the prisoner to conclude that someone had spoken, implicating him in the conspiracy. Rattled, Farrell was escorted out of the Castle to dwell on what he had heard. By 3 January 1883, Robert Farrell offered to give evidence against the conspiracy, now eager to 'break this gang up':[176]

> *He went to inspector Kavanagh and told him from his interview with myself and Mr Mallon, he was sure that someone had turned traitor and had given us information which had led to my questions. He further said that he did not intend to be left in when others were turning informers, and then made a statement which he signed, giving full details of the conspiracy and the name of those engaged from time to time in carrying its objects.[177]*

Farrell told Kavanagh all he knew, describing the Invincibles as an assassination club and listing their hierarchy as James Carey, Daniel Curley, Joseph Brady and James Mullet.[178] Farrell traced his own involvement in

Fenianism to 1876, and his membership of a Dublin circle of the IRB, presided over by Dan Curley. Farrell stated that Curley had recruited him to an inner circle within Fenianism, the purpose of which was to assassinate Government officials on the island of Ireland, and named Joseph Brady and Timothy Kelly as fellow members of this inner circle. He named brothers

Robert Farrell, the first Invincible to crack under questioning.

Dan and Patrick Delaney as Invincibles, and told of the latter having led the failed attempt on Judge Lawson's life.

Importantly, Farrell also recounted the Invincibles plot against Forster, and how they had sought to assassinate him at Queen's Bridge, en route in his carriage from Phoenix Park to Dublin Castle. They had waited for him at the quays, near John Street. The car was to be stopped by waiting Invincibles upon the signal of a tailor named Henry Rowles. Joseph Brady and Timothy Kelly were waiting, planning to smash open his carriage door and assassinate the Chief Secretary with knives. However, Carey, who was to identify Forster's carriage to the assassins, mistook the cab, and the Chief Secretary unwittingly escaped a violent death.[179]

Despite his earlier claim to have been exceedingly drunk on the night of the attempted assassination of Denis Field, Farrell now recalled, to the detectives' surprise, a deeper plot, to assassinate William Barrett alongside Field:

> On the evening of the attack on Mr Fields, Mr W.G. Barrett, wine merchant, Westland Row, was also to have been murdered by a man named Molloy, Peter Street, a clerk who is about twenty three years of age, Daniel Curley, Joseph Mullet, [Michael] Fagan, a smith in Fagan's, Great Brunswick Street ... Joe Hanlon and George Smith, a bricklayer, Ringsend ... Mr Barrett was to be murdered while passing from his office, in Westland Row to the railway station as it was known when he left to go home. The way it was to be done is this: Joe Mullet was to hand [Barrett] a letter and while taking it, Mullet was then to seize him by the hands and Molloy was to do his work. On that evening, the 27th November 1882, Joe Mullet summoned a meeting, to be at Kennedy's public-house, Duke Street, at four o'clock. I was there, so was Molloy, Larry Hanlon ... Joe Mullet and others. There were knives or daggers there. I did not see them, but Molloy told Mullet that there was a name on his which he got taken off. Mullet checked Molloy for speaking so. We then went, I and Hanlon,

from Kennedy's bar by way of Grafton Street, to corner of Great Brunswick
Street, where we met Tim Kelly. Kelly and Hanlon then left me and went to
Westmorland Street, and I went to Westland Row where I met Dan Curley.
He asked me had I a revolver. I said not. He said he had two and that he'd
give me one. We then went to Merrion Street, to the Merrion Hall where
he gave me the revolver. I asked him what I was to do with it, and what
did he mean? He said, 'Joe will tell you.' We then went back to Westland
Row, where we met Joe Mullet and Molloy ... Mullet said to Molloy when
opposite Hunters in Westland Row, 'Here, Molloy, put Barrett on the letter
and I will hand it to him, and I will then grasp his hands and then do you
your work.[180]

Additionally, Farrell identified Brady, Kelly, Joseph Hanlon and Myles Kavanagh as implicated in the attempted assassination of Denis Field.

Having taken Farrell's statement, Inspector Kavanagh passed his informant to Inspector Mallon. Farrell told Mallon that, while he was willing to co-operate, he could not go to the Castle to give further information to Curran, as other Invincibles were watching who had been summoned to the Castle, and how many times, to sniff out possible informers. A meeting was therefore arranged at Curran's home in Terenure, the prisoner being shuffled into the grounds in heavy darkness. In Curran's living room, Farrell swore to the accuracy of his statement, testifying on the organisation of his Dublin Fenian circle and his recruitment to the Invincibles. Curran was exceedingly interested in this last point, and Farrell implicated several men in conspiracy:

Daniel Curley told me in his own house in Mount Street, about eighteen
months ago, that there should be an inner or confidential circle founded, to
consist of the cream of the organisation. Daniel Curley told me it was not
necessary for any man, already a member, to be resworn. I first thoroughly

understood that this inner circle was to carry out assassinations when Daniel
Curley directed me to be at the Quays at Stapleton's public house at Ellis
Quay, and to endeavour and seize and stop the Chief Secretary's horse as the
carriage was passing to the Castle ... I saw Henry Rowles, Daniel Curley,
Peter Doyle ... Joseph Brady, John Dwyer, Thomas Dwyer, Timothy Kelly,
William Moroney ... Daniel Curley told me that if I stopped the horse Tim
and Joe would do their work.[181]

Farrell's evidence was of great interest to the investigation, yet importantly he was not in Phoenix Park at the time of the assassinations of Cavendish and Burke, and he was nowhere near Denis Field. All he could offer regarding the May assassinations was a meeting with Joe Brady at Wrenn's tavern opposite the Castle, on 6 May 1882. Brady inquired when he would be available that evening, as something needed to be done. What this was, Brady did not say.[182] Farrell could not get off work, and he was dismissed by Brady. The inference was clear, though – that Brady was a principal actor in the Phoenix Park assassinations.

Curran listened as Farrell related what he knew of the previously unknown attempt on Barrett, stating that he had been instructed by Joe Mullet to meet him at Duke Street on that day. At Duke Street, he was instructed to make for Westmoreland Street, with Laurence Hanlon. From there, he went to Brunswick Street, where he met Daniel Curley. With Curley, he then met Joseph Hanlon, Michael Fagan, Joe Mullet and George Smith.

Mullet stated that if the assassination squad was interrupted by police, Farrell was to open fire, as a struggle would take place. Curley commented, 'It will be a good job if we can finish both tonight,'[183] clearly meaning Barrett, and the other team waiting on Field across the city.

Farrell finally came to the attempted assassination of Judge Lawson. He testified to meeting would-be assassin Patrick Delaney in a Dublin pub, recalling:

I met Pat Delaney at Kevin Street at about half past three or four o'clock, and had a drink in Corrigan's public house ... Delaney asked me if I had heard of anything strange lately, I said not, and he replied I would hear of something soon, he looked wild and mad like. I heard of the attempt on Judge Lawson, and the arrest of Delaney next day.[184]

Farrell's evidence was clear and damning – an assassination society operating within Fenianism existed as suspected, now confirmed by evidence from a member of its circle.

With this evidence in hand, Curran went to see Edward George Jenkinson, to demand the immediate arrest and detention of the suspects. The Assistant Undersecretary for Police and Crime was away, however. He next presented his evidence to the Attorney General. Curran was told that his evidence, while interesting, was inadequate, but it was agreed that the time had come to arrest the Invincibles. Jenkinson disagreed, however, favouring a maturation of the investigation, to gain greater more detailed information and additional arrests. Curran was not prepared to give up, and next he went to the Viceroy, John Poyntz Spencer, over the heads of the Dublin bureaucracy. This time Curran received satisfaction, as the Viceroy authorised immediate action against the Invincibles:

Upon consideration of the contents of Farrell's disposition, and of the various facts within my knowledge ... I came to the conclusion that as the matter stood no Government official, nor Judge, nor indeed anyone in authority, was safe from assassination when these men were at large ... Lord Spencer's orders were that if I thought I had a good case I was to act on my own discretion. I did act on my own discretion ... I signed warrants for the arrest of every man whom I knew to be an Invincible in Dublin.[185]

On the night of 12 January 1883, Dublin Metropolitan Police and G-men raided the homes of suspected Invincibles. Initially, seventeen Invincibles were arrested, and in the following days, this number grew to twenty-six. Those arrested included James Carey, Joseph Mullet, Joseph Brady, Thomas Martin, Robert Farrell, Joseph Smith, Timothy Kelly, William Moroney, Edward McCaffrey, Henry Rowles, James Mullet, James Fitzharris, Joseph Hanlon, Daniel Curley, John Dwyer, Laurence Hanlon, Peter Doyle, Myles Kavanagh, Peter Carey, Patrick Whelan, George Smith, Edward O'Brien, Michael Fagan and Thomas Caffrey, along with the already imprisoned Patrick Delaney. James Carey was indignant and threatened to sue John Adye Curran for slander and false imprisonment.[186] *The Freeman's Journal* reported on 13 January:

> *The atmosphere of the city was thick with rumours asserting that the police authorities intended in the course of the night or early morning to make raids simultaneously in various parts of the city ... it was observed about midnight that police on the usual beats were few and far between, and this fact of course lent substance to the rumour 'that something on a grand scale was about being executed ... everything was suspicious and surrounded with unusual mystery and anti publication precautions ... Dame Street was occupied for a considerable time by an unusually large number of marines and ordinary constables ...*[187]

On Saturday, 20 January, twenty-one prisoners were taken from Richmond Gaol to Green Street Courthouse, Dublin. A crowd gathered outside, but they were kept away from the courthouse by a large cordon of soldiers and police.[188] The twenty-one were charged, despite a serious lack of real evidence, with plotting to assassinate Government officials. The Invincibles could have looked on happily, believing that the charges against them would be thrown out of court. There was, however, in the dock, the ominous

Police struggling to maintain public order outside Green Street Courthouse as the trials begin.

empty seat of Robert Farrell.[189] All knew that this could only mean one thing – Farrell had turned Queen's evidence. On appearing in the witness box to testify against his former comrades,

> *There was an expression of suppressed rage that crossed the prisoners' faces when they observed him calmly enter the box to be sworn … Once or twice the bitterness of the prisoners towards the witnesses was manifested … Brady with a degree of determination that may be easily imagined exclaimed 'you are a liar!' James Mullet, when identified declared the witness to be a 'liar and a scoundrel.'*[190]

In the witness box, Farrell repeated what he had said to Curran, detailing what he knew of the conspiracy and the various assassination attempts, and saying he had received his orders from Curley. He testified on his past activities as a Fenian, and recounted hearsay regarding the attack on Field.[191]

Throughout his evidence, which was by no means conclusive or definitive, the Invincibles jeered, booed and laughed loudly.

On 27 January, the prisoners were moved to Kilmainham Gaol, in the Dublin countryside. The court case would be moved to the nearby Kilmainham Courthouse, avoiding the need for strong security against large crowds, and reducing the possibility of a rescue attempt. On 3 February, the trial began of eight of the prisoners, under a Mr Keys and a Mr Woodlock. To the charge of killing Burke and Cavendish on 6 May 1882, Joe Brady and Edward O'Brien made an audible laugh, much to the chagrin of the magistrates. The defendants all denied any involvement, and refused to recognise the legitimacy of the Court.

The prosecution unveiled their star witness, William Lamie. Lamie told nothing of any relevance to those attending the Kilmainham Courthouse proceedings. While Farrell's evidence was merely circumstantial, Lamie's, in legal terms, was worthless. When challenged, he could not give definitive dates, and seemed to be simply name-dropping leading Fenians and Invincibles. Lamie was, in fact, being used as a means to secure the execution of his brother-in-law Joseph Poole, for the assassination of the Fenian informer John Kenny, and much of his narrative was directed to Poole. This was seriously inappropriate, given that Poole was not present at this trial. Lamie did, however, tie Poole to Curley, Brady and Mullet:

> He attended meetings of the secret brotherhood in [Dublin] at various places, amongst them at Cuffe Lane, where his brother in law, Joe Poole occupied the position of [Centre] ... In Cuffe Lane many meetings were held. Daniel Curley attended them. Afterwards meetings took place in Peter Street, and there together with Poole he met Brady and Moroney ... witness recollected the murder of Kenny in Seville Place. It was after this murder [he] was arrested, and [Lamie] then became centre. He attended a meeting also held in the house 51 York Street. It was a centre council meeting ... five persons were present including Michael Fagan [and] Joseph Mullet.[192]

None of this was damning evidence, and its irrelevance was not lost on the Court or the media. The prosecution had certainly proven that the prisoners were connected to Fenianism, but it had not proven a connection to the Phoenix Park assassinations.[193]

The prosecution produced John Fitzsimons, who regaled the courtroom with his discovery of the surgical knives in the loft of Carey's house in South Cumberland Street. A number of other witnesses clearly identified Brady and McCaffrey as having been in Phoenix Park on the day of the killings, but again this was circumstantial – there were multiple reasons for anyone to be in the park.

Meanwhile, desperate to break the Invincibles conspiracy, John Mallon sought to sow seeds of doubt in the minds of the prisoners, one chronicler recalling:

> The object was to bring the prisoners to implicate one another, and their fears and their suspicions of treachery were most cunningly played upon. They were exercised in a small yard apart, and meetings were arranged between particular comrades, in circumstances, which allowed their talk to be overheard. A possible witness against them, who was supposed to be in safe hiding across the Channel, was pushed for a moment through the door of the exercise yard, and as suddenly withdrawn. By word and suggestion they were made to feel that they had been betrayed on every side, and above all, that the chief traitors were of their own number. Amongst the six-and-twenty who had been placed in the dock not all were worth prosecuting, but it was fixedly resolved to bring the ringleaders to justice, and, if possible, to send the actual murderers to the gallows upon the testimony of their own Companions.[194]

With this in mind, Mallon had increasingly marked Myles Kavanagh. Kavanagh, the cab driver, hated Skin the Goat, and knew that Skin the Goat and Mallon were quite intimate, Skin the Goat having driven for

Trials begin of 'The Murder League in Dublin', from newspaper *The Graphic*, 3 February 1883.

Mallon previously. John Mallon was well aware of this, and worked it to his favour. Kavanagh, alone, would look on with dread in the Kilmainham exercise yard, as Mallon showed little interest in him, and spoke to Skin the Goat in the far distance. Patrick Tynan recalled a further story:

> [Mallon] *knew that there was a personal difference between the car-drivers ... a matter of long standing dispute. One morning they were both brought from their cells, and taken to the prison courtyard. Kavanagh's outside car was there, and Mallon told him to get up on the box and drive around the yard ... During the time Kavanagh was driving around Mallon engaged* [Skin the Goat] *in conversation. Mallon purposely assumed an air of great mystery and*

THE INVINCIBLES

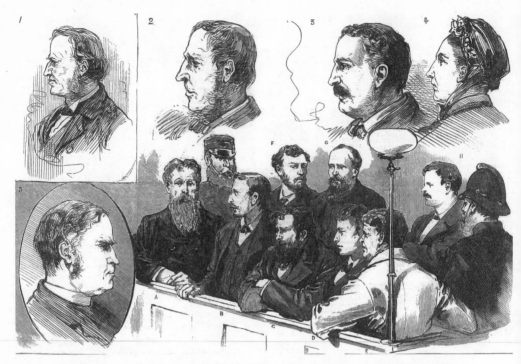

The prisoners in the dock at Kilmainham Courthouse, along with 1. John
Fitzsimons, who found the knives; 2. George Godden, the park ranger
who witnessed the getaway; 3. and 4. Stephen and Sarah Hands; and 5. Dr
Webb QC, senior counsel for the defense. *The Graphic*, 10 February 1883.

earnestness while talking and listening to [Skin the Goat's] *replies, the subject
they were discussing having no reference to politics … He ordered Kavanagh
down, and told Fitzharris to take his seat upon the car and drive round. With
a look of triumph on his face, Mallon commenced taking notes of the imaginary
information, furtively watching the effect on Kavanagh, to whom he did not
speak …* [Mallon] *used* [Skin the Goat] *as a trap to weaken Kavanagh and
to induce him to become Crown witness.*[195]

Mallon had ordered that Kavanagh and Peter Carey were to be put together.
Both men were taken to the infirmary, where they were to be seen by Dr
William Carte, the Gaol physician. They were left alone in a room together:

There was some oak panelling in the passage outside Dr Carte's door, and a small section of this was removed, upon the instructions of [Mallon], *and replaced by a sheet of perforated zinc. It had all the appearance of an ordinary scheme of ventilation. Mallon took up a position on the hidden side of the panelling and metaphorically glued his ear to the perforated zinc. What happened was exactly what he had speculated for.*[196]

Alone, Kavanagh and Carey spoke of the Phoenix Park assassinations, describing the event and naming those involved, including Kavanagh's part in driving Brady, Kelly, Delaney and Caffrey out of the park afterwards. Mallon was hiding behind a vent the whole time, listening and taking notes. He noted with interest that Kavanagh and Carey were both willing to turn informer against the remaining Invincibles.

Using what he learned from this, Mallon convinced Kavanagh that he knew everything about the conspiracy, and that Skin the Goat had told him everything he needed to know, making Kavanagh's execution inevitable. The cab driver was broken. Mallon feigned disinterest in his desire to turn approver, telling him that he knew enough already, and leaving him to stew. Returning later, Mallon appeared to have a change of heart and listened intently to what Kavanagh had to say. Mallon took Kavanagh on a cab, retracing the route that the cab driver had taken with the Invincibles following the assassinations:

Police Inspector Smith showing the knives found in the loft of Carey's house.

Early one morning after Kavanagh had turned Queen's evidence, Mallon
took the informer out of prison, put him in a trap and drove him over the
whole route he had taken on the day of [the assassinations] ... *The object of*
this was to test him as thoroughly as possible, to piece his statement together in
sequential order, and to gather material for picking up whatever tiny threads of
corroboration there might be available.[197]

From Kavanagh, Mallon now had definitive evidence of the involvement of
the prisoners in the assassinations. Kavanagh's freedom lay on one precon-
dition – he had to give evidence for the prosecution. On 10 February 1883,
Myles Kavanagh took to the witness stand in Kilmainham Courthouse:

Never did the mention of a single name cause greater emotion than the call
of the first witness – Michael Kavanagh. A murmur of sensation rose in
the Court, and the prisoners shared in the excitement. The utterance of the
unexpected name changed their whole demeanour. Whispered words were passed
from one ear to the other. Last week Kavanagh was in the dock; now under the
protection of the Crown, he appeared as an informer.[198]

Kavanagh testified that he had been sworn into the Invincibles by Tim Kelly,
and had been allotted the task of 'driving the boys' from any operation they
undertook.[199] He said that, along with Patrick Delaney, he had driven Kelly
and Brady to the Viceregal procession on Dame Street on 6 May 1882. Here
they had identified John Poyntz Spencer, the new Viceroy. Later that evening, Kavanagh brought Brady and Kelly, with two others, to the scene of the
assassinations, entering through the Islandbridge gate and making their way
to the George statue, where the men got off his car.

Kavanagh's evidence placed Carey and Smith in the park, waiting by the
roadside prior to the assassinations. He also recalled the presence of Joseph
Hanlon, and remembered Brady mentioning Skin the Goat, and noted his

arrival in the Phoenix Park in preparation for the assassinations. Kavanagh then detailed the route he had taken, to get the assassins away at speed from the scene of Cavendish and Burke's deaths.

If this was not enough to infuriate the Invincibles watching and listening in the dock, Kavanagh now revealed the details of the botched Field assassination, implicating Brady, Kelly, Daniel Delaney and Joseph Hanlon in the plot. The appearance of the cab driver in the dock was a major breakthrough in the prosecution case against the Invincibles, as one newspaper noted:

> With the production of the evidence of Kavanagh, it is believed that the Crown authorities have played their best card and the testimony to be received at the subsequent hearings of the Phoenix Park murders and the Frederick Street inquiries will be all utilised in collaboration of the testimony of Kavanagh and the other approvers.[200]

Efforts to crack more of the prisoners continued, and the next to provide evidence was Joe Smith, the man who had identified Burke in Phoenix Park to James Carey. Smith confirmed much of Kavanagh's testimony, implicating Skin the Goat and Carey.

The noose was tightening around the Invincibles' necks; all that was now needed was a leading figure in the conspiracy. Mallon strongly desired to break one of the main Invincibles languishing in the gaol – either Curley, Brady, Carey or Kelly. Among these prisoners, word was spread that each of the others was singing like a bird. None would cooperate, but the stress weighed heavily on their minds. Separated and isolated within the prison complex, each increasingly wondered if the others were speaking to Mallon. Mallon recognised that Carey was growing ever more nervous as to his fate, and increasingly led Carey to believe that Dan Curley had begun to inform on the Town Councillor:

It was supposed that Carey was willing, if not eager from the outset to be the
Judas of the party, but the facts were otherwise ... He had inside him a kind of
stubborn pride and all the Irishman's instinctive horror of the role of informer.
He refused to speak until he felt the rope around his throat ...[201]

Mallon worked on consolidating this lie of Curley's betrayal by using Carey's wife, Maggie. Meeting her outside the prison, he led her to believe that Curley was revealing all he knew about her husband's activities within the conspiracy. The policeman now allowed correspondence between Mrs Carey and her husband, knowing Maggie Carey would stress to the prisoner the necessity of speaking up before Dan Curley saw to his execution.

As he languished in his bare prison cell, psychological warfare was perpetrated against Carey. He was disturbed by the noise of footsteps creeping along the floor, 'between the lights, before the sun has completely set and a tiny while prior to the actual necessity for artificial illumination.'[202] The grill covering the spy hole in his cell door was left open. Looking out, Carey could see policemen with papers under their arms walking into the cell opposite. John Mallon following shortly afterwards, then Crown solicitor George Bolton, then prison guards carrying a small desk and paper under their arms.

Stewing in his cell, Carey wondered who was talking. Thinking of Farrell and Kavanagh, he was convinced someone had turned approver. Later, he was led to believe that Curley was in that cell, and Mallon taunted Carey on his imminent demise courtesy of his confederate:

... at first he was indignant ... for along with his lifetimes detestation of an
informer he dreaded the doom that would always remain suspended over him as
chief traitor to his comrades; but the belief planted in his weak mind, that it was
a race between Curley and himself decided the issue.[203]

Carey finally cracked, and offered to tell all.

... the great campaign of history making has fizzled miserably out. Ambition and glory attaching to the stealthy removal of political opponents and the law-givers has surrendered to a craving for self-effacement and the repudiation of heroics. Nemesis is rampant and lives must be sacrificed to her.[204]

Mallon feigned disinterest – what Carey had told him was all well-known, he said, and he already had enough evidence from Curley. He left Carey in his cell, his mind racing as to his demise and Curley's betrayal.

This, of course, was all nonsense. Curley had refused to give any information to Mallon: 'those who knew him would as soon believe that Robert Emmet offered to turn informer, as Daniel Curley ... he had always been a true, honest fearless nationalist'.[205]

The next day, Mallon returned to Carey's cell, now with a change of heart, listening intently to what Carey had to tell him. Of particular interest to Mallon was confirmation that Patrick Egan had been involved in the conspiracy, principally in terms of funding. Mallon suppressed this information in deference to his friend.[206]

Behind the scenes, the authorities discussed the use of Carey as an informer. John Adye Curren was wholeheartedly against his employment, holding that the Crown prosecution already had enough evidence to secure the conviction of leading Invincibles, including Carey, while other small figures in the conspiracy would be brought over. He was, however, overruled:

Counsel for the Crown took a different view – I do not say wrongly. They were of the opinion that the fact of a man of Carey's position turning [informer] *would be a warning to all who might in future engage in similar conspiracies.*[207]

According to contemporary commentator Tighe Hopkins, Carey had been overwhelmingly stubborn, refusing all appeals to him to become an informer against his comrades. Refusing to talk throughout the hearings at Kilmainham Courthouse, it was the testimony of Myles Kavanagh that finally moved Carey to testify on his role in the Invincibles:

> It was supposed that Carey was willing, if not eager, from the outset to be the Judas of the party, but the facts were otherwise. He was less a hero, I think, than any of his associates in the plot, but he had in him a kind of stubborn pride and all the Irishman's instinctive horror of the role of informer. He refused to speak until he felt the rope at his throat. It was the damning evidence of Kavanagh that finally unnerved him, and forced his lips to save his neck. But even then it was hard to fetch the truth from him.[208]

Between Mallon relentlessly playing on Carey's nerves, and the impact of Kavanagh's testimony, Carey finally cracked and turned approver. As a principal figure in the conspiracy, he was to give damning information on the Invincibles to the police investigation. Carey's fate was sealed. He would forever be remembered with infamy in Irish history, his name a derogatory term throughout the nineteenth and early twentieth centuries, as Patrick Tynan recalled:

> The man was now sold over to his wretched destiny. He, who the previous day had before him a patriot's death, was now steeped in the slime of poisonous treachery, and his name stained for generations ... by one fell stroke he had precipitated himself from virtue to infamy ...[209]

Carey was shuffled from Kilmainham Gaol to the Courthouse next door, and left in a room to stew in his thoughts. He was nervous and shaky, and drank some brandy before making his appearance on the witness stand.

Contemporaries in Kilmainham Gaol recalled that from the outset, Carey was difficult and edgy, knowing the potential death he faced. Ushered from his room, he made his way into the courtroom and up towards the witness box. His former comrades looked on in shock and disgust, seeing plainly that one of their leaders had betrayed them. Unable to look at them, Carey faced the wall, as James Mullet forced his way to the front to summon his solicitor:

> *At first breath of the execration the small man, whose entrance was the signal for the commotion, hesitated, recoiled, and would have fled in craven terror but for the official hand upon his arm. So, with an obvious effort, which plainly racked his nervous energies he braced himself and mounted the table. As he took the steps he shouted, in a shrill, piping treble, casting a furtive glance, which it would be hard to describe. Containing as it did, both the elements of cowardice and exultation, to one corner of the dock, 'I was before ye's, after all Dan.'* [210]

The Invincibles began shouting abuse at the witness, calling him a scoundrel, a thief and a liar, forcing intervention from the judges. Skin the Goat, particularly vocal, denounced him as a perjurer for money, while Joe Brady gave him an icy stare, his eyes full of anger. One commentator recalled, 'Had Joe Brady, who glared at him, and stretched forward towards him, been able to reach him, I believe he would have been torn to pieces, for Brady was a powerful young fellow; he was for all the world, like a tiger on a spring.' [211] Dan Curley reacted with little surprise, remaining silent, while Pat Delaney loudly declared, 'There is the man I may thank for my whole misfortunes in life from my childhood up.' [212] Carey responded to the cries, holding that 'he was no informer, and had got no one arrested'. [213]

Outside the Courthouse, as word spread among the Dublin working class of Carey's treachery, strong feeling rose against Carey and his family. One newspaper reported:

The hatred against Councillor Carey among the lower orders in Dublin,
increases in intensity, and it may safely be said that nothing at all approaching
it, has ever been displayed towards anyone individual ... Mrs Carey is guarded
by police when going to early mass and her children dare not show themselves
out of doors. Were it not for the police and marines who guard her residence
there can be little doubt it would be attacked. In conversation with a person
some day before her husband became an approver, Mrs. Carey said 'if anything
happens to my husband, I can give such evidence that can incriminate the very
highest among them.[214]

Carey's evidence, elicited bit by bit to an eager audience, summoned up a vivid image of a secret Fenian conspiracy to assassinate leading Government figures in Ireland. The graphic detail was almost underlined for listeners by the 'calm and callous precision'[215] of his narrative. He outlined Fenian history and ideology, stating that he had joined the Invincibles for the good of Ireland. He described the popular outrage at the coercion policy employed by the Government, and said that he became convinced of the Invincibles' methods 'when coercion was in full force, when the popular leaders were in prison, when any man might be thrown into prison at a moment's notice, and kept there without trial'.[216]

Carey described leading Fenian John Walsh's visit to Dublin to found an assassination society. He identified several of the prisoners in the dock as implicated in the conspiracy, naming Curley, Brady and Mullet as leading Invincibles. He declared that their aim was 'in the first place to make history, and in the next place to remove all the principal tyrants in the country'.[217] Asked what 'removed' meant, Carey replied that it meant assassination.

Carey next minutely detailed the failed attempts on Forster's life, implicating several prisoners in the dock. He claimed that nineteen attempts had been made on the former Chief Secretary's life, each one marred by ill-luck.

Carey coolly described how the leading politician was to be 'removed', and several attempts to stop his carriage as it passed through Dublin. According to one observer:

> *Horses were to be shot and the occupants of the carriage and any bystanders who interfered were to be disabled. The witness's calm manner when talking about the removal of the Chief Secretary was indescribable.*[218]

Carey described how Mrs Frank Byrne had smuggled the knives into Ireland, and implicated John Walsh, Patrick Sheridan and Captain McCafferty. This mention of Mrs Frank Byrne and PJ Sheridan caused immense sensation, given their high rank within the Land League, Frank Byrne's connection to Parnell regarding the so-called Kilmainham Treaty being particularly politically sensitive.

Of equal sensation, although more melodramatically, Carey named a mysterious individual whom he called 'Number One', who allegedly held the sinews of war and directed operations for the Dublin directory. As to the movements of this mysterious individual, Carey said that the last time he had seen Number One was at Blackrock railway station, Dublin, in October of the previous year. Here, this shady individual told Carey of the disappearance of the knives. This Blackrock connection was of interest to the ongoing police investigation, as Number One was apparently making for Kingstown, a major seaport commercially used by travellers to Britain. Investigations would extend to England on this point.

Mrs Frank Byrne was arrested in London under instruction from the Home Secretary, as a suspect in the Phoenix Park assassinations. From investigations made in London it was learned that she had been associating with known Fenians operating in Britain. Mrs Byrne had been approached by Scotland Yard the night before she was arrested, and it was found that she had £200 in her possession, purportedly to aid the escape

James Carey in the witness chair, observed by other members of the conspiracy.

from Britain of Fenians implicated in the Invincibles conspiracy. Stopped with this money in her possession, as a woman, she was not searched. Aware that the police were closing in on her, she gave this money to Patrick Tynan's wife, who made her way to France to meet up with her husband and Frank Byrne. Under instructions from Howard Vincent, head of London's CID, Tynan was to be watched, but he mysteriously disappeared.

Mrs Byrne was quickly conveyed to Dublin, accompanied by four Scotland Yard detectives. Arriving at Kingstown in total secrecy, her face hidden under a veil, she was then taken by train to Westland Row Station, where she was met by several police officers and placed into a cab. Arriving at Dublin Castle, Mrs Byrne was questioned for several hours on her and her husband's roles in the Invincibles conspiracy.

She was next conveyed to Kilmainham Courthouse. It was intended that Carey would identify her in court, leading to a full charge of complicity in the conspiracy. However, on examination, Carey claimed not to recognise her, stating that the woman who had brought him the knives used in the assassinations, who operated under the name of Mrs Frank Byrne, was not the woman sitting before him. Released, she made her way to London and then to America, where she joined her husband.

Carey laid out in detail preparations leading to the assassinations of 6 May of the previous year, and 'a pin could have been heard to drop'[219] in the Courtroom. *The Freeman's Journal* lamented: 'Never before in the whole history of crime has a scene more dramatic or calculated to move the public mind with amazed horror been enacted than that which Kilmainham Courthouse witnessed.'[220] Carey admitted that he had collected the knives for the assassins, and had suggested their use against Burke. Carey held that Edward McCaffrey was not in Phoenix Park on the day of the assassinations; he listed in detail who was, however, identifying Brady, Curley, the Hanlon brothers, Kavanagh and Skin the Goat, among others.

Carey methodically described how Joe Smith had pointed Burke out to him, identifying him as the Undersecretary. Carey had then pointed Burke out to the assassination party, Joe Brady having been appointed as the actual assassin of the Undersecretary. Carey described in detail how he had been told to get out of the park by Brady. He made his way out to join Smith, who had also been dispatched, and looked back to see the Invincibles walking in formation.

He described in detail how Burke and Cavendish had walked through the first three Invincibles – Curley, Fagan and Hanlon – toward Brady and Kelly, the former three turning and walking behind them. From 200 yards away, Carey said he saw Joe Brady attack Burke. Consolidating his narrative, Carey outlined a conversation with Daniel Curley after the assassinations, implicating Brady as Burke's assailant. Brady looked on in silence through all of this, picking his teeth with the stump of a pencil. In the aftermath of the assassinations, Carey received the knives from Number One. Under instructions, they were broken and burned by Carey's brother Peter, supervised by Joe Brady. Carey added smilingly that he 'would have kept them as national relics or sent them to the exhibition of Irish relics'.[221]

Inquiries into the mysterious Number One had led detectives to the door of Patrick Tynan at Peckham Rye, London. This investigation was aided by Peter Carey, who parallel to the testimony of his brother, identified Tynan as a stranger who had seemingly played a leading part in the conspiracy.[222] Curran urgently issued a warrant for Tynan's arrest, seeking to bring him to Dublin for questioning under Section 16 of the Coercion Act:

> *Patrick Joseph Tynan, formerly of Kingstown in Ireland, and lately of Peckham, London, on the 6th day of May in the year 1882, feloniously and wilfully and of his malice aforethought did kill and murder Lord Frederick Cavendish and Thomas Henry Burke in the Phoenix Park and said district.*
>
> *These are therefore in her majesty's name, requiring and commanding you and each and every of you, on sight or receipt hereof, without any delay to search for and apprehend the body of the said Patrick Joseph Tynan. And him so found to bring before me, or some other of her majesties justices of the peace that he may be dealt with according to law. And for doing so this shall be your warrant. Given under my hand and seal, this second day of March 1883, at the Dublin Metropolitan Police Court, Inn's Quay, South Side.*
>
> *John Adye Curran*[223]

The railway station at Blackrock, where 'Number One' was last seen.

Tynan could not be located by police either in Ireland or England. He had seemingly gone to France with Frank Byrne, where he was reported to be following British Prime Minister William Gladstone at Cannes. While neither Byrne nor Tynan could be arrested in France, their presence near the Prime Minister necessitated surveillance, provoking fears that they might try to assassinate him. A detective, disguised as a Russian prince, was briefed to befriend the two men and invite them onto his yacht. The plan was to kidnap them and deliver them back to Britain.

In Westminster Parliament, Carey's revelations on the role of PJ Sheridan in the Invincibles conspiracy were met with astonishment, and were highly embarrassing for the Irish Party. Pointing to the earlier Kilmainham Treaty, John Eldon Gorst MP, of the Conservative Party, urged the Liberal Government to make no further concessions to the Irish Party,[224] although until the facts all came out, he was of the opinion that Parnell was entirely ignorant of the inner circle of the Invincibles. He did, nevertheless, demand some kind of explanation from the Irish leader, or a disclaimer at the least of his relationship with Sheridan. Sir R Maxwell MP, however, was less conciliatory. He put forward a point of order as to Carey's claim that PJ Sheridan was a leading Invincible, and asked for clarification on Parnell's associations with the Land League organiser.

From the opposition benches, alongside murmurings from the Government benches, Parnell was reminded that figures politically close to him were engaged in the Invincibles conspiracy. Sheridan's name increasingly cropped up, alongside those of Frank Byrne and Thomas Brennan, who under the terms of the Kilmainham understanding were to aid him in suppressing agrarian violence in Ireland. This was extensively seized upon by the British newspapers, which noted that Parnell had offered Sheridan to the Government, by means of the so-called Kilmainham Treaty, in order to quench the agrarian crisis. Conservative MP John Gorst stated:

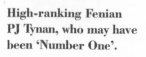

When they looked at the revelations which had recently taken place at Kilmainham Courthouse, and saw the kind of associates the Government were at one time prepared to take into their confidence, in order to procure the pacification of Ireland, the house will admit that a little anxiety on the subject was not altogether misplaced.[225]

High-ranking Fenian PJ Tynan, who may have been 'Number One'.

Gorst further argued that the Government had been horribly wrong in dismissing the coercive policy of William Forster in favour of conciliation. This conciliation, he asserted, had led to the assassinations of Cavendish and Burke in Phoenix Park. The Government had now been forced into a political U-turn, reverting to William Forster's policy of coercion. The new, draconian Coercion Act represented a firm means

Courtroom sketches from the *Illustrated London News*. Clockwise from left: Patrick Delaney, Myles Kavanagh giving evidence, Kavanagh's cab, James 'Skin the Goat' Fitzharris, Joe Brady.

of pacifying Ireland, ruling her by the sword rather than the velvet glove. William Forster was flattered by Gorst's appraisal of his former strategy, and embittered by his Government's dealings with Parnell. Offended by the so-called Kilmainham Treaty, and enraged by the attempts to assassinate him, he was scathing in his attack on Parnell, to the point of accusing him of responsibility:

I wish to state that, in my opinion – and I believe that it will be the opinion of many others – no mere disclaimer of connection with the outrage will be sufficient. We have had disclaimers before; I am told that James Carey even wrote a letter of condolence to Miss Burke on the murder of her brother. Do not let the hon. Member suppose that I charge him with having planned any murder, or with complicity with murder. But I wish there to be no mistake that this I do charge [Parnell] *and his Friends with. He and they allowed themselves to continue the leaders – he the avowed Chief – of an organization which not merely ostensibly advised and urged the ruin of those who opposed them, and avowed that doctrine of 'Boycotting,' which was to make life almost more miserable than death, but which set on foot an agitation, which organized or promoted outrage and incited to murder, of which the natural result and outcome was murder, and* [Parnell] *ought to have known this to be the natural outcome. It is very hard for me to understand how he did not know it, and how he did not separate himself from it altogether, and disavow and denounce it. Now, let me illustrate my meaning. We have heard of cases in which Gentlemen get into this House, and get out of it, by bribery. Very often the candidate or the Member is not found guilty of bribery himself. What happens is this – that he gives money, but takes very good care not to know what are the acts of bribery. But the bribery becomes rampant; and it is very hard, I believe, in some cases to say that these candidates have not known very well what were the means by which they hoped to get a seat in the House.* [Parnell] *was not merely in the position of a candidate; he was also in the position of the Chairman of an Election Committee. He was the man who, more than any other, derived advantage and power, until we took it from him – power by help of this terrorism. What I say is – he has to show us how it was that he did not find out that this terrorism was so used, and what steps he took to find it out, or what steps he took to discourage it; but we know that he took none, and we know that he remained content to reap the advantages of this agitation.*[226]

The following day, Parnell responded to the charges of the former Chief Secretary, implying that Carey's evidence could not be relied upon, and that there was no connection, however small or circumstantial, between his associates and figures close to Parnell. Parnell denied all of the charges directed at him, distancing himself completely from the conspiracy. However, at the same time, Parnell understood that Forster's charges could potentially regain ground for Parnell with his Irish-American audience. On the offensive now, he delivered one of the greatest speeches of his career. He did not have to justify himself to an English audience, he argued, directing his reply to the Irish people, whom he claimed did not require him to prove that he was not an accomplice to conspiracy:[227]

> *To refer to the evidence which is now being given before the Courts at Dublin ... I will just refer to it so far as to state what the evidence actually was – I mean the evidence which is supposed to throw suspicion on some members of the Land League – as having connected them with these terrible assassinations in the Phoenix Park. Now, Sir, the statements that were made in that direction were made by the approver Carey. There is no need to comment upon that fact, beyond saying that they were statements not of fact, but of belief, of the belief of others. They are three in number. Firstly, Carey swore that he had met a person in the garb of a priest, that he was introduced to him as Father Murphy, and that this man informed him (Carey) that he was going down into the country to form a branch of the 'Invincible' organisation. Carey then said that he was afterwards informed – but he did not say by whom – that this Father Murphy was Mr Sheridan of Tubbercurry. Secondly, Carey swore that some amongst his comrades believed the money came from America, but others believed it came from the Land League. This, again, the House would bear in mind, was only a statement of belief, and the House will acquit me of any desire to comment on this evidence. I simply quote it to show what the evidence really was, and I am*

*perfectly satisfied to allow the House to draw its own conclusions. Thirdly,
Carey swore that a woman, whom he was informed was Mrs. Frank Byrne,
wife of the Secretary to the English Land Confederation, had brought him
weapons. That, too, is hearsay evidence. I wish to point out again that all
these statements of Carey's would not have been admissible in an ordinary
case, and would not have been admitted here were it not that this was a
case of conspiracy, and were it not that he had sworn that he heard these
statements made by some amongst the prisoners who were charged with
being participators in the conspiracy. That evidence, I say again, was only
hearsay evidence; and, so far as we have gone, the third statement – that
the woman who brought the weapons was Mrs. Frank Byrne – has been
abundantly disproved, for when Mrs. Byrne was brought over to Dublin
for identification, Carey failed to identify her, and she was discharged by the
Detective Department with abundant and profuse apologies.*[228]

As to Sheridan being offered to the Government as a mediator to appease
the violence, Parnell again denied the charge. He shifted the blame for this
to Captain William O'Shea, husband of his lover, who had stated that:

*I myself know nothing about the organisation of the Land League; but I told
Mr Forster that I had been informed by Mr Parnell the day before that if the
Arrears Question were settled, that organisation would explain the boon to
the people, and tell them that they ought to assist the operation of the remedial
measure in the tranquillising of the country. I added that Mr Parnell had
expressed his belief that Messrs. Davitt, Egan, Sheridan, and Boyton would
use all their exertions, if placed in a position to do so, to advance the pacification
of the country, and that Mr Sheridan's influence was of special importance in
the West, owing to the fact that he had been the chief Land League organiser in
Connaught, while Mr Boyton had held a similar appointment in Leinster.*[229]

This indicated, according to Parnell, that he had no part in offering Sheridan to the Government as a mediator; it had simply been suggested privately on account of his involvement in the Land League and alongside the names of several leading individuals. The Irish leader next pointed to a Government memorandum, which had been based on O'Shea's statement to Forster. He demanded to know why the other names O'Shea had mentioned – Davitt, Egan and Boyton – were not included in the memorandum. For Forster, O'Shea had not told him this, although this was denied by O'Shea. Parnell concluded that the names were deliberately omitted to implicate him in conspiracy. Forster, increasingly lambasted by the Irish benches, would now face the wrath of Parnell. He compared the former Chief Secretary to James Carey, but said that the former Chief Secretary was worse, as at least Carey had informed to save his own life:[230]

Call him back to his post. Send him to help Lord Spencer in the congenial work of the gallows in Ireland. Send him to look after the secret inquisitions of Dublin Castle. Send him to levy the payment of blood money. Send him to raise the taxes which an unfortunate and starving peasantry have to pay for crimes not committed by them. All that would be congenial work for him. We invite you to fill up your ranks, and send your ablest and best men to push forward the task of misgoverning and oppressing Ireland. For my part, I am confident as to the future of Ireland. Although her horizon may appear at this moment cloudy, I believe that our people will survive the present oppression, as they have survived many and worse ones. And although our progress may be slow, it will be sure; and the time will come when this House and the people of this country will admit once again that they have been mistaken – that they have been deceived by those who ought to be ashamed of deceiving them – that they have been led astray as to the right method of governing a noble, a generous, a brave, and impulsive people; and that they will reject their present Leaders, who are conducting them into the terrible course which, I am sorry to say, the Government appears to be determined to enter – that they will reject those guides and Leaders with just as much determination as they rejected the services of [Forster].[231]

While the British Parliament debated the aftermath of Carey's revelations, the Magistrates' Court hearing at Kilmainham was concluded on 19 February. The prisoners would be further examined in six weeks' time at Green Street Courthouse, Dublin. Meanwhile, one of the prisoners, Henry Rowles, had died on 18 February, while in custody in Kilmainham Prison. Rowles had been suffering from regular epileptic seizures. He had been out in a small exercise yard within the prison alongside Brady and Moroney, who rushed to his assistance when he fell in the yard, consumed by a fit. Brady grabbed him as he fell and tried to revive him, but this was against prison rules, and he and Moroney were taken away back to their cells. Falling on the ground, it was noted that Rowles frothed at the mouth:

When he would be taking the fit he would raise his right hand over his head, and then bring it down in front of him. His whole body would work. The right leg would remain straight all the time, and the left leg would work. The right eye was fixed, and the left eye was closed.[232]

Henry Rowles, who died in custody in Kilmainham.

In order to conclude the cause of death, a post mortem was conducted in the gaol, headed by the County Coroner, Mr Harty, and representing the Crown, Samuel Lee Anderson. Interviewed as to his knowledge of the death of Rowles, Gaol Doctor William Carte concluded that the cause of death was congestion of the brain caused by epileptic fits. In his testimony to the post mortem, Carte recalled his final meeting with the Invincible:

> He found him lying on a bed in a room in the central hall of the Prison. On inquiry he learned that he had a faintness or weakness in one of the exercise yards. Witness questioned him and examined him. And came to the conclusion that he had an epileptic form of convulsion ... Witness also directed that he should be removed to the infirmary, where he would be more comfortable, and would be better attended.[233]

Concluding that Rowles was dying, Carte allowed his wife to visit him in Kilmainham Gaol, but Rowles was so ill, he did not recognise her. Mrs Rowles and her family complained bitterly to the Gaol authorities that they had not been informed about his condition until the last minute. Rowles had become ill on Wednesday, with his condition worsening by Friday, but the family was not informed until 9am on the Sunday morning. In the presence of his wife and sister-in-law at the Gaol infirmary, after a brief period of consciousness, Henry Rowles drifted off into a coma, dying at seven o'clock that day, Sunday, 18 March. The family was allowed to remove Rowles's body to the family home at Fishamble Street, and he was buried at Glasnevin Cemetery on Wednesday, 21 March 1883. Responding to statements that the State had in fact properly informed Henry Rowles's family of his declining condition, his eldest son, Henry Rowles Jr, noted in a letter to *The Freeman's Journal*:

In regard to a statement which appeared in the Freeman on the 19th inst.
In reference to my late father, I have to ask you to allow me to make two
corrections. It is stated that the family got timely notice of my father's illness
and that he remained conscious until the last. The family did not get notice
until 9 o'clock on Sunday morning, and then though we went at once, we found
my father unconscious and he remained in that condition (unconscious) until
he died at ten minutes past seven o'clock in the evening. I may add though, it
would appear that on Saturday evening, when my brother went to the prison,
with his father's clean clothes, no intimation was given him of his illness.[234]

Meanwhile, the remaining prisoners shuffled each morning to and from
the Courthouse under heavy guard, due to crowds gathering outside the
prison in support of the prisoners,[235] and the danger of a rescue attempt:

The prison vans containing the nineteen persons for trial will be guarded by
sixteen mounted constables and about twenty policemen and marines who
will be seated on cars. There will be in addition a strong escort of cavalry
from Islandbridge barracks; and along the route by which the accused will be
conveyed groups of marines will be stationed at short intervals. The approaches
to Green Street and Halston Street, leading to the front and back entrances of
the Courthouse, will be guarded by cordons of police, who shall be instructed to
allow no person to pass but those showing tickets of admission or summonses as
jurors, and the professional engaged for the accused.[236]

Within Green Street Courthouse, tremendous preparations were undertaken, for what would be the undoubted trial of the century. It was expected
that there would be a huge turnout of reporters from across the world.
Sections of the Courtroom were allocated for their comfort. Eight stenog-
raphers were to be placed to either side of the dock, where the prisoners
would sit. A special area was allocated for artists, who would sketch the

prisoners for the illustrated newspapers. Such were the growing numbers of applications from newspapers that it had been decided that the reporters would be selected by lottery, with some exceptions, allowing up to sixty reporters the right of attendance.

The imposing facade of Kilmainham Gaol.

THE TRIALS

5

JOE BRADY

At Green Street Courthouse on 11 April 1883, Joe Brady was the first to be tried for the assassinations of Burke and Cavendish. He stood before Judge O'Brien, known colloquially as 'hatchet face':

> No trial in my experience attracted to it any anything approaching the almost
> feverish excitement which centred upon this case. I remember that the prisoner
> was conveyed from Kilmainham prison under a mounted escort of military and
> police, with armed police and marines following in cars. In a second vehicle
> were the four informers, James Carey, [Robert] Farrell, William Lamie and
> Michael Kavanagh.[237]

The prosecution was led by Attorney General Andrew Marshall Porter, assisted by Solicitor General James Murphy and Peter O'Brien. Drawing on Carey's testimony at Kilmainham Courthouse, and the evidence secured in Kilmainham from Kavanagh, Delaney and Smith, the Attorney General opened by asserting to the jury that the Invincibles were an

assassination committee, motivated by
a desire to establish an Irish Republic
outside the authority of the Crown.[238]
Waiting in an isolated room in Green
Street Courthouse, Carey was called to
the witness stand. Dublin Reporter JB
Hall recalled:

*The calling of Carey as a witness created
a sensation far exceeding the earlier
scene at Kilmainham. Knowing him
as nearly everyone in Court had done as a*
Town Councillor and a citizen of repute,

Joe Brady, as depicted in the
Illustrated London News.

*with a reputation for ostentatious piety, there was something indescribable
in the effect his presence produced, and with every head stretched forward,
and breath almost held, the scene was striking, indeed. He spoke slowly and
calmly as he had done at the preliminary hearing. During his evidence he
had occasion to look straight at Brady, and their eyes met, and I can never
forget the look of scorn, contempt and hatred with which the prisoner fixed his
piercing eyes on the informer. Carey quickly shifted his position and looked at
him no more until leaving the table he was brought face to face with him and
received the same appalling look.*[239]

In the witness stand, Carey repeated the damning evidence he had given
at Kilmainham Magistrates' Court, implicating Brady in the assassinations in the park, and in earlier assassination attempts on Forster.[240]
With the departure of Forster, Carey described how the attention of
the Invincibles turned to Thomas Henry Burke. He vividly illustrated
how several Invincibles waited in Phoenix Park on 5 May, the day
before the assassinations, planning to take the life of Burke in reprisal

for British policy in Ireland, administered by the Undersecretary. Asked who these men were, Carey indicated Brady, Curley, Kelly, Caffrey and Patrick Delaney.[241] Carey again noted that Brady had made his way to the Undersecretary's residence, but finding he was not present, left the scene. In Carey's narrative, he, Brady and Kelly met at Kingsbridge, with the object of assassinating Burke. Discovering that Burke had left Dublin Castle earlier, they abandoned the plan until the following day. Carey mentioned a parcel, containing knives, carried into the park by Brady:

Murphy:	*whom did you see the parcel with?*
Carey:	*Joseph Brady.*
Murphy:	*Were you told by him what the parcel contained?*
Carey:	*No, it was not necessary!*
Murphy:	*Did you know what it contained?*
Carey:	*Yes.*
Murphy:	*What kind of parcel was it?*
Carey:	*It was a newspaper parcel – enclosing – what I knew.*
Webb:	*I object!*
Murphy:	*How did you know it?*
Carey:	*Because we had it arranged that there were certain things to be brought there.*
Webb:	*Arranged with whom?*
Murphy :	*Pardon me a moment. Had you made any arrangement? You said earlier that you were there watching for Mr Burke. What were you to do with Mr Burke?*
Carey:	*To assassinate him!*
Murphy:	*Was Joseph Brady one of the four directing men at this time?*
Carey:	*He was.*[242]

According to Carey, Joseph Brady was responsible for carrying the knives and carrying out the assassination of Burke. The knives, he continued, wrapped in the paper parcel, were in his pocket on the morning of 6 May 1882, and in Phoenix Park prior to the assassinations at a quarter past seven. Carey recalled, after the assassinations, a conversation with Brady:

> 'Is it true,' said I, 'what I heard that it was Lord Frederick Cavendish that was along with Mr Burke?' 'I don't know,' said he, 'and only for himself, he would not be the way he is;' and then he described it. I asked him was it true what I heard that when the thing was done he was so cool as to wipe the knife in the grass and he said, 'Yes. [243]

It was noted that during the delivery of his testimony, Carey had reason to look at Brady, who cast a damning look on the informer. Carey shifted his position, turning his back on Brady and facing the wall.[244] The prosecution now moved on to the details of the conspiracy:

Murphy:	*Had there been any knives brought to your house by any person?*
Carey:	*There had in February.*
Murphy:	*Had there been other weapons? Had there been rifles and revolvers?*
Carey:	*Yes, two rifles, four revolvers and ten knives.*
Murphy:	*Ten knives?*
Carey:	*Yes!*

Carey testified that prior to the assassination he was in Wrenn's public house with Brady, Kelly and Caffrey. He told of how Curley and Brady had previously tried to see and identify Burke at the Castle several times, but had failed. Arriving at the park aboard Skin the Goat's cab with George Smith, the informer identified Brady, Kelly, Patrick Delaney and Thomas Caffrey as riding on Myles Kavanagh's car. As explained to the earlier Magistrates' Court, after Smith had identified Burke to the assassination party of seven, Brady told Carey to get rid of Smith and to leave the park.

Carey and Smith made their way, in Carey's narrative, to College Green. At nine that evening, he met Curley at Holles Street and an hour later met Brady at Denzille Street. He was then told that Cavendish had been assassinated, along with Burke. Brady claimed not to know if the man with Burke was indeed Cavendish, but said that regardless, 'only for himself he would not be [dead]'.[245] According to Carey, Brady described in detail how he had assassinated Burke, telling how Cavendish hit him on the face with his umbrella, and ran into the middle of the road, where he 'finished him off'.[246]

In cross-examination, Brady's defence, composed of Dr Webb, Richard Adams and DB Sullivan, sought to undermine Carey's testimony. Brady's barrister wanted to portray Carey as a dangerous, unscrupulous hypocrite, who lied his way through life. To this end, Carey was questioned as to his religion, a subject that made the informer visibly uncomfortable:

Webb:	*Carey, are you a man who makes any profession of religion?*
Carey:	*No; Not a 'profession' of it.*
Webb:	*You make no profession of religion?*
Carey:	*No.*
Webb:	*What is your point by emphasising the word profession?*
Carey:	*I could not tell what you mean.*
Webb:	*Pray Sir, don't attempt to bandy words nor chop logic with me. I ask you a simple question. Do you make any profession of religion?*
Carey:	*I am a professed Roman Catholic.*
Webb:	*Are you a member of any religious sodality in the Church?*
Carey:	*I am not.*
Webb:	*Were you ever a member of any religious sodality?*

Carey:	I was.
Webb:	Were you a member of a sodality in 1881?
Carey:	I was.
Webb:	Were you a member of a sodality in the year 1882?
Carey:	For a portion of it.
Webb:	When did you cease to be a member of that sodality?
Carey:	When I was arrested.
Webb:	Was it one of the rules of that sodality that you should meet every Friday?
Carey:	No.
Webb:	What was the rule as to your meetings?
Carey:	I have not got the rules by heart.
Webb:	I did not ask you for the rules, I only asked a question as to what the rules for meeting were. They were to be once a month?
Carey:	[No answer]
Webb:	Now why do you not answer the question at once? Had you a rule as to the periods on which you were to receive Holy Communion?
Carey:	[No answer]
Webb:	Had you, Sir?
Carey:	Yes, once a month.
Webb:	And while you were a member of the sodality did you receive the Holy Communion once a month?
Carey:	Not every month.
Webb:	Did you receive it at times?
Carey:	I had the honour.
Webb:	Did you receive the communion in the month of March 1882?
Carey:	I did.
Webb:	Did you receive communion in the month of May 1882?
Carey:	I did.[247]

Having established this, Dr Webb sought to destroy Carey's character, citing his leading role in the Invincibles conspiracy as a means to sway the jury against his testimony. The informer declared under pressure that all of his actions were performed under compulsion:

Webb:	*Were you not one of the prime movers in the murder of Mr Burke?*
Carey:	*I was not.*
Webb:	*Weren't you the paymaster of the assassins?*
Carey:	*Under compulsion.*
Webb:	*I don't ask you as to being under compulsion.*
Carey:	*I took the post, but did not mark the consequences.*
Webb:	*Was it under compulsion that you received the Holy Communion?*
Carey:	*No.*
Webb:	*Was it under compulsion that you joined the society?*
Judge O'Brien:	*Which society do you mean? Was it the religious or the other one?*
Webb:	*the other society.*
Carey:	*No.*
Webb:	*You joined it of your own free will and pleasure?*
Carey:	*Not knowing its ramifications at the time.*
Webb:	*Have you not sworn already that the object of that society was to remove tyrants and to make history?*
Carey:	*Yes, the object was told to me afterwards.*
Webb:	*Did you never say that before you were sworn a member you were told the object of the society was to make history?*
Carey:	*I was told afterwards.*[248]

Webb now drew on Carey's Fenian past, and his position as a leading figure on a Fenian vigilance committee, pointing out how Carey had presided over a rule demanding the death of informers, while all the time a practising member of a religious sodality. Webb secured from Carey a declaration that he had been delegated to identify Burke as he entered the park, and furthermore that he had suggested the use of knives against the Undersecretary. Carey lamented, 'Oh, I could swear a lot more things. I'm only telling half the things that happened, just according as they were asked me. I am more friendly to you than you think, Mr Webb. Bear that in mind.'[249]

Carey was followed by Myles Kavanagh, who repeated his Kilmainham testimony, citing the presence of Brady, Tim Kelly, Thomas Caffrey and Pat Delaney in Phoenix Park on 6 May 1882. Kavanagh could confirm this, having driven them to the park.[250] According to Kavanagh, Brady had paid him £3 in total for the cab ride, and had sat by Kavanagh's right shoulder as they made their escape from the scene of the assassinations.

This evidence, however, was later contradicted by an independent witness, George Godden, who testified that Brady was in the park on 6 May, on Kavanagh's cab, but could only identify him to Kavanagh's left shoulder. This discrepancy was seized upon by Brady's defence, who noted that if Brady was to Kavanagh's right, Godden could not have seen him in the park, as his view would have been obstructed.

Next on the stand was Joseph Smith. Like Carey and Kavanagh before him, he could place Brady in the Phoenix Park on 6 May.

Robert Farrell's evidence was entirely circumstantial. He recounted how he had been recruited into the Invincibles conspiracy by Daniel Curley, a known associate of Brady. He could place Curley and Brady together on several occasions, mingling with other Invincibles charged in connection with the assassinations, including Kelly and Laurence Hanlon. Farrell noted that he had been involved in an earlier attempt to assassinate Forster, in a conspiracy that Brady was certainly a member of, and Curley was a captain of. He recalled that at a meeting of the Invincibles at Brunswick Street in Dublin on 28 March 1882, which included Brady, Kelly, Curley, Daniel and Patrick Delaney, Laurence Hanlon and Peter and James Carey.

Farrell's narrative was controversial, however, given that in the Star Chamber inquiry, he had stated under oath that he never knew Brady, despite his evidence indicating involvement with Brady on several occasions prior to the assassinations. Furthermore, Farrell was not in Phoenix Park on the day of the assassinations, and was not connected with any of the Invincibles on that day. Equally in legal terms, Farrell's evidence in no way proved Brady's membership of the Invincibles. Brady's barrister concluded:

The only evidence that this man had given that Brady was a member of that inner circle is that he saw him on the streets with a variety of other men. Brady has not been brought into privity with any criminal organisation whatever, and I submit the existence of this criminal organisation has not been proved by anything this man has said. All that this man has said is this – that Curley – a third party, a stranger – said to him – 'there is to be a number of picked men that are to watch what is going on at the castle; will you be one of them? I will be your right hand man, and you will be my left.' That is all that has been established, but there is an enormous abyss to be jumped when they ask the jury to jump at the conclusion that this society, which from the terms of it, for aught I know, might have been an honest one, for it is perfectly consistent with what he said, that he acknowledging himself to be a member of that ... should attempt to bring the prisoner at the bar into privity with a criminal organisation of which he is not proved to be a member and of which the only evidence of proof is that he and a dozen others, or score of others as it might be, was in a certain street at a certain time, or on a certain bridge at a certain time, and that months and months before the alleged crime, and with no necessary or even natural connection with it, I submit that he cannot say what passed between him and Daniel Curley with no living person present except the two of them in Curley's house, with Brady, for all I know, a hundred miles away.[251]

This was argued by Dr Webb's supporting counsel, who criticised Judge O'Brien for entertaining Farrell's narrative:

As Dr Webb has pointed out, the present indictment is not for a conspiracy – it is solely for the murder of Mr Burke. What has your Lordship already done? You have admitted the evidence of the object of that conspiracy, and now the Crown seek in a charge against a man, not for conspiracy, but for murder, to extend to this case a law which applies to cases of conspiracy alone. And they ask you to receive against the prisoner evidence of every act done by that society even before there is evidence that this particular murder was planned or contemplated. I say it would be a novelty and it would be most prejudicial to the interests of the prisoner if you were to allow these questions now to be answered. The result would be, I submit, to let in upon this inquiry into a charge of the murder of A. B. vast number of by issues as to other crimes, real or imaginary, which may be alleged to have been committed or contemplated.[252]

However, Brady's presence in the park was corroborated by further independent witnesses, including William Meagle, suggesting his involvement in the May assassinations, and overriding doubts as to the accuracy of Farrell's testimony. Dr Webb's opening remarks to the jury painted Farrell as a perjurer, greatly weakening the prosecution case:

One of the effects of a crime like this was that it awakened in the mind of the whole community what had been called 'a sense of wild justice of revenge,' and there was a cry for punishment: there was an impulse for immediate vengeance. Society itself turned savage. The law itself was in danger of becoming lawless; and justice forgets her emblem, throws away the scales, tears the bandages from her eyes, strikes wildly with her sword, and suddenly transforms herself into vengeance ... The evidence by which this crime was supported was as portentous as the crime. No man who listened to the evidence

of Farrell, Kavanagh or Carey would to the day of his death forget the perjury,
the disregard of every law, human and divine; the shamelessness and the
atrocity not only avowed, but avowed as one of the most honourable and
ordinary transactions in life. Farrell was obliged to admit that all he swore to
before was false. The pure waters of the fountain of truth were contaminated by
the breath of a man like that. Whatever injury there might arise to society from
unpunished crime, there would be an infinitely worse evil by the encouragement
of triumphant perjury. It was almost idle to speak of James Carey. He knew
no words of his could kindle the feelings of indignation and horror which must
agitate the breasts when they remembered what he swore, he the prime mover
of this conspiracy ... its concoctor; one of its directors; the man who first suggested
the knives ... who according to his own confession was the paymaster to the
assassins, the man who set his victim, and gave the signal; the man whose last
words as he left the gang were, 'mind it is the man with the grey suit.'[253]

Webb asked the jury to consider how they could believe the evidence of the main prosecution witnesses. He wondered, if men such as Carey could sacrifice Burke and continue their daily lives, embedded in religion, could they not also sacrifice Joe Brady, to save themselves? The defence presented evidence that tended to suggest Brady's innocence, at all times pondering the question of who should be relied upon for testimony – dishonourable men such as Carey or Farrell, or honourable, independent parties?

One of these independent parties was Annie Meagher, who swore to Brady's presence in her uncle Christopher Flynn's home on Britain Street at the time of the assassinations, leaving at five past eight in the evening. This story was corroborated by Flynn, who knew Brady and worked at the same stonecutter's, and had been jailed during the Star Chamber inquiries for refusing to co-operate with Curran's questions over the leading Invincible. However, Flynn's wife Ann diverged from script, revealing that the story of Brady's presence in their home was untrue.

William Meagle testified to Brady's presence in the park on 6 May 1882, and had witnessed him engaged in a scuffle with Undersecretary Burke. Asked whether he could be sure of this, Meagle said he could recognise the prisoner if he were amongst a thousand men. Alongside Meagle, George Godden told the prosecution what he had seen in the park, vividly describing Kavanagh's cab speeding past him away from the scene of the assassinations, and clearly seeing Joseph Brady sitting in the cab.

Brady's fate was sealed. The jury took forty minutes to deliberate, then returned and pronounced Brady guilty of the assassinations of Cavendish and Burke. The prisoner remained erect, showing no emotion, although prior to the verdict it had been noted that he grasped the woodwork on top of the dock with both hands.[254]

O'Brien:	*Joseph Brady, you been found guilty upon cumulative and overwhelming evidence, such as to preclude any intelligent person from entertaining a doubt of your guilt of this most dreadful crime ... For the life you have taken your own life is forfeited. You have now after a lapse of so long a period of time, having all the advantage of a deliberate and fair trial, and of the highest and most zealous advocacy that the profession of law could furnish, been found guilty and have to follow your victims to eternity.*
Brady:	*I am not the first that has been sworn against innocently.*
O'Brien:	*I think it my duty to declare that I entirely concur in the justice and the propriety and the necessity of the verdict which has been pronounced. (His lordship now assumed the black cap) The sentence of the Court upon you Joseph Brady, is that you be taken from the bar of this Court, to the Prison in which you were last confined, and thence be taken to the gaol of the County of Dublin, and on Monday, the 14th day of May,*

in this present year, you be taken to the common place of execution in the gaol, and there be hanged by the neck until you are dead, and that your body be buried in the precincts of the Prison; and may God have mercy on your soul.[255]

Bowing to his counsel, Dr Webb, in thanks,[256] Brady now left the court-room. A girl in the front of the gallery, said to be Brady's girlfriend, was visibly shaken and weeping, his father 'a pathetic sight'.[257]

Joe Brady is returned to Kilmainham Gaol from the courthouse after receiving the sentence of death.

6

DANIEL CURLEY

Within a couple of days of Brady's trial came that of Daniel Curley. A republican of pronounced enthusiasm and ardour, he appeared at Green Street Courthouse on 16 April 1883, ferried there under heavy escort from Kilmainham Gaol. According to *The Irish Times*:

> He was respectably attired in a tweed suit, the same which he had worn in Kilmainham Courthouse. When he was brought into the dock a stir of curiosity and interest occurred amongst the audience, and his appearance was closely scrutinised by every eye. He advanced quietly to the front of the dock, with self possession placed his hat on one of the two seats, and gripping the bar with both hands stood drawn up to his full height for a couple of minutes ... He showed no symptoms of agitation save that when first he grasped the bar his hands slightly trembled.[258]

For the third time, Carey was employed as prosecution witness. The public showed somewhat less interest now, having become accustomed to his narrative and appearance. Ever the showman, it seemed as though

Carey was aware of this sudden drop in attention – he now introduced a new element to his well-trodden evidence, alleging that the convicted Brady had said that Burke and Cavendish were talking about an attempt on Forster's life, just as Brady grabbed Burke. This certainly seemed to reawaken interest in Carey's narrative. His story was decidedly told with a desire to convict Curley, speaking of his leading role in the Invincibles and his receiving of monies for the use of the Dublin directory.

Dr Webb, acting in Curley's defence, again questioned Carey on his involvement with religious sodalities, seeking again to portray Carey as unscrupulous and hypocritical. Having pointed this out, he began a heated interrogation of the informer:

Webb:	*Were you not a murderer?*
Carey:	*I was not, I shed no blood.*
Webb:	*You shed no blood?*
Carey:	*I thought it was playing at Soldiers.*
...	
Webb:	*Tell me Sir, who was it first suggested knives?*
Carey:	*I don't know. I suggested daggers.*
Webb:	*Was that playing at Soldiers?*
Carey:	*Yes it was.*
Webb:	*Then these meetings held in your house were not for the purpose of assassination?*
Carey:	*Well I think not.*[259]

Webb was left slightly bemused. Having heard from Carey that he was just 'playing at soldiers', he now moved to the earlier attempts on Forster's life, hearing from Carey that there were twenty attempts on Forster, which he was a party to. Webb continued:

Webb:	*Was it not your intention to murder him?*
Carey:	*Well indeed I would not call it murder at all, to remove him.*
Webb:	*You would not call it murder? And at the time when these things were going on, were you a member of a sodality?*
Carey:	*No.*
Webb:	*When did you cease to be a member of a religious sodality?*
Carey:	*Of course that is your standing point.*
Webb:	*Don't dare to address me, Sir.*
Judge O'Brien:	*Answer the question.*
Webb:	*When did you cease to be a member?*
Carey:	*On the 12th of January 1883.*
Webb:	*Then you were a member during the whole of 1882?*[260]

Webb had walked Carey directly into contradicting his earlier statement, endeavouring to sow doubt in the jury's mind. He continued to berate Carey for his involvement in religion and the taking of the Eucharist, while at all times 'steeped to the lips in blood'.[261] Webb sought to debase Carey's argument that he was simply 'playing at soldiers', challenging him on his earlier involvement in Fenianism, dating back to the Fenian rising of 1867. Carey was increasingly becoming nervous, his earlier frivolity now gone in the tense courtroom. His nervousness was accompanied by an increasing recklessness, as Curley's barrister leaped to and from Carey's Fenian past, his religion, and the twenty assassination attempts he had taken part in against Forster. He gave Carey little time to think, and the strain was evident:

Webb:	*In the presence of God and when a question of life or death is at issue, do you say that Mr Forster deserved assassination?*
Carey:	*I say he deserved no great love from any Irishman.*
Webb:	*Did he deserve to be assassinated?*
Carey:	*As I have said already, I would not like to see him going to Heaven.*

Webb:	*And you absolutely carry your vengeance beyond this life into the next world?*
Carey:	*I would not like to meet him there.*[262]

Carey now became more boisterous, laughing toward Webb and Curley. Webb asked him if he was taking the proceedings seriously, and if he took Curley's trial as a laughing matter. Carey responded sarcastically, in reference to Curley, 'No, too serious for some.'[263]

Following Carey came Robert Farrell, who outlined Daniel Curley's leading role in Fenianism, citing his activity as a Fenian centre in Dublin. Farrell described himself as a member of Curley's Dublin circle, having been recruited into the Invincibles personally by Curley, and having attended several meetings chaired and organised by the prisoner. Farrell, who had earlier perjured himself at the trial of Brady, was a weak-willed figure. He was cross-examined by Richard Adams, who sought to cast doubt on the reliability of his evidence and his character:

Adams:	*You believe it your duty to tell the truth when you were sworn?*
Farrell:	*Yes.*
Adams:	*You were sworn to tell the truth at the investigation in the Castle before Mr Curran?*
Farrell:	*Yes.*
Adams:	*Did you swear before Mr Curran, 'I don't know a man named Daniel Curley ...' Is that Daniel Curley now at the bar?*
Farrell:	*Yes.*
Adams:	*And do you know him?*
Farrell:	*Yes; But I did not want to let on that I was belonging to any organisation.*
Adams:	*Did you swear you did not know Daniel Curley?*
Farrell:	*Yes.*

Adams:	*Was that false?*
Farrell:	*Yes.*
Adams:	*Was it a lie?*
Farrell:	*Yes.*
Adams:	*Was it perjury on your oath?*
Farrell:	*Yes.*[264]

Having established that Farrell was a perjurer, Adams now set out to portray him as an opportunistic money-grabber, selling information to the highest bidder. The informer was asked what money he expected to receive from the Government for his information, the insinuation being that the more sensational his evidence was, the greater his reward:

Adams:	*Did you get any money?*
Farrell:	*No.*
Adams:	*Do you expect any?*
Farrell:	*Well, I expect I won't be put out on the street, at the mercy of the World.*
Adams:	*Do you expect any money?*
Farrell:	*I expect I will be looked after. I do not know what will become of me.*
Adams:	*When you were examined by Mr Curran, you had nothing to expect?*
Farrell:	*No, but I was compelled to do what I did, and a certain prisoner not here now said 'do as I tell you or else.' That is hard.*
Adams:	*But do you expect now to be put on the streets?*
Farrell:	*No.*
Adams:	*How much money do you expect?*
Farrell:	*If I get £80 or £100 I won't refuse it.*

Adams:	*How much do you expect?*
Farrell:	*I have not entered into any engagement.*
Adams:	*What would be a fair price?*
Farrell:	*£42,000 or less. (laughter)*
Adams:	*And before you expected to get anything you did not know Dan Curley?*
Farrell:	*I have told you I did not want to mention his name.*
Adams:	*If you got £2000, how many of them would you know?*[265]

After Farrell came Myles Kavanagh, who testified to Curley's presence in Phoenix Park on 6 May 1882. The cabman graphically illustrated the build-up to the assassinations, describing how Brady, Fagan and Kelly, along with Curley, eagerly awaited Carey's identification of Burke. This evidence was later corroborated by Joseph Smith.

James Carey's younger brother Peter was next called to the witness stand. He had claimed to be a member of the Invincibles and known to Curley for four years, but was never a part of the leading hierarchy controlling the Dublin directory. According to the younger Carey, Daniel Curley had been highly suspicious of Myles Kavanagh. Fearing that the cabman would co-operate with the State investigation into the assassinations, Curley had suggested to Peter Carey that he should be killed, and told the younger Carey to watch him:[266]

Peter Carey.

Murphy QC:	*What did you say about Kavanagh in the presence of the prisoner Curley and the others?*
Peter Carey:	*I was told –*
Murphy:	*Don't mind what you were told. Tell us what you told them after you had seen Kavanagh and spoken to him?*
Carey:	*I told them that Kavanagh the cabman was as good as gold. Curley said 'why didn't you go further with him?' I said I did not like, for fear they might blame me.*
Murphy:	*What did Curley say to that?*
Carey:	*He told me I should have went further to find him out.*
Murphy:	*What further did he say about Kavanagh?*
Carey:	*That Kavanagh should be wiped out.*[267]

Like Brady before him, Curley's fate was sealed. Deliberating for just over forty-five minutes, the jury returned a verdict of guilty against the Dublin carpenter. Curley was afforded the right to make a speech from the dock. He declared that he was innocent of the charge levied against him, and had been the victim of paid informers who had callously sent him to his death:

Curley:	*I will say distinctly that I am not guilty of the charge I am accused of. I had some remarks to make, but it was not until I heard your Lordship's charge that I determined to say this – that it is a biased unreasonable charge.*
O'Brien:	*Daniel Curley –*
Curley:	*You will excuse me, my Lord, if I say a few words … with reference to the identifications made after the imprisonment and the acts of the informers. At the time I was identified, all the parties were prepared to identify me. There were twelve or fourteen of us brought into the yard, and I was on the extreme left, and then I was ordered to come and stand in the centre of the line.*

*On another occasion a warder was ordered to stand at the rear
of the man – Joe Mullet – for identification. These are the points
that are unreasonable. These are the points that I have spoken to
the Counsel on. There are several other matters that I would wish
to remark upon; but there are other people awaiting their trials,
and of course, to meet the same fate – I expect. Not that I fear
death – I never courted it; I deny the charge; I say between myself
and God this minute that the two men who identified me as being
at the Polo ground, know I was never there. I was not near the
place. I was not in the Park on the 5th of May. You will have to
be very cautious, my lord, about the informers. I don't seek redress.
Of course I expect no mercy. I don't pray for pardon. I expect none
from the British Government; they are my avowed enemies ... I
know the position in which I am standing here. I am standing
on the brink of the grave. I will speak the truth ... I admit I was
sworn into the Fenian organisation twelve years ago; when I was
only twenty-two years of age, and from that time to the present
I worked openly in the organisation. I was let into a number of
their secrets, and I will say here today that I will bring them to
my grave faithfully and truly; and as to my own life, if I had a
thousand lives to lose, I would rather lose them sooner then bring
to my grave the name of informer and that I should save my life
by betraying my fellow man ... I am a member of the Invincible
society – undoubtedly, unhesitatingly.*[268]

Sentenced to be executed within four days of Joseph Brady, on 18 May
1883 at Kilmainham Gaol, Curley was ushered away from the dock. As he
left, Curley loudly announced toward those in attendance, 'Good bye all.
God save Ireland.'[269]

7

TIMOTHY KELLY

Timothy Kelly was tried on 19 and 20 April, at Green Street Courthouse. The building was surrounded by plain-clothes and uniformed police and military marines, with every passage and doorway heavily guarded.[270] The approvers in his trial would again be Carey, his brother Peter, George Smith, Myles Kavanagh and William Lamie:

> *Timothy Kelly being put forward dropped quickly into his seat at the corner of the dock, folding his arm on the iron rail. His full lack lustre eyes and a slight hectic on his cheek bone imparted to his pale, soft face an anxious look, which became intensified by the appearance of intermittent wrinkles on his forehead.[271]*

Once in the dock, Kelly was surrounded by two gaolers and two police constables, while marines stood in front of the dock at either side.[272] Opening the case for the prosecution, the Attorney General stated that Kelly was, 'from the very circumstances of his youth and his activity a prompt, willing and ready agent' of the Invincibles conspiracy, and that he had been in Phoenix Park on 6 May 1882, acting as one of the assassins.[273]

Kelly remained aloof throughout the proceedings, although it was noted that he had aged somewhat since the proceedings in Kilmainham Courthouse, the strain of imprisonment showing in his face.[274] *The Irish Times* reported that 'he was in no measure abashed or confused, but looked with interest about him, attentively regarding the proceedings and scrutinising any countenance that struck him in his cool survey of the occupants of the Court'.[275]

The first witness to be called was again Robert Farrell. He testified that Kelly was an active member of the Invincibles, involved in every assassination attempt on William Forster. As he had done in the trial of Daniel Curley, Farrell recalled a litany of Fenian activity and painted Kelly as an active associate of the convicted Joe Brady:

> *I know the prisoner at the bar, and have known him for about three years. I was a member of the Fenian organisation and had met the prisoner at meetings of that body … I remember a meeting at Victoria Bridge where I met Curley, [Kelly], Brady and a man named Rowles amongst others. They were walking up and down in twos and threes. [Kelly] was repeatedly with Joe Brady.*[276]

Farrell said that they were there for the purpose of assassinating William Forster. Daniel Curley instructed Farrell to stop the Chief Secretary's coach when it neared the bridge, so that the assassins could carry out their mission. Having failed on this occasion, the Invincibles left the scene.

Farrell was, however, a dangerous witness for the prosecution to rely upon. It had already been proven in the Joseph Brady case that he had perjured himself, and this fact was seized upon by Kelly's defence, led by DB Sullivan. Sullivan sought to portray the former Fenian as a notorious liar, a man who could not be relied upon in a case where a young life was hanging in the balance:

Sullivan:	*Farrell, how often have you committed perjury?*
Farrell:	*How often?*
Sullivan:	*Yes.*
Farrell:	*Once.*
Sullivan:	*How many falsehoods have you sworn on the gospels?*
Farrell:	*I swore on my examination at Dublin Castle that I was not a Fenian and that I did not belong to the Invincibles.*
Sullivan:	*Both were perjuries?*
Farrell:	*They were lies, yes.*[277]

Drawing on his earlier admission during Brady's trial, repeated at Curley's trial, that he had lied under oath to John Adye Curran at the Star Chamber inquiry, Sullivan once more extracted from Farrell an admission that he had lied:

Sullivan:	*When were you first examined on oath in connection with this business?*
Farrell:	*On Friday 29th December 1882 at Dublin Castle, before Mr Curran.*
Sullivan:	*You were sworn to tell the truth?*
Farrell:	*Yes.*
Sullivan:	*You were asked on your oath if you knew Daniel Curley the carpenter?*
Farrell:	*Yes I was.*
Sullivan:	*What was your answer?*
Farrell:	*I said I did not.*
Sullivan:	*Was that true?*
Farrell:	*It was not true.*
Sullivan:	*Were you asked if you knew Joseph Brady?*
Farrell:	*I was.*
Sullivan:	*Did you swear that you did not?*

Farrell:	*I swore that I did not. It was a falsehood.*
Sullivan:	*Were you asked if you belonged to an illegal society?*
Farrell:	*I was.*
Sullivan:	*Did you swear that you did not?*
Farrell:	*I swore that I did not. That was also a false oath.*
Sullivan:	*Were you asked if there were illegal meetings in York Street?*
Farrell:	*I was, and I swore that there was not. I swore that I would tell the truth honestly.*
Sullivan:	*And did you?*
Farrell:	*I told lies.*[278]

The defence had successfully created doubt over the accuracy of Farrell's testimony under oath, but Kelly would be placed in the park by James Carey, who testified that he saw Kelly, alongside Brady, advancing on Burke and Cavendish. This evidence was corroborated by Thomas Huxley, a gardener formerly in the employ of Edward Cecil Guinness at Farmleigh house, who could easily confirm that Kelly was one of the men he saw in the park on 6 May 1882, following the assassinations. Huxley recalled that he saw a group of men close to the scene of the assassinations, on his way into Dublin through the park:

> *In May last I was in the employment of Mr Guinness at Farmleigh, Castleknock. On the evening of the 6th of May I came into town by the park and after crossing the road at Castleknock, I noticed a group of men at the second clump of trees on the road near to Dublin ... When first I saw them they appeared to be conversing, and as I approached they separated and walked about.*[279]

Huxley's evidence, however, was rather sullied when it emerged under cross-examination that he had been paid £8 and £7 by John Mallon on two separate occasions after he had sworn his deposition:

Sullivan:	*Have you got any money recently?*
Huxley:	*Yes.*
Sullivan:	*From whom?*
Huxley:	*From Mr Mallon.*
Sullivan:	*The Chief of Detectives?*
Huxley:	*Yes.*
Sullivan:	*How much?*
Huxley:	*£8 – about a fortnight ago. I got £7 from him seven or eight weeks ago.*
Sullivan:	*Since you swore your deposition?*
Huxley:	*Yes, I got no other money.*
Sullivan:	*Did you expect no other sum of money?*
Huxley:	*No. I would not refuse it.*

The defence submitted that Huxley had been paid for false evidence. Re-examined by the prosecution, Huxley claimed the money had been paid to him as expenses connected to a move to England for his own safety, and that there was no truth in the suggestion that he had been corrupted.

Timothy Kelly's older brother Patrick provided an alibi, stating that Kelly had remained in the family home all day on the Friday and Saturday. According to Patrick's version of events, Kelly had read the paper in their home after arriving from work. The two went to a public house around 6.30pm, and then went to a friend's house in Aungier Street. The friend in question was Simon Reid, who testified that the Kelly brothers had come to his house at 7.30pm, just at the time of the assassinations. This story was confirmed by three other witnesses – Patrick Reid, brother of Simon, James McConn and Paddy Neville, all of whom were old school friends and claimed to have been with Kelly that evening. However, Kelly's work supervisor, John Brown, claimed that the apprentice Kelly usually worked from 6am to 8.30pm each day, but had not been at work on the afternoon of 6 May 1882.

Closing the case, the prosecution put to the jury that Kelly had been an active Invincible, involved in all previous attempts at assassination; and that his presence in the park had been noted by informers within the conspiracy and corroborated by independent witnesses. To this, the defence replied that the evidence of the informers should be ignored on the basis of infamy and perjury, while the evidence of identification of Kelly in the park was utterly unreliable. Given that Kelly's life was in the balance, if there was any shadow of a doubt over his guilt, the jury must rule not guilty.

On examining the evidence, the jury could not reach a verdict, many sympathising with the youthful prisoner:

> The twelve 'good men and true,' at last entered after an hour and ten minutes and slowly filled their seats. Silence was called and the clerk of the Crown held up his hand for the issue paper. He saw, however, that it was blank, and handed it back to the foreman; then putting the formal question, said 'gentlemen, have you agreed to your verdict?' the foreman answered 'we have not ... your lordship charged us that we could find that he was in the Park – if there was some more evidence that he was in the Park. We are not clear about it.'[280]

The jury was dismissed, and Kelly was returned to Kilmainham Gaol. Onlookers recalled that he seemed intensely relieved as he left the dock, waving and smiling at friends and family.

Three days later, Kelly was again arraigned at Green Street Courthouse. The outcome was the same, with the jury divided on the evidence of Kelly's presence in Phoenix Park. Kelly was again returned to Kilmainham Gaol, while the Court mused on an unprecedented third trial.

8

MICHAEL FAGAN

Michael Fagan was originally from Westmeath, but lived in Dublin, working as a blacksmith for John Fagan of Brunswick Street. He was twenty-four years of age and illiterate, and lived in an artisan cottage in Buckingham Street, on the northside of the city. A leading figure in Dublin Fenianism, he had acted as centre of a Fenian circle previously, connected intimately with James Mullet and Daniel Curley.

Fagan pleaded not guilty to the charge of murder. As in Kelly's case, the prosecution, headed by Peter O'Brien, said that Fagan was present throughout the Invincible conspiracy, had been involved in all attempts to assassinate Forster and was in Phoenix Park on 6 May 1882. While the case again relied on the testimony of informants, it was to be legitimised by two new independent witnesses, Michael McKeon and Thomas McEneny, compositors for *The Irish Times*. McKeon, who had declined to testify until forced to do so by the judge, claimed to know Fagan and to have seen him in the park, near the nine acres, on the day of the assassinations.

McEneny, called to the stand, was uncooperative, refusing to testify:

McEneny:	*No power can make me give evidence.*
Judge O'Brien:	*Come on to the table Sir!*
McEneny:	*I refuse.*
O'Brien:	*Come on to the table Sir!*[281]

Judge O'Brien's patience snapped, and McEneny was made to come to the Judge's bench. He was given the Bible to swear upon, but threw it to the floor without taking an oath. O'Brien was furious with McEneny's contempt of court, and now threatened him with twelve months' imprisonment. McEneny relented, and corroborated McKeon's testimony, saying he had met Fagan eight months prior to the assassinations, at a public house in Fleet Street near *The Irish Times*, in McKeon's company. He had met him several more times between then and the assassinations, and was familiar with his appearance.

The statements of *The Irish Times* compositors were verified by Fagan's boss, John Fagan. While unable to place him in Phoenix Park on the day of the assassinations, he noted that Fagan had mysteriously not been in work on that day, or on 27 November, the day of the attempt on Denis Field. John Fagan expressed surprise, however, that Michael Fagan was in the dock as a prisoner, being able to offer on his behalf a good character reference as an honest and sober man.[282]

James Carey proved more amenable than the independent witnesses, and reiterated his version of events, again stating that Fagan was one of the seven men who had walked in column towards Cavendish and Burke. Fagan watched Carey intently, laughing and dismissive of the informer's evidence. On behalf of Fagan, Richard Adams cross-examined the witness, following the by-now established strategy of sowing doubt in the minds of the jury as to Carey's testimony and character. Adams successfully cornered Carey into a declaration that the assassination of Burke was legitimate, as the oppressed had a right to assassinate their oppressors:

Adams:	*Do you know the ten commandments ...? Are you aware one of them is thou shall not kill?*
Carey:	*Perfectly.*
Adams:	*Are you aware that murder is forbidden by the faith you belong to?*
Carey:	*I am quite well aware of that.*
Adams:	*Would you be glad to remove tyrants now?*
Carey:	*No trouble at all.*
Adams:	*Are you at this moment anxious to remove tyrants?*
Carey:	*I am not in a position.*
Adams:	*Are you at this moment anxious to remove tyrants?*
Carey:	*The wish might be farther to the thought.*
Adams:	*Would you desire to have the opportunity?*
Carey:	*What is the use in my saying I would? They should always be removed.*
Adams:	*Whom do you mean by tyrants at this moment?*
Carey:	*Anyone who tramples on the rights of the people.*
Adams:	*Is there anyone in the Government now you would be anxious to remove?*
Carey:	*I don't know anyone, they are less guilty now than Mr Burke.*
Adams:	*Yes. Was Mr Burke a tyrant?*
Carey:	*Yes: Only for him Mr Forster would not have got all the tips.*
Adams:	*You do not consider it a crime to remove Mr Burke?*
Carey:	*Not the slightest!*
Adams:	*Nor a sin? Do you consider it a sin now?*
Carey:	*I may have altered my mind ... These were no sins and you will not get any more answers from me![283]*

Alongside Carey, the usual informants were to be used to convict Fagan. Joe Smith placed the prisoner in the park on the day of the assassinations, standing near Skin the Goat's cab. Smith alleged that he had seen Fagan with other Invincibles in Brunswick Street throughout April 1882. Carey had told Smith at the time that they were on 'business', a reference to conspiracy to assassinate. However, Smith had earlier claimed that he did not know Fagan until he saw him in Kilmainham Gaol, and that he had only thought he had seen the prisoner in Phoenix Park on 6 May 1882. Smith's evidence brought little new to the case, especially as he had left Phoenix Park before the assassinations took place, and the evidence he did give was clearly circumstantial.

Smith meandered from his original testimony, however, directly contradicting Carey in two ways. Firstly, according to Carey's narrative, Smith had been employed to identify Burke to the waiting Invincibles, but now, for the first time, Smith exclaimed that Carey was perfectly familiar with Burke's appearance, and so he was not needed. On a second point, Carey had stated that Edward McCaffrey had not been in the park on 6 May 1882, and had in fact been working that day. He had said that following the assassinations, a council of Invincibles was held, in which events at the park were detailed by all involved. While McCaffrey was at this meeting, he had nothing to say, as he knew nothing of the actual events in the park. Smith now placed McCaffrey in the park on 6 May.

Carey was recalled, and adhered rigidly to his story, implying that Smith was lying. Only being able to speak for himself, he said, he had not seen McCaffrey in the park, and as far as he knew, he was not there. Prompted by the Attorney General, however, Carey did allow the possibility that McCaffrey was behind Skin the Goat's cab when he went to the assassins to identify Burke.

Carey's younger brother Peter now took the stand. He confirmed the existence of an assassination society operating in Dublin. He said that his duties included taking care of weaponry, which he termed 'tools', with Dan

Curley instructing him when and where they were needed. While this was tantalising stuff, it had little to do with the events of 6 May 1882, and many were aware that Peter Carey had not witnessed the assassinations, and unlike Smith, had not actually been in Phoenix Park. The younger Carey detailed a plot to assassinate Forster at St Mark's Church, Brunswick Street, on Easter Sunday of the previous year. On this occasion, he saw Joe Mullet, Carey, Caffrey and Michael Fagan. Failing on the Sunday, the group returned to Brunswick Street the following day. Forster failed to arrive, and they tried a third time on the Wednesday, but again there was no sign of Forster:

> *The attack was to be made at Mark's Church, and Brady was to come round to my place and give me any tools they had, and I was to make away with them in a bag, up to another place, so I stopped in my own house looking out the window until after seven o'clock, when I saw James Carey and Peter Doyle ... Peter Doyle called me ... James told me I would have to be at Mark's Church at ten o'clock that night. I went there and saw the same men with others there again ... Between that evening and the night I saw there the two Delaneys, Joe Brady, Joe Mullet, Michael Fagan, Edward O'Brien, George Smith, Dan Curley and Tim Kelly.*[284]

Thus, according to the younger Carey, Fagan was a key Invincible, involved in earlier attempts at political assassination, and there was no reason to believe that he was not in the Phoenix Park on 6 May of the previous year. Peter Carey could place Fagan amongst leading Invincibles on several occasions, such as the Brunswick Street plot, when he understood that the Invincibles were out to assassinate the Chief Secretary.

Robert Farrell next took to the witness box. He described the Invincibles as an assassination society based on and within Fenianism. Like Carey, he could place Fagan among leading Invincibles on several occasions, intending to assassinate the Chief Secretary. However, Farrell was also not in Phoenix Park on the day of the assassinations, and his evidence was therefore nothing more than circumstantial.

That Fagan was involved in conspiracy was beyond doubt. Following his arrest, a police raid on his home had discovered materials relating to the collection of money for Fenianism, including a small book divided into columns under the headings 'C' and 'M', which the Dublin Metropolitan Police thought might stand for 'civil' and 'military',[285] accounting the amount of £26.9s.6d. Fagan's defence never sought to deny that he was a Fenian, and admitted that he was in the Phoenix Park on 6 May 1882, but denied that he was actually part of the assassination group who had waited on Burke. The defence, led by Mr Byrne, contended that evidence would show that Fagan had left the park before 6pm, having met McKeon and McEneny. According to Fagan's alibi, he was in fact on D'Olier Street at twenty minutes to seven, en route to a house on Walworth Road. Fagan's brother-in-law, William Scully, testified that he had a drink with Fagan and a man named Fox around ten minutes to seven. A further witness, a lady named McMahon from Liverpool, who had been staying with her daughter Jane at the house in Walworth Road, recalled that Fagan had been in her daughter's home that evening, until ten o'clock, and could not possibly have been in Phoenix Park.

McMahon's evidence was challenged, however, on the basis of her son-in-law, Arthur Forrester, also of Walworth Road. Forrester had left Ireland in the wake of the establishment of Adye Curran's Star Chamber inquiry. McMahon said that he had lost his job as a paper reader and moved to England, although when asked his address she could not recall it. To the court, this was extremely suspicious, particularly when the prosecution put it to McMahon that Arthur Forrester was a Fenian centre, and that on the day of James Mullet's arrest relative to the Bailey assassination, he and his wife were with him and taken into custody, her husband ultimately evading arrest as a fugitive. Furthermore, it emerged that Forrester had been arrested previously in England, for possession of revolvers linked to Fenianism. McMahon's daughter, Jane Forrester, corroborated her mother's testimony, but was forced under oath to admit that her husband and Mullet were friends and would meet regularly. While this was largely inconsequential, the fact that Mullet was a leading Fenian, and that Forrester was obviously connected to some unspecified Fenian activity, tended to undermine Fagan's alibi.

Despite this, however, the defence had a strong case. Closing arguments stated that Michael Fagan had been implicated in the conspiracy by informers such as Carey, Smith and Kavanagh, all of whom had admitted their parts in the assassinations. Fagan had left the park, meeting William Scully, Mrs McMahon and Forrester, an alibi confirmed by independent witnesses, Fagan having as much right as any other citizen to be in Phoenix Park on that momentous day. Pleading with the jury, his representation asked them,

> ... as sensible and Christian men to pause before they convicted [Fagan], who could not speak for himself and could only be heard through the medium of his advocate – before they sent a man to his doom upon the evidence of a man like James Carey, who defamed the most sacred rites of his church, for the purpose of concealing from man the blackness of a heart that could not be hidden by the all seeing eye of heaven.[286]

The fact that Fagan was a Fenian should not affect the case, it was argued, as he was not being tried for treason felony and membership of a secret society, but for involvement in the assassinations of Cavendish and Burke.

By 27 April, the jury had decided Fagan's fate. He was found guilty of the assassinations of Lord Frederick Cavendish and Thomas Henry Burke. Showing little emotion as the jury announced their verdict, he looked to his solicitor, indicating that he expected nothing else from the court.

Judge O'Brien asked Fagan if he had anything to say as to why he should not be executed. Standing up, Fagan hit the dock with his hand, exclaiming that he was a Fenian and would die a Fenian, but that he was not guilty of these crimes:

> Fagan: *I am not guilty Sir; I have nothing to say but that I am not guilty. I am not guilty except by being a Fenian; I might be guilty and I will die one ...*
>
> Judge O'Brien: *Michael Fagan the jury have found you guilty, and it was impossible for them to have arrived at any other conclusion. Your guilt has been made clear to demonstration, and no reasonable being can entertain any doubt as to it. Not only were you a member of this conspiracy – not only did it appear that you were taking in several of those murderous proceedings. But your presence at the scene of the crime was established upon the evidence of persons who were most reluctant to give evidence against you ... I shall only make one observation, and that is as to your awful fate. This is a dreadful lesson to all persons against those secret societies into one of which you entered under the corrupting influences of someone who had lured you into it.*[287]

Judge O'Brien sentenced the third Invincible to death by hanging, to be carried out at Kilmainham Gaol on 28 May 1883.

9

'SKIN THE GOAT' – JAMES FITZHARRIS

'**S**kin the Goat' was tried on Monday, 31 April, at Green Street Courthouse. His somewhat unusual appearance drew attention from observers:

> *His appearance is more remarkable that that of any of the other prisoners …*
> *He is a man of about fifty years of age, and is of the middle height. The hair on*
> *his head is of an iron gray colour, but his moustache and beard is quite sandy.*
> *Heavy brows overhang a pair of small, bright, twinkling eyes, which in their*
> *turn surmount a nose which at some time or other must have been broken.*
> *His clothes are rather shabby, and around his neck he wears an old red cotton*
> *handkerchief with the pin of which he is in the habit of picking his nails.*[288]

The defence argued that there was no proof that Fitzharris was actually a member of the Invincibles, that his presence in Phoenix Park was simply in pursuit of legitimate business as a cab driver, and that he was unaware of the intentions of the assassins. Representing Fitzharris, McInerney held that the case had been prejudiced from the beginning, with the story of the assassinations played over and over again through the media and the previous trials. This reversed the principle of being presumed innocent until proven guilty, and placed a difficult onus on the defence. McInerney said that the defence would not be putting forward any witnesses, but requested the right to make a final speech. Judge O'Brien denied this, saying there was no precedent for such a request.

Opening the case for the prosecution, given the publicity surrounding the trials and the well-worn testimony of several figures implicated in the assassinations, there was little need for the Attorney General to revisit what had already been established. He did, however, state that anyone implicated in the conspiracy was guilty of the crime. The prosecution, therefore, was setting out to make the case that while Fitzharris had not actually killed anyone, he was an accomplice to the assassinations. Rehashing the origins of the Invincibles society, the Attorney General sought to illustrate that Skin the Goat was involved in attempts on the lives of Forster and Burke. He said that Fitzharris had recruited Joseph Smith into the Invincibles, as a means of identifying Thomas Henry Burke.

Having outlined the case against Skin the Goat, the prosecution called its first witness: Joseph Smith. According to Smith, he first met Fitzharris at the Lower Castle Yard of Dublin Castle, asking the whereabouts of a man named Cummings. According to Smith, Fitzharris claimed that Cummings had left a stick in his cab, and he wished to give it back to him. Smith introduced Skin to Cummings, but noticed that he received no stick. Withdrawing to a public house, the three men began drinking. Cummings left early, and Fitzharris asked some questions regarding Thomas Henry Burke and his regular habits. A couple of days later, Fitzharris met Smith at Wrenn's tavern opposite the Castle and here, according to Smith, he introduced him to James Carey.

Smith said that on 6 May 1882, he met Daniel Curley and Joseph Brady with James Carey at Wrenn's tavern. Leaving the pub with Carey, they headed towards Parliament Street. He saw Fitzharris's cab, with Joseph Hanlon on board, and Fitzharris drove the cab to Phoenix Park. Sitting with Carey in the park, waiting for Burke, Fitzharris lay against his cab, reading a newspaper. When Burke arrived, Fitzharris drove Smith and Carey to the other party of Invincibles.

James Carey was called once again as a witness. He recounted some of the nineteen attempts on Forster's life, and Fitzharris's alleged role in the attempts to kill the Chief Secretary. On 18 April 1883, Carey said, he met Skin at Pembroke Quay with a number of other Invincibles, waiting for Forster. In Carey's narrative, this attempt on the former Chief Secretary's life was a failure due to Henry Rowles failing to signal his approach. Fitzharris had driven his cab toward Forster's, the intention being to block and stop the cab on a received signal, Invincibles then boarding the carriage and assassinating the Chief Secretary. In another attempt on Forster's life, Carey said he had driven in Fitzharris's cab toward Brunswick Street, carrying knives to meet with waiting Invincibles. On 6 May 1882, Carey confirmed Smith's evidence of driving to the park in Skin's cab. On spotting Burke, they made their way to the advance party on Kavanagh's cab to point him out.

James 'Skin the Goat' Fitzharris.

The younger Carey brother, Peter, confirmed James Carey's evidence that Skin the Goat was at the meeting on Pembroke Quay, seeking to kill Forster. Peter Carey repeated that Skin's role was to block Forster's carriage at John Street, facilitating the assassination. Recalling this attempted assassination, Carey recollected that Skin had been despondent at it failure. Skin stressed that had he had weapons, he would have killed Forster himself. Peter Carey also stated that Skin had told him all about the assassinations of 6 May 1882, naming Joe Brady and Timothy Kelly as the actual assassins.

Robert Farrell, also appearing as a Crown witness, offered little to incriminate Fitzharris. Despite having been sworn into conspiracy, Farrell had stated on oath that he had never before seen Fitzharris until imprisoned in Kilmainham Gaol. Myles Kavanagh, however, called to the stand after Farrell, could identify Skin as the second cab driver in the park, driving the second group of Invincibles away at speed.

The testimony of the informers was somewhat diluted by testimony from three independent witnesses, including Daniel Booth, a cab driver working on the evening of the assassinations. Booth had been hailed at Westland Row, his passenger headed for the Hibernian School in Phoenix Park. Booth recalled seeing Fitzharris's cab near the cricket ground, his horse facing the Phoenix monument, Skin sitting on the grass, smoking. However, Booth said that no men were around Skin or speaking to him, and this evidence was confirmed by a second independent witness, Joseph Neill, who had been passing through the park that evening.[289] These statements supported the defence line that Fitzharris was in the park on legitimate business, rather than Invincibles activity.

This position was ridiculed by the prosecution, who said it was entirely unbelievable that Fitzharris knew nothing of the Invincibles conspiracy, and was simply employed by the same men on several occasions of attempted and actual assassination. For this to be proven, however, the jury had to believe in the reliability of the evidence given by the approvers. With regard to this evidence, Murphy, on behalf of the prosecution, asked a rhetorical question: If the approvers were correct that Skin had driven them to and from Phoenix Park, and if Fitzharris was indeed engaged in legitimate business, why did he not leave when he saw the assassinations? Why did he wait, and bring some of the group on a prearranged route to safety? Answering his own question, Murphy said it was because he was an Invincible himself, a player in the conspiracy.

Weighing up all of the evidence, the jury eventually decided that Skin the Goat was not guilty of the charge of complicity in the Phoenix Park assassinations of 6 May 1882. Despite this verdict, however, Fitzharris was not released. The prosecution wanted to try him again, on another charge, so he was returned to Kilmainham Gaol.

The second trial of James Fitzharris began on Tuesday, 15 May 1883, on the charge of being an accessory to the Phoenix Park assassinations. The prosecution, this time represented by Solicitor General John Naish, sought to prove that Fitzharris was indeed an Invincible, an active participant in conspiracy, and not merely in Phoenix Park that day on legitimate business.

As in the first trial, the first witness against Skin was Joseph Smith, who reiterated his earlier evidence. James Carey on this occasion lacked the bravado of his former performances, and when the name of Joe Brady was mentioned, he was seen to show emotion. Carey brought little new to Fitzharris's second trial, but under cross-examination he said that he had paid Skin the Goat the usual fare for journeying to the park, and that to his recollection he was not an Invincible. Joseph Hanlon again told of being in Phoenix Park on 6 May 1882, having been driven there by Fitzharris with Carey and Smith, whom he claimed not to have known before that journey. Separating from Brady, Kelly, Caffrey and Delaney, Hanlon recalled leaving the park with Curley and Fagan on Skin's carriage, although he was not sure that Curley had given the driver orders where to go. Peter Carey followed once more, narrating the failed attempts on Forster's life, and recalling in great detail what Skin had allegedly told him of what he had seen of the assassinations. This, one newspaper lamented, was a horrible piece of sensationalism.

Following the four approvers came four independent witnesses – William Meagle, John Cummins, Patrick Murray and Daniel Booth – all of whom testified that Fitzharris was in the park on 6 May 1882. However, they could not prove that Skin was not in the park on legitimate business. The defence argued that the Crown case had failed to prove Fitzharris's complicity in the assassinations. On this occasion, the jury disagreed, and James Fitzharris was found guilty of complicity. Judge O'Brien sentenced him to life imprisonment:

> *James Fitzharris, you have been found guilty of this crime. You were charged with the crime of murder and acquitted; but the crime of which you are now being convicted differs in no respect of the moral guilt from that of murder. The death of Mr Burke and Lord Frederick Cavendish was principally owing to your act, for, if you had not corrupted the man Smith, who had been employed at the Castle, the crime might not have been committed. Your life was saved by the merciful spirit of the law, against which a large part of that life had been spent in plotting. But the inexorable necessities of the law, as well as of justice, demand that for your crime you be sentenced, as I now sentence you, to penal servitude for the remainder of your life.*[290]

Briefly taken to Mountjoy Prison in Dublin, Skin was then taken to Britain, where he would remain in prison until 1899. Recollecting visiting Skin the Goat in Maryborough Gaol in 1897, the Irish MP James O'Connor noted:

> *He was known for many years as the drollest and wittiest jarvey in Dublin. How his car driving colleagues came to call him 'Skin the Goat' I do not know,*

but by that sobriquet he was distinguished in his popular profession. He is the least changed in appearance of his prison companions, and though he must be at least seventy years of age, he is as straight as a young soldier, and as full of fun and merriment as a sailor ashore.[291]

Released with Laurence Hanlon on a ticket of leave in 1899, the two made for Dublin on 23 August, arriving at midnight. Despite having just been released from seventeen years in prison, no car could be found, and the two walked from Inchicore to Joe Mullet's home in Bridge Street. James Fitzharris died in poverty on 7 September 1910, having spent his last days in a Dublin workhouse. He is buried in Glasnevin Cemetery.

10

THOMAS CAFFREY & PATRICK DELANEY

The trial of Thomas Caffrey, on 2 May 1883 at Green Street Courthouse before Judge O'Brien, lasted a little under one hour. Caffrey was tried alongside Patrick Delaney, who admitted being in the park on Invincibles business, and leaving in Kavanagh's cab, but not to the actual assassinations. Arriving in Court, the prisoners were not accompanied by their solicitor Gerald Byrne, as they did not intend to fight the case against them.

In the dock, Caffrey and Delaney looked worn, sickly and haggard, the rigours of Kilmainham Gaol etched on their faces. Unlike Caffrey, Delaney had provided valuable information on the conspiracy while under lock and key, identifying leading figures including Patrick James Sheridan, Thomas Brennan, Patrick Egan and Frank Byrne, all associated with the Land League and Fenianism.

O'Brien: *Patrick Delaney, you stand indicted that you, on 6th May 1882, feloniously, wilfully and of your malice aforethought, did kill and murder one Thomas Henry Burke. How say you? Are you guilty or not guilty?*

Delaney: *I am guilty of being in the Park, but I did not commit the murder.*[292]

Judge O'Brien demanded that Delaney plead either guilty or not guilty to the murder charge, and Delaney confirmed his culpability. Explaining to the judge why he should not be executed, Delaney amazingly claimed not to have known what the Invincibles stood for. He portrayed himself as an innocent, foolishly drawn into the conspiracy by more cunning men, and only taking part in operations under fear of death. On his attempted assassination of Judge Lawson, he claimed that he had been selected to carry out the operation by Mullet and Brady, but preferred not to assassinate the notorious judge. He had been willing to go to gaol rather than die for disobeying orders and violating his oath. Delaney claimed to have known that Lawson was protected by security, and claimed that in order to avoid killing him, he purposely alerted his entourage, drawing attention to himself and facilitating his capture. Delaney pleaded with Judge O'Brien not to execute him, declaring:

My Lord – I was drawn into this without knowing what it was about. I was brought into it at first foolishly – I was taken away from my work to go there. I was ordered there, and I had to obey the order or take the consequences. I had to go to the Park. I was at the scene of the murder, and saw what took place, but I took no part in it. For my own sake I went on to Kavanagh's car. He speaks the truth, and so does Carey. And I say what is the truth. I took no active part in the murder. It was Brady and Kelly who committed the murders and no other persons …

... My Lord, about Judge Lawson's affair, it was me that saved Judge Lawson's life. I was put on to shoot Judge Lawson, and the only way I had to get out of it was to draw McDonnell's attention to me, and I preferred to go to prison sooner than commit it.[293]

Despite Delaney's guilty plea, Judge O'Brien decided that he must be executed, as 'if he were present, and there with the intention of taking part in the murder, it was all the same whether or not he actually struck Mr Burke or not. In either case the punishment for the crime was death, and sentence of death should be passed.'[294] Placing the black cap on his head, O'Brien said:

See what you have brought yourself to – see the misery and ruin you have brought on your wife and children by this conspiracy. I have but one duty to perform, and that is to pronounce on you the sentence that the law demands and requires on your plea of guilty. And I do order and adjudge, that you be taken from the bar of this court to her majesty's prison in Kilmainham ... and that on the 2nd day of June next, you be taken to the common place of execution, within the walls of that prison, and that you be hanged by the neck until you are dead and may the Lord have mercy on your soul.[295]

Placing his hat on his head, Delaney nodded to Judge O'Brien, made a word of thanks and was ushered from the dock by prison officers, disappearing from view.

Thomas Caffrey, 'a somewhat sloppy, careless, self-neglected kind of fellow',[296] was next arraigned before Judge O'Brien. While not involved in the actual assassination of Cavendish and Burke, he was determined to plead guilty:

My Lord, I have to say, standing here on the brink of my grave that I did not know what was going to happen twenty minutes or half an hour before,

I was ordered to go there and if I did not go there my life would have been taken. That is all I have to say my Lord.[297]

Caffrey was something of a hanger-on, described by historian Frederick Bussy as:

… a fairly average specimen of the Irish 'omadhaun' and was so regarded by his companions. A fellow who would pull a car out of a ditch and could be trusted to keep a pipe alight or mind the coats at a fight, kick an objectionable stranger, or run a mile with a message, so long as there was a drink at the end of the task.[298]

Like Delaney, Caffrey said he had only gone to Phoenix Park under threat of death. He had not known what he was to be used for until twenty minutes before the actual assassinations, therefore repudiating the accusation of intention to assassinate. Yet despite this, and despite his not having been an assassin, Caffrey, like Delaney, was sentenced to death. He was to be hanged at Kilmainham Gaol on 2 June:

I have no means, Thomas Caffrey, of judging the truth of the statement you have now made. However, I do not desire to be understood as necessarily conveying that statement is untrue. You are a terrible example of the consequence of your crime. I know nothing whatsoever of you except that I assume I am right in concluding that you have been drawn into this crime – that you have brought yourself to this friendless and deplorable condition by having become a member of a secret society whose object was assassination. Your fate is an additional reason for all persons of your class and station to at once come out of this wicked conspiracy, this awful destructive system of secret conspiracy that has carried ruin and desolation into many a home in this country.[299]

Although Delaney had been tried and charged on the same day as Caffrey, and for the same misdemeanour, Earl Spencer reprieved the former and not the latter. This was seen as peculiar, given the similarities between the cases against Delaney and Caffrey. Both men had accompanied Kavanagh as he drove the assassins away from the park. While Caffrey had admitted guilt, Delaney had given Mallon information regarding the conspiracy, and was rewarded thus. No reprieve would be granted to Caffrey, although Frederick Bussy hinted that he would not have been executed for the assassinations had he not been implicated in further transgressions. What these misdemeanours may have been has unfortunately been lost to the passage of time. Bussy, however, hinted at a connection to incidents at Barbaville, County Westmeath, and Loughrea, County Galway.

On 2 April 1882, William Marlowe Smyth, landlord of Barbaville House in Westmeath, was returning home from church in his carriage, with his wife, sister-in-law and a Lady Harriet Monck. They had just entered the grounds of his estate, when the coachman spotted a number of men with rifles, faces blackened, opening fire. The carriage was riddled with a haze of bullets. Smyth survived, but his wife was shot in the head and died instantly.

At Castledaly, Loughrea, on 6 June 1882, a landlord and Resident Magistrate, Walther Bourke, was killed by five IRB men. Bourke had possession of estates at Curraleigh, near Claremorris in County Mayo, and Rathasane, County Galway. He was notorious within his estates at this time of heightened agitation, demanding rent of his tenants that they could not afford to pay, and ultimately serving eviction notices on them. *The Freeman's Journal* recalled of his relations with his tenants that 'during the whole land agitation they and he have been a little short of open war'.[300] Such was the repugnance Bourke was held in that he 'seldom went out without protection, and was not unarmed, even when attending mass'.[301]

Returning from a holiday in England, Bourke was protected by two uniformed British soldiers armed with Winchester rifles. Making his way to his farm, he met John Newell, a local IRB centre and farm labourer, and the two men chatted for a while. The following morning, accompanied by a British dragoon soldier for his protection, Bourke went to Gort, seeking eviction papers upon his tenantry. Travelling home from Gort, he was ambushed at Castledaly and killed along with his escort and his horse, shot by assassins concealed behind a wall. John Newell's son, Marcus, recalled that the slugs used against the landlord were in his father's pockets the previous day.[302]

In both these cases, the weapons used were rifles and of a good class. Mallon connected them to Thomas Caffrey and Michael Fagan:

> *They found their way via Dublin, through Dan Curley. They were consigned to a family connection of Curley's as 'stir rods,' and some of them were consigned to Loughrea by Caffrey, while others were taken to Barbavilla by Fagan.*[303]

While Mallon could not be sure of Caffrey's exact involvement in the assassination of Bourke, he was convinced that Fagan had been one of the men involved in the attack on Smyth in Galway, as well as in further attacks in Tubbercurry, County Sligo.

11

EDWARD O'BRIEN & PETER DOYLE

The trials of Edward O'Brien and Peter Doyle, on charges of conspiring to assassinate public figures, were held on 11 May 1883. Arriving in the dock, it was noted that Edward O'Brien looked pale and wretched, Victorian prison life clearly disagreeing with him. O'Brien offered a plea of guilty, and Judge O'Brien sentenced him to ten years' penal servitude.

Peter Doyle also pleaded guilty to the charge of conspiracy, but requested to be allowed to bring forward a character reference. He argued that he had been brought into the conspiracy by smarter persons and, on learning its objective,

Edward O'Brien.

withdrew from the society. Judge O'Brien indicated that he had a problem with this, as Myles Kavanagh had said in his testimony that he had been inducted into the conspiracy in Doyle's company. The character witness would be John Brown, his employer, who stated that on the day of the assassinations, Doyle was at work. Brown described Doyle as a conscientious worker and a man of good character, who was working on 5 and 6 May 1882, and could not therefore have been involved in the assassinations. Judge O'Brien took the opportunity to condemn Brown for having so many Fenians and those with Fenian sympathies in his employment, opining that all bosses should take measures to avoid men of these opinions in their employment.

Judge O'Brien said that, given Doyle was not in Phoenix Park on 6 May 1882, he would grant the prisoner an exception, but he could not help but remember Kavanagh's assertion that he had been introduced into the Invincibles conspiracy by Doyle. To this, Doyle noted that he had not introduced Kavanagh into conspiracy to assassinate. Taking all of this into account, Peter Doyle was sentenced to five years in prison.

Peter Doyle.

12

JAMES MULLET, WILLIAM MORONEY & LAURENCE HANLON

James Mullet was tried for involvement in the attempted assassination of Denis Field. Judge O'Brien noted that he had been implicated as a leading figure in conspiracy, for over a year, to assassinate leading Government officials repugnant to the nationalist cause. Mullet pleaded guilty to the charge of conspiracy, but as he was incarcerated at Kilmainham on the day of the Phoenix Park assassinations, he could not be implicated in them. Judge O'Brien noted, however, that Mullet was a principal in the conspiracy. He had been involved in the planning of the attack on Denis Field and William Barrett, and was also a central individual within Fenianism. For Judge O'Brien, this called for firm punishment:

You were in custody on the 6th of May, and for some time previous, and it is impossible therefore, for me to impute to you, at least any external part in the dreadful tragedy of that day. But that is all that can be said in extenuation of your part in this conspiracy. You were one of the principals who organised it, and you remained in authority until you were arrested. You were one of those who planned the murderous attack on Mr Barrett, according to which it was arranged that a letter should be presented to him, and that he should then be seized by both hands and stabbed to death in the public streets ... you also planned or took part in planning the attack on Mr Field; and there is a great deal more known about you in that transaction than has been disclosed to the public ... By your influence and superior position you have led others into an abyss of crime and I must pass on you the extreme measure of the law, which, however, does not indicate the punishment you deserve, and that is that you be kept in penal servitude for ten years.[304]

On the same day as Mullet, William Moroney was also tried for conspiracy to assassinate leading Government officials. Moroney pleaded guilty, and also received a sentence of ten years' penal servitude.

Laurence Hanlon was next called to the dock, accused of attempting to kill Denis Field. Hanlon refused to plead guilty, loudly declaring that he was looking forward to his trial and was innocent of the charge. Opening the case against him, Crown prosecutor James Murphy noted that the attack on Denis Field had been particularly savage, and was the incident that had ultimately served to break the Invincibles conspiracy. The prosecutor narrated the details of the case of Michael Walsh in Galway, whose trial for the killing of a policeman had been the catalyst for the attack on Field and the attempted attack on Barrett. The attacks were portrayed as attacks on the operation of the rule of law in Ireland:

Jurors true to their God, their consciences and their duty gave verdicts in accordance with justice, and Mr Field and Mr Barrett were amongst these. The Invincibles thought they could portray themselves superior to the law, paralyse its force and deaden its arm – they felt perfect safety on account of their apparent immunity after the crime of the Phoenix Park.[305]

It was also recalled that Hanlon was a cousin of Daniel Curley, and with his brother Joseph had joined the inner circle of the Invincibles, becoming active participants in its machinations. Robert Farrell would again play a leading role in the prosecution case, telling the jury that Hanlon had narrated to him how two groups of Invincibles had sought to undertake simultaneous assassinations of Field and Barrett. One, under Joe Mullet, waited at Westland Row for Barrett, while the other, including Hanlon, waited for Field, eventually attacking him near to his home:

The prisoner and Tim Kelly went up from Westmorland Street in advance or close to Mr Field. Joe Brady and Daniel Delaney had gone up to the corner of Hardwicke Street on Kavanagh's car and waited until [Hanlon] gave the signal with a handkerchief. Mr Field was knocked down, brutally stabbed and feigned death. Then Brady and Kelly escaped on the car; Delaney and [Hanlon] escaped by another route, and the whole party met again that evening ... The prisoner accounted for the escape of Mr Field by stating that three persons were looking on and mentioned that Tim Kelly lost his hat. Farrell became informer – he knew nothing of the Park murders – he told all within his knowledge as to the prisoner's narrative. Kavanagh was arrested, and through that young man they discovered all about the assassinations of Lord Frederick Cavendish and Mr Burke. The evidence of the approvers would be borne out by independent witnesses, and there would be independent testimony to prove that Hanlon was on the scene of the attack.[306]

Denis Field was called to the stand – not to testify against Hanlon, but to describe the dreadful details of his attempted assassination. Field was noted to have recovered from his injuries, but he recalled in graphic detail the attempt on his life, the courtroom falling into weighty silence:

> *He said that he left his place of business on the 27th November 1882, at a few minutes to six o'clock, and was walking along Sackville Street to his residence in North Frederick Street. He did not see any car near to his residence. When coming up to his own door, he was engaged, with stooped head endeavouring to unfasten a button at the lower part of his coat. He felt a hand placed on his right shoulder, and the words, 'you villain,' were uttered in a low tone. He looked up and saw a couple of men in front of him. Looking the reverse way he saw two more. He received two blows on the back by what he felt was a sharp instrument ... After that he fell on his back and cried out 'murder, murder,' for several moments. He saw four men on the kerbstone. There were frequent blows aimed at him; he recollected warding off some. When he was prostrate a blow was aimed at his heart. He put up his arm and a knife or sword cane went right through it. He seized the weapon, which he found to be a three sided sword cane. He parried it with his umbrella. He got a severe blow, which cut through his jaw and right through his tongue and another in his left cheek. He lay as if dead, and saw his assailants looking at him as he lay powerless, and one by one they departed.*[307]

Laurence Hanlon was sentenced to penal servitude for life, eventually being released in 1899.

13

TIMOTHY KELLY

Timothy Kelly was tried for a third time at Green Street Courthouse on Monday, 7 May 1883. Prior to the case, one newspaper captured the mood of the political establishment when it described the results of Kelly's previous trials as 'unsatisfactory'.[308] Another paper was more to the point:

> *The cheek given to the vindication of the power of the law in Ireland by the disagreement of two juries as to the guilt of Timothy Kelly, has been fully compensated for by the pleas of 'guilty' entered yesterday by Delaney and Caffrey. What amount of truth there may be in the statements made by those wretched men as to their non-participation in the plot against Mr Burke's life until, in fear of their lives, they obeyed the order to join the expedition to the Park, is a question on which it is not necessary to pronounce any opinion. The important point is that those in charge of the prosecution have succeeded so completely in laying bare the secrets of the vile gang by which the Phoenix Park murders were carried out, that not withstanding the support given them by the*

*sympathy of the lower classes in Dublin and the manifest ease by which evidence
for an alibi can be got up, two of those engaged in the murder have recognised
that it was hopeless to attempt to resist the proofs of their complicity in the
crime. It may be fairly hoped that some sobering effect will be produced even on
the most depraved section of the Irish population by the double confession and
condemnation witnessed in Green Street yesterday.*[309]

Behind the scenes, John Mallon had extensively lobbied Earl Spencer with
a view to bringing Timothy Kelly to trial for a third time. Spencer was lean-
ing towards leniency, as two carefully selected juries had failed to reach a
decision on the evidence presented. However, Mallon told the Viceroy that
Kelly had admitted his involvement in the assassinations while at Kilmainham Gaol. If this was true, it must be wondered why this information was
never used in Kelly's three trials – there is no mention of his supposed confession in the court records. Kelly had not given Mallon any information
implicating his associates within the conspiracy, and showed no desire to
become a witness for the prosecution. On Mallon's word, Spencer agreed to
press for an unprecedented third trial.

Kelly arrived in the courtroom quite merrily, meeting looks toward
him with a wink and a smile. He looked disinterested, being tried for a
third time with exactly the same evidence and witnesses as before. Wearing an overcoat with a pink handkerchief, he was observed to lean against
the bar of the dock, gazing at the jurors and the observers in the gallery.
Bussy reports emotionally on the young Invincible in the dock, recalling
him as a 'slip of a boy, rather tall and thin, with a good stamp of features,
but somewhat pale'.[310]

Attorney General AM Porter opened the case for the Crown, illustrat-
ing the details of the Invincibles conspiracy, endeavouring to characterise
Kelly as a leading player. According to Porter's narrative, Kelly was Joe
Brady's right-hand man – whenever Brady was engaged in Invincibles

activity, Kelly was beside him. Porter outlined how he would prove that Kelly was one of the assassins in Phoenix Park on 6 May 1882, and how he fled on Kavanagh's car from the park. Kelly, sitting in the dock, listened attentively, but remained unconcerned. Looking to a Kilmainham Gaol warder sitting beside him, he indicated for a piece of paper, and receiving it, Kelly:

> ... *hastily scribbled a few words, carefully folded, what was evidently intended for a note. For he endorsed it on the outside, and concealed it in the palm of his hand.*[311]

Aware that he was being watched, Kelly indicated that he would like the note to be given to Fred Gallagher, a journalist standing near the press box. Many in the court wondered what was passing between the Invincible and the journalist. Gallagher opened the note cautiously, read it and gestured to Kelly, folding the note back and placing it in his pocket. Increasingly, rumours circulated as to what Kelly had written to Gallagher. Was it a confession? A final note? An escape plan? Frederick Bussy met Gallagher at the luncheon interval of the case. His curiosity getting the better of him, he pleaded with the journalist to tell him what was in the note. Gallagher was happy to comply, as Bussy reports:

> *'It's a shame the poor fellow cannot get out to do a little bit of business for himself – so he's asked me to do it for him,' and he handed me Kelly's paper. It contained a request that Gallagher would put a shilling for him on some horse that was running in a race taking place that day.*[312]

Kelly's horse did not win. Gallagher and his staff, along with a number of warders, reportedly backed the same horse, following Kelly's lead, and lost a great deal of money.

The first witness against Kelly was Robert Farrell, who as before recounted the background to the Invincibles conspiracy, and the failed attempts to assassinate Forster. Farrell said he had known Kelly for some years, and had met him at Fenian meetings in Dublin. Recalling an attempt on Forster near Victoria Bridge in Dublin, he recalled seeing Kelly in the company of Joe Brady. He described on another occasion seeing Brady and Kelly dismount a cab together, meeting other Invincibles at a Fenian meeting. Farrell boarded the cab later on, with Kelly and Brady, and they followed another cab towards the Viceregal Lodge, and back out of the park, the implication being that they had been following the Chief Secretary.

After Farrell came Peter Carey, in whose narrative Kelly was an active figure in the Invincibles conspiracy, a conspiracy that was explained to him by his brother James. He recalled an attempt to assassinate the former Chief Secretary at St Mark's Church in Brunswick Street, where he was told to wait until the arrival of Joe Brady and Tim Kelly, the men who would carry out the assassination. According to the younger Carey, this pattern was repeated three times. Cross-examined by Kelly's defence, Carey said:

Carey:	*I attended about five or six meetings for the purpose of murder. If the person sought was caught he would have been murdered.*
Smith:	*Would you have committed murder?*
Carey:	*I would have helped it anyway. The object of the organisation was to wipe out or remove parties. I felt no horror at it. I thought it was the right thing to do.*[313]

Myles Kavanagh recalled that he had been sworn into the Invincibles by Tim Kelly, whom he believed to be active in the conspiracy. He testified that Kelly had called on him on 5 May 1882, and he took Kelly to Phoenix Park in his cab. On the morning of the assassinations, Kelly had again ridden in Kavanagh's cab, to the home of Joseph Brady at North Anne Street, picking up the convicted Fenian. Making their way to North King Street, they collected Pat Delaney and Thomas Caffrey, and then stopped for a time at Wrenn's public house, opposite Dublin Castle. Kavanagh said he drove Kelly on two occasions that day to Kelly's yard in Thomas Street, where Delaney worked, and back to Wrenn's again.

Leaving Wrenn's around five o'clock, Kavanagh drove Kelly with the other three men to Phoenix Park, entering through the Islandbridge gate. When Smith had spotted Burke, Kavanagh drove Carey and Smith nearer to the Phoenix monument, where he saw Kelly, along with Brady and other Invincibles.

Following the assassinations, Kelly, Brady, Delaney and Caffrey mounted his cab and left by their elaborate route via Chapelizod, skirting the outskirts of the city to avoid detection. Kavanagh testified that Kelly dismounted at Palmerston Park to get the tram, making his way to a Prisoners' Aid Society meeting in Dublin city.

Under cross-examination, Kavanagh was quizzed on his alcoholism. He recalled that on 6 May 1882, he was under the influence, having consumed four alcoholic drinks prior to leaving for Phoenix Park, and three upon his return. Kavanagh asserted, however, that he was sober enough to recall the events and to drive the men to and from the park, and when Kelly had approached him on the morning of 6 May, he was entirely sober. This admission, however, was a significant knock to the prosecution case – one of its key approvers had now admitted to being under the influence of alcohol when the actual assassinations had taken place, calling into question his entire testimony on the day's events.

The fourth approver in the case against Timothy Kelly was James Carey. He arrived with a swagger, flinging his hat under the witness chair. In swearing the oath, he took the bible into both his hands, theatrically kissing it as the oath was repeated. Carey brought little new to the case, his story by now having been repeated and reported on several times. Regarding his relationship with Timothy Kelly, however, he was rather vague, testifying that he had seen the prisoner on several occasions alongside Joseph Brady. Carey recalled an article in Dublin newspaper *The Freeman's Journal* on 3 May, advising that in order to reform what was undoubtedly a rotten system, the Castle administrators needed to be cleared out from the administration. Many took this as a call for their summary removal by physical force.

As to Kelly's involvement in the Phoenix Park assassinations, Carey could place Kelly with Brady, whom he recalled held the knives in a parcel in his pocket. He identified Kelly as an active figure in the conspiracy, known to himself and the mysterious Number One. Carey would assert that along with Brady, Kelly was one of the actual assassins of 6 May 1882, although Carey himself was some yards away from the assassinations as they took place.

Cross-examined by Kelly's defence, Carey held it was no sin to assassinate the Undersecretary; he acted horrendously under the terms of the Coercion Act, administering a brutal system, imprisoning his own people and overseeing wholesale evictions throughout the countryside.

Despite strong outbursts from James Carey, the Crown approvers brought little new excitement to the case, all of their evidence having been heard before. All were surprised, however, by the arrival of a new approver, who had agreed in Kilmainham Gaol to testify against Timothy Kelly.

This was Joseph Hanlon, older brother of Laurence Hanlon. He had made a deal in Kilmainham Gaol, granting him a pardon in return for taking the stand against Kelly. Looking at Kelly as he took the stand, Hanlon looked despondent, and he took the oath upon the bible in a barely audible tone. Joseph Hanlon was first cousin to the condemned Daniel Curley, and his brother Laurence had staunchly refused to give any information to the police – he had received penal servitude for life. There was an expectation that Joseph would face a similar fate to his younger brother.

Laurence Hanlon's sentence, however, had clearly unnerved him, and he now wished to save himself from incarceration or execution, as he stated under cross-examination by Kelly's defence:

McInerney: *Is this your first appearance on the table here?*

Hanlon: *Yes. And I am sorry to come here at all. I was compelled to do it.*

McInerney: *Who compelled you to it?*

Hanlon: *To save my own life.*

McInerney: *To save your own life you came here to testify against Tim Kelly?*

Hanlon: *I could not help it. I expect my life will be saved. I can't say whether I am pardoned now. I think I am.*

In prison, Hanlon had indicated that he wished to strike a deal, and was willing to give evidence if necessary against other Invincibles. Hanlon's offer of evidence was welcomed by the Kilmainham authorities, and Crown solicitor George Bolton was summoned to meet him in an isolated room in the gaol. Bolton received a detailed deposition of Hanlon's involvement in the conspiracy, and what he had seen in Phoenix Park on 6 May 1882.

According to Hanlon, he had been recruited into the Invincibles by a man named John Dwyer, who had not been arrested in relation to the conspiracy. Following his initiation as an Invincible, he claimed to have been instructed to go to Brunswick Street, to St Michael's Church. This was clearly for an attempt on the life of Chief Secretary William Forster. At Brunswick Street, Hanlon saw Brady, Kelly and Robert Farrell. At Brunswick Street the following night, he met the same three again, this time along with Pat Delaney, Joe Mullet and Peter Doyle. The men were instructed to act as if they did not know each other. For another attempt to assassinate Forster, Hanlon was armed with a revolver, stationed at the quays near an esplanade, along with Brady, Curley, George Smith and

Michael Fagan. For yet another attempt, near Kingsbridge train station around the end of April 1882, Hanlon again met Brady, Kelly, Curley, Carey and others.

Hanlon told Bolton that he was in Phoenix Park at the time of the assassinations of Cavendish and Burke, alongside Timothy Kelly,[314] whom he testified was one of the actual assassins.

Examined now by Attorney General AM Porter, Hanlon described in detail the journey from Wrenn's public house in Dame Street to Phoenix Park:

Porter: *Did you know the prisoner, Tim Kelly?*

Hanlon: *I did.*

Porter: *Did you see him there that day?*

Hanlon: *I did.*

Porter: *At Wrenn's?*

Hanlon: *I did. I know Kavanagh the Cabman. I think it was in the Park I first saw him that day. I saw Tom Caffrey and Pat Delaney at Wrenn's.*

Porter: *Did you see Brady, Kelly, Caffrey and Delaney at the same time?*

Hanlon: *I could not say at the same time. We left Wrenn's to go to the park between four and five o'clock.*

Porter: *How did you go?*

Hanlon: *In Fitzharris' cab. Brady told me to go in the cab. James Carey and Smith got into it also. We drove to the park.*

Sensational new prosecution witness Joseph Hanlon.

The cab stopped up a short distance above the Gough statue. We there got out and stood about the road. We saw a polo match. I moved about and was at both sides of the road. I cannot say where Carey and Smith went. I separated from them. Curley came afterwards and I was speaking to him. I went by myself up to nearly opposite the Viceregal Lodge on the left hand side of the road.

Porter: *Whom did you find there when you went up?*

Hanlon: *Joe Brady, Tim Kelly, Tom Caffrey and Pat Delaney. Curley was not there then, but came in about ten minutes afterwards. I think he came before Fagan. There were none there but the seven. When I joined them first, Kavanagh was there with the cab, and he went back on the road in the direction of the Gough statue. We were all waiting there about two hours. We were lying on the grass or moving about from one side of the road to the other. I recollect Kavanagh's car coming back with James Carey and Joe Smith on it. I saw them both wave their handkerchiefs. The car came up and James Carey, Curley and Brady were standing with me. James Carey said – 'mind the man in the grey suit.' Smith was told by Curley to get off the car, and I do not know what became of him. After a short time Carey walked towards Island Bridge. About the same time, Curley, I and Fagan walked away. Before that Joe Brady said that we might go on down the road – 'that four were enough.*[315]

In Hanlon's narrative, as earlier described by Carey at Kilmainham, the four men walked in the direction of the Parkgate entrance to the park, passing Cavendish and Burke. Hanlon now tried to look back, but was prevented by Curley. They turned around, Hanlon noting that the two men had crossed in between Brady and Kelly, Delaney and Caffrey. Looking back, he saw the bodies on the ground:

Joe Brady was getting on [Kavanagh's] car, and the other three were on the car at the time. We were just stepping into [Skin the Goat's] cab at the same time. Curley, Fagan and I got into it in silence.[316]

Driving into town with Hanlon, Curley dropped a number of letters into some newspaper offices; these were the cards that Carey said Curley had left the day following the assassinations. Making their way into Trinity College, they then withdrew.

Independent witness Thomas Huxley, gardener at Farmleigh House in Phoenix Park, repeated his evidence that he had seen a group of men at a clump of trees near to the Phoenix monument, while walking towards town with a friend, Fred Fielder, sometime after 6pm that evening. Kelly was one of the group whom the gardener recalled scattering on their approach, desiring not to be seen. Fielder, however, could not identify Kelly as one of that group, and this was an hour before the assassinations took place. Huxley further admitted from the dock that he had seen Kelly at the divisional inquiry in Kilmainham Courthouse the previous January, and, aware that there was a reward for information, was there to oblige.

Another independent witness, George Mottley, could offer no better evidence. Mottley, who had a hat-making premises on Redmond Hill, testified that he had seen Kelly talking to Myles Kavanagh on Dame Street, three hours before the assassinations took place. Mottley recognised Kavanagh, as he was a regular customer and had purchased a hat from him that morning.

John Brown, Kelly's work supervisor, was again called before the Court. His evidence was used to confirm the testimony of Carey, Smith and Kavanagh, that the Invincibles had waited from late in the morning through to evening for Burke's arrival in the park. As noted in the earlier trial, according to Brown, Kelly was in work from 6am to 8.30pm on Friday 5 and Saturday 6 May. On cross-examination, however, it was admitted by

Brown that Kelly was often absent from work due to poor health. While the prosecution evidence was not definitive, it argued that, given Kelly's clear relationship with other leading Invincibles, particularly the convicted Joseph Brady, and given his presence in the narratives of Kavanagh and Carey, as eyewitnesses in the Phoenix Park at the time of assassination, his guilt was clear.

As attested to by his brother at his earlier trials, Kelly's alibi was that he was sick on the Friday and had been forced to return to bed, his illness carrying over to the Saturday. This story was confirmed by John Farrell, a work colleague of Kelly's, who swore to having seen him sick in bed on the Friday before the assassinations. His brother Patrick, again called to the witness stand, said he had returned from work on the evening of 6 May 1882 between five and six o'clock, and found his brother home, feeling poorly and having not returned to work. Patrick and Timothy visited a friend's house in Aungier Street, arriving at the home of Simon Reid at 7.30pm, the time when the assassinations took place. Patrick Kelly departed Reid's house, and next saw Timothy at eleven o'clock.

Simon Reid, interviewed next, took up Kelly's movements from a little after seven o'clock. Leaving for Webb's store in George's Street to purchase trousers, he left Kelly at the corner of Dame Street around eight o'clock, returning to Webb's to make the purchase. Another witness, Charles McGowan, again placed Kelly within the Aungier Street area, recalling that he saw him near Bishop Street at twenty minutes to eight, making his way to Shannon's public house. Some of this testimony, however, was met with confusion, as neither brother could say who the trousers were for. They claimed that although differing in height and weight, they often wore the same clothing.

Kelly's mother, Mary, next took to the witness stand, looking extremely pale-faced and anxious. She corroborated her son Patrick's story, saying her son Timothy had stayed home from work, feeling poorly, having attended on Saturday morning. Confirming Brown's statement that Kelly had regularly been absent from work due to illness, she said her son suffered from epilepsy and had been to the hospital on several occasions recently. Timothy Kelly did indeed suffer from epilepsy, but nevertheless, Mary Kelly was intensively cross-examined by the Attorney General, seeking to find holes in her testimony:

Porter: *What was the name of the last doctor who treated him?*

Mary Kelly: *I can't tell, there has been so many. He has been at the Adelaide Hospital.*

Porter: *Tell me any doctor that saw him in April or May 1882?*

Mary Kelly: *I cannot say.*

Porter: *Or the name of that hospital?*

Mary Kelly: *He was attending the hospital, but not in the hospital.*

Porter: *Can you tell me the name of any doctor that saw him in the spring of '82? Or any hospital he was in?*

Mary Kelly: *I cannot say, he was in so many. He was treated by Dr O'Leary.*

Porter: *How long is he dead?*

Mary Kelly: *A good many years.*

Porter: *You can't give me any more information on this point.*

Mary Kelly: *No.*[317]

Mary Kelly's evidence on this point gave little benefit to her son, except to clarify that he suffered with epilepsy, something the defence would hold made him a rather unlikely assassin. However, a further independent witness, Patrick Purcell, offered something more substantial.

Purcell was a fellow apprentice coachbuilder, working under John Brown and, like Kelly, active in the Prisoners' Aid Society. Purcell said he met Kelly at Britain Street, at approximately four minutes to eight, and the two went to Mooney's public house in Middle Abbey Street for drinks, and then to the Prisoners' Aid meeting for eight o'clock. Thomas Sheridan, a colleague of Kelly's who had been speaking to Purcell, testified to this detail, recalling that Kelly arrived at five minutes to eight, going for a drink with Purcell. Sheridan recalled that as he left them, he looked toward the clock on the General Post Office, noticing it had just struck eight. Kelly was then seen at the Prisoners' Aid meeting, from 8pm or 8.15 until 10.45.

Purcell's evidence was important, as Kavanagh had described under oath the rather convoluted route he had driven after the killings, leaving Kelly at the Palmerston Park tram station near to eight o'clock. Thus it was impossible for Kelly to have met Purcell at Britain Street at four minutes to eight. Purcell's version of events was confirmed by other attendees at the Prisoners' Aid Society meeting, including William Bardon and Simon Doyle, who recalled Kelly arriving in the meeting room between eight o'clock and a quarter past eight on the evening of the assassinations. It was up to the jury to decide who was telling the truth – the independent witnesses or the conspirators.

Kelly's barrister, Mr Sullivan, summing up the defence case, declared that Kelly had not received a fair trial. He had been tried on two previous occasions, with for the most part the same witnesses, and asked similar questions, and on both occasions the jury could not come to a verdict. Sullivan reminded the jury that the details of the Invincibles conspiracy had been told on several occasions. It had been recorded in countless newspaper articles, and was familiar to even the most uneducated in society. He mused on whether a society of assassins would choose a boy, not even in his twenties, suffering with epilepsy and St Vitus' dance. Carey and Farrell had alluded to the selection of the cream of Fenianism for the ranks of the Invincibles, and Sullivan wondered aloud whether a young boy would be eligible for that status:

Whatever misapprehensions or mistakes at first there might have been felt concerning the origin of the crime, they now knew that it had its springs deep down in the heart of secret societies, established in Ireland, England and in America. They knew that those who came to organise that deed of blood came from secret political societies in the North of England, in the United States: and they sought out here not novices, not young inexperienced boys, not those who were all but children, not the epileptic youth, not the young lad afflicted with St. Vitus' Dance. No, they established their organisation amongst those whom James Carey called the cream ... of the Fenian conspiracy, He was selected himself because he was well-known for his fidelity! Fidelity to whom? Consistency to what? Because he was an old and hardened conspirator, and possibly much worse than that: and amongst men of that class – men of the model of James and Peter Carey – amongst the officers of the Fenian organisation, amongst its 'B's and its centres ... from amongst these were its ranks recruited ... When these men earned the character that they claimed, the character of desperate and reckless men, the Prisoner at the bar was a child at his mother's side.[318]

Sullivan noted that, while Kelly was undoubtedly associated with Brady and other Invincibles, this did not constitute involvement in the Invincibles conspiracy. Regarding Farrell's testimony, he noted that the informer had only asserted that he saw Kelly with known Invincibles. A key proof of Kelly's innocence was the testimony of Purcell and Sheridan, who could place him in Dublin city between five minutes to eight and eight o'clock, making his supposed journey from Phoenix Park on Kavanagh's car an impossibility.

The defence now went on the offensive. Sullivan said that the prosecution witnesses – Farrell, the two Careys, Kavanagh and Hanlon – were all tainted and infamous, and he pleaded with the jury to have nothing to do with the informants. Sullivan reminded the jury that Farrell was guilty of perjury, and had admitted this previously in court. Furthermore, Farrell was a sworn member of the Fenians and of the Invincibles, and had been involved in several attempts on William Forster's life.

As for James Carey, a man who had himself chronicled nineteen attempts on Forster's life, Sullivan could not comment on his evidence, describing him as a 'human vampire', 'a creature devoid of any vestige of humanity – the head and front of all these diabolical deeds'.[319] Carey was the vilest of all men, continued Sullivan, steeped to the lips in blood, who committed sacrilege to the Catholic sacrament of Eucharist and his sodality. He appealed to the jury to ignore all that Carey had said.

Kavanagh, Sullivan said, was a perpetual drunkard, who had admitted that he had taken alcoholic drink before driving the assassins to and from Phoenix Park. Peter Carey was decried as a scoundrel, no better than his brother, while Joseph Hanlon, Sullivan claimed, had only taken to the stand to avoid execution – his evidence should be regarded as that of man who felt the rope around his neck. He concluded:

If there was any man in that [jury] box who considered that a conviction in this case was necessary for some temporary state necessity or some great political object, if any man in the box felt that for such an object that young man must die … It might be that by the word pronounced at the end of this case, the doom of the prisoner was fixed, and that in the pale grey morning to come, the bell would toll preceding his death. If such a word were pronounced, never again would such a weak frame, and pleading anxious face, be seen by them … Yet shall they meet again, nor would they tarry long. For even the strongest amongst them, life's dream would soon be passed and ever terrible then would be such a meeting for him who would stand not guiltless of his brother's blood – not guiltless because he allowed passion and vehemence to influence his reason, and prejudice to overcloud his judgement. But might he not hope for them all a happier meeting in that spirit land to which

time hurried them with quick feet, where their highest claim to the mercy
they would all require, would be that they had dealt justly, honestly, and
mercifully with the life of the prisoner of the bar.[320]

Shortly after four o'clock on 9 May, Judge O'Brien summed up the evidence for the jury, saying that there was enough independent evidence against Kelly to secure a conviction irrespective of the evidence of the informers. The jury then withdrew. As Kelly was ushered away from the dock, he noticed a friend and, raising his hand, he turned his thumb upside down, circling his neck and clucking his tongue. It was painfully obvious to all that he believed his execution was imminent.

Twenty-seven minutes later, the jury returned to a courtroom full of suspense. As the foreman of the jury stood up, Kelly stared intently, loudly exclaiming to a gaoler beside him that he was willing to bet a bob they would hang him. In his third trial, Timothy Kelly was found guilty of assassination. Kelly stated in a very loud voice that he was innocent of the charge. He thanked his defence team, then waited to hear Judge O'Brien passing sentence of death:

Timothy Kelly on this, the third trial, you have been found guilty on evidence
as clear and certain as possibly could be, and as it was on both the former trials.
Justice, certain and slow, though delayed and obstructed, as it may be for a time,
has at last, in your person, reached one of the principals in this great crime. Pity
for your youth and your unhappy fate forbids me from dwelling on your part
in that great crime, or from saying one word that would aggravate the painful
position in which you now stand.[321]

Putting on the black cap, O'Brien told Kelly he was to be executed at Kilmainham Gaol on 9 June 1883, his remains to be buried, unmarked, within the confines of the prison walls for all eternity.

14

JOSEPH MULLET

J oseph Mullet appeared at the dock in Green Street Courthouse, again before Judge O'Brien, charged with the attempted killing of juryman Denis Field. Mullet, aged twenty-four, refused to recognise the legitimacy of the Court, and refused to plead. This drew the wrath of Judge O'Brien, who repeatedly insisted that the prisoner enter a plea to his courtroom. The Dublin Invincible replied with louder refusals, frustrating O'Brien to the point that he instructed a plea of not guilty be registered. Mullet waived his right to be defended in the trial, and sat in the dock with his arms folded, showing contempt for the now-infamous Judge.

The Attorney General opened the case against Joseph Mullet, saying that the prosecution would seek to prove that Mullet was a very considerable figure in the Invincibles conspiracy, who exercised a powerful influence in the organisation. The Attorney General said that he was lucky not to have been charged in connection with the Phoenix Park assassinations, as there was ample evidence of his complicity in the conspiracy to assassinate Thomas Henry Burke. He charged Mullet with being one of the principal organisers of the attempted killing of Denis Field, going so far as to claim that the prisoner had actually ordered the killing, while waiting at West-land Row in Dublin for juryman William Barrett.

Robert Farrell would be employed as Crown witness, supported on this occasion by William Lamie, who would identify Mullet as the organiser of the Field attack. These approvers would be followed by the Carey brothers and Myles Kavanagh. Among evidence to be used against Mullet were a knife and sheath and a revolver, discovered in his home by police and identical to weapons used by Delaney in his failed attempt to assassinate Judge Lawson.

The prosecution would establish Mullet as a dyed-in-the-wool Fenian, drawing on a number of documents found in his possession when arrested. These documents included receipts for money, and scraps of paper detail-ing payments to individuals referred to by initials. It was contended that these initials referred to Joseph Brady, Daniel Curley, Michael Fagan and Andrew Forrester. A diary would also be produced in which Mullet con-demned Parnell as a fraud, believing that he would ultimately betray the cause of Irish independence. With reference to the crisis in Ireland, Mullet had remarked in this diary that the British Government were guilty of crime in Ireland and deserved retribution.

Robert Farrell took the stand, questioned for the Crown by Senior Coun-sel Peter O'Brien. Farrell said he had known Mullet for three years, regu-larly meeting the prisoner in James Mullet's pub in Dorset Street. While this was largely circumstantial, Farrell could identify Mullet as a Fenian centre, having met him on several occasions at Fenian meetings, including a centre meeting in Aungier Street, Dublin, attended by Michael Fagan, Sylvester Kingston and William Lamie. Farrell listed in Joseph Mullet's regular company Joe Brady, Timothy Kelly, Daniel Curley, Peter Doyle, Michael Fagan and Edward O'Brien.

According to Farrell, following the arrest of Daniel Curley under the Coercion Act, Mullet took charge of the Invincibles, directing operations and giving orders to Farrell, under the alias of 'Fisher'. Farrell testified that the day prior to the attempted killing of Judge Lawson, he had received instruction from Mullet to be in Merrion Square the following evening. Farrell was unable to comply with this instruction, but he once again recalled meeting Patrick Delaney at Lower Kevin Street, acting pensive.

Farrell said that the day prior to the attempted assassination of Denis Field and William Barrett, he had been instructed by Mullet to be at a public house on Duke Street at four o'clock the following day. Farrell told Mullet he would be unable to attend, to which Mullet implied that should he not turn up, he would be killed. Farrell therefore thought it wise to go. Meeting Mullet and a number of other men at Duke Street, he was instructed to go to Westland Row. They separated into groups, and Farrell made for a little street behind Trinity College, meeting Mullet and Joseph Hanlon. Mullet told him that he would soon see a scuffle, and that Farrell's job was to shoot any policeman that might interfere. Mullet held an envelope addressed to William Barrett and, on seeing Barrett, Mullet would walk towards him and stop him by handing him the envelope. This was the sign for a man named Molloy to kill him. Barrett did not arrive, however, and the group dispersed, intending to meet again the following day to wait for Barrett. Farrell, however, failed to arrive the next day, and claimed to have resigned from the Invincibles in December 1882.

Mullet was allowed to question Farrell, and drew on his admitted perjury to Curran, extracting a suggestion from Farrell that he would perjure himself to save his life.

Joseph Mullet.

O'Brien now interrupted and demanded clarification from Farrell, and Farrell, with O'Brien's approval, stated that he had misunderstood the question and would never perjure himself under oath.

Peter Carey was next to take the stand, testifying that Mullet sat on the Dublin directory of the Invincibles and that he had met him several times at Brunswick Street for the purpose of the political assassination of William Forster. Carey said that the directory was broken up around October 1882, due to the ongoing State investigation, but Judge O'Brien dismissed his evidence on this point:

Mullet: *You say the council was broke up?*

Carey: *Yes.*

Mullet: *About what date?*

Carey: *About August; no, the latter end of October.*

Mullet: *Of the Invincibles?*

Carey: *Yes, while I was on it.*

Peter O'Brien: In reference to this breaking up, what was said about it?

Carey: *It was said things were getting too hot.*

Judge O'Brien: Was the prisoner present when this was said?

Carey: *No, he was not.*

Judge O'Brien: Then this is not evidence![322]

James Carey, following on from his brother, also said that he had seen Mullet at Brunswick Street, but he could not verify whether he was actually a member of the Invincibles, or if he was there on Invincibles business.

The next witness was Myles Kavanagh, the cab driver, who recollected seeing Mullet at Pembroke Street while driving the convicted Brady and Kelly. Questioned by Peter O'Brien, he could not remember whether Mullet had actually spoken to these two on this occasion. On the day of the attack on Field, Kavanagh recalled driving Brady and Delaney to Hardwicke Street, where he saw Tim Kelly and Laurence Hanlon. As Field was attacked, the group made for his cab, Dan Delaney urging him to pick up speed amid cries of murder. They made for Ringsend at speed, and stopping at the Ringsend Basin, the weapons were dumped in the river. Kavanagh could not, however, say that he had seen Mullet that day.

Kavanagh was followed by William Lamie, who, like Farrell, could identify Joseph Mullet as a Fenian centre and as having attended a council of Dublin centres, which included Michael Fagan. According to Lamie, the meeting was held at a tailor's house in Aungier Street, and was chaired by Mullet. It was agreed here to set up a vigilance committee to deal with suspected informers within the movement, and the question of Joe Poole, Lamie's brother-in-law, was brought up. A complaint had been made against Poole, according to Lamie, and Mullet suggested that the question of Joseph Poole's allegiances should be brought before the vigilance committee.

Lamie described two different funds used for the maintenance of Fenianism – civil money and military money, the former for the day-to-day expenses of the Fenian organisation and the latter to procure weaponry. Lamie testified that he paid Mullet civil money, receiving receipts in Mullet's handwriting under the pseudonym 'Salmon'. Lamie recalled meeting Mullet at a further arranged meeting, this time at Glasnevin Cemetery, in the presence of Dan Delaney and Michael Fagan. Importantly, he contended that Robert Farrell was also there.

Thomas Scallon, an independent witness, identified Mullet as attending a public house he had worked in, recalling Mullet as the principal man among a group that included Curley and the Delaney Brothers.[323] This aligned with Farrell and Lamie's testimony as to Joseph Mullet's leading role in Fenianism and his association with key Invincibles.[324]

Following Lamie came Acting Police Inspector Peter Priestley, who had previously arrested Fagan on behalf of the Dublin Metropolitan Police.

Priestley had also accompanied Acting Police Inspector Joseph Warmington when he arrested Mullet, and he described in detail the materials found upon the prisoner.

Taking the witness stand, Warmington deposed that he had arrested Mullet in a police raid on his home at 6 Temple Cottages, Dominick Street, on 12 January. Mullet's home was extensively searched by police officers, Warmington discovering a six-chambered revolver, fully loaded, hidden in a drawer in his bedroom, along with two cleaning rods. A knife and a sheath were also found among his personal items. Mullet denied any knowledge of the weaponry, insisting that it had been planted.[325] Warmington aroused much excitement in the courtroom by producing the revolver for the benefit of the prosecution, the gun being identified by Constable Patrick Brennan as similar to that used by Delaney in the attempt to assassinate Judge Lawson.

Joseph Hanlon, former Invincible, testified that on the day of the attack on Judge Lawson, he had met Mullet with other Invincibles at Merrion Square, and later met him in a public house along with Brady, Kelly and Fagan. Increasingly, these depositions made under oath by independent witnesses, combined with the testimony of approvers, were shoring up the notion that Mullet was indeed involved in conspiracy, yet there was nothing to prove that he was an active participant in the Invincibles. Furthermore, there was now an active discrepancy in the case – the evidence of one of the independent witnesses could no longer be corroborated.

John Fagan, who had worked with the convicted Michael Fagan, had deposed to John Adye Curran that he had frequently seen Mullet coming to his place of work with Laurence Hanlon to meet Michael Fagan. He had stated on oath that the man whom he believed to be Joseph Mullet had a hunchback, as Mullet had. Now in the witness box, however, he could not be sure of Mullet's identity:

Fagan: There was a man named Michael Fagan in my employment. I could not swear that I used to see the prisoner coming to my establishment to see him.

Peter O'Brien: Used he come to your establishment?

Fagan: I would not like to say that he did, or he did not, sir.

Peter O'Brien: Did you swear it before?

Fagan: I did not see the prisoner at the time. I only saw his photograph.

Peter O'Brien: Didn't you know him to have a hunchback?

Fagan: No.

Peter O'Brien: Did you say this – 'I recollect Joseph Mullet, the hunchback, coming frequently to look for him.'?

Fagan: I did.

Peter O'Brien: Did you recollect at the time that he had a hunchback?

Fagan: Mr Curran told me he had.

Peter O'Brien: Did you swear this – 'I recollect Laurence Hanlon coming to my place to look for him.' Was that right?

Fagan: No.

Peter O'Brien: Was your information read to you?

Fagan: It was.

Peter O'Brien: Did you sign it?

Fagan: I did.

Peter O'Brien: Is it true?

Fagan: No.

Peter O'Brien: Did you swear it?

Fagan: Allow me for a moment. I am very willing to tell what I know. I was shown two photographs, my lord. They were very indistinct, and I said I thought I knew him. Now the reason why I don't know the prisoner at the bar is this. [Michael] Fagan had a brother in law, who I believe, is not at all unlike [Mullet]. I never saw the brother in law to know him until

after I was sworn, and I found then that he was so like him,
that I could not undertake to say which was which …

Peter O'Brien: *Does he resemble this man at the bar?*

Fagan: *Yes.*

Peter O'Brien: *Has the brother in law a hunchback?*

Fagan: *He has not.*

Peter O'Brien: *Listen to your former evidence – 'I recollect Laurence Hanlon*
coming to my place and looking for him, and I recollect Joseph
Mullet the hunchback coming in frequently to look for him.' Did
you swear that?

Fagan: *I suppose I did it, if it's down there. I only spoke at the time from*
the photograph, and they both did look alike, but I could not
swear now.

Judge O'Brien: *How did you come to describe him as Mullet the hunchback?*

Fagan: *I did not. It was Mr Curran, my Lord!*[326]

John Fagan was temporarily dismissed, until the accuracy of his information could be confirmed. This idea that Curran had intimated to Fagan what to say prejudiced the case against Mullet, necessitating the calling of John Adye Curran to the witness stand. Curran could not recall whether he had suggested to Fagan that Mullet had curvature of the spine, but he was adamant that Joseph Mullet was the man that Fagan was familiar with, holding that Fagan, on oath in his presence, had identified Mullet from a photograph. Judge O'Brien declared that Mullet and Michael Fagan's brother-in-law were not similar in appearance, and concluded that John Fagan's evidence was false.

With Mullet refusing to make a defence, before summing up the case, the judge asked him if he had any statement to make as to why the jury should find him not guilty of involvement in the attack on Denis Field. Mullet replied:

I will make the statement I intended to make at the commencement with respect to my refusing to plead ... First I objected either to plead or defend myself, or be represented by counsel on the grounds that our case had been prejudiced by English public opinion and through the press and in the senate; for from the day on which we were arrested up to the present there has hardly appeared any edition of the press that did not contain a leader or a speech of a minister, in which we were held up to public execration as 'the murderers in Kilmainham,' or the 'Kilmainham murderers.' There has been a slight variation in the form of the words used latterly – Sir William Vernon Harcourt ...[327]

Mentioning the British Home Secretary was anathema to Judge O'Brien. Believing Mullet to be reflecting on the attitudes and behaviour of others not relevant to the trial, the judge refused to allow Mullet to proceed with his speech. Mullet protested his right to voice his opinions, but O'Brien refused to give Mullet an opportunity to denounce the court and those who had prejudiced his case, and Mullet then refused to speak. He would not comment on the evidence produced, merely saying that the prosecution had commenced unfairly, and he would allow it to finish unfairly.

Judge O'Brien noted to the jury that Mullet was charged with involvement in the attempted killing of Denis Field, and that while not actually involved in the attempt on Field's life, he had planned it. According to O'Brien, this made Mullet as guilty as an actual offender in the eyes of the law. The questions to be considered by the jury were therefore: Was Mullet associated with those who committed the attack on Field – namely Brady, Kelly and Laurence Hanlon; and had the prosecution proved his involvement as a leading figure in conspiracy? The jury returned after fifteen minutes' deliberation, with a verdict of guilty. Mullet was sentenced to life imprisonment, O'Brien concluding:

Joseph Mullet, the jury have found you guilty of the attempt to murder Mr
Field. Those who perform their duty, a public duty, at the command of the
law must and shall be upheld by all the power and majesty of the law. Your
instrument in this crime has been sentenced in this Court for his part in it, and
I must at least, sentence you, who planned the crime, to the same punishment –
namely to be kept in penal servitude for life.[328]

Leaving the dock, Joseph Mullet loudly declared: 'If I can't get justice here, I will get it somewhere else, or other people will get it for me.'[329] Mullet was taken to Mountjoy Prison in Dublin, and then removed to England.

Finalising the trials of the Invincibles, 'true bills' – a declaration that a grand jury found there was enough evidence to justify a prosecution – were returned against Laurence Hanlon, James Mullet, Joseph Mullet, George Smith and Daniel Delaney for the attempt on Denis Field. A further true bill for conspiracy to murder was returned by the jury on Laurence Hanlon, James Mullet, Joseph Mullet, Edward O'Brien, Edward McCaffrey, Peter Doyle, George Smith, Thomas Doyle, William Moroney, Daniel Delaney, Thomas Martin and James Fitzharris. For the assassinations of Cavendish and Burke, true bills for murder were returned against Edward McCaffrey and Edward O'Brien, with Skin the Goat found to be an accessory following the act.

As to the other individuals implicated in the Invincibles conspiracy but remaining outside of Britain and Ireland, the British State considered the issuing of charges against them, hoping to force their extradition to stand trial for involvement in the conspiracy. This consideration became a reality when Judge O'Brien, via a grand jury, issued true bills against Sheridan, Tynan, Byrne and Walsh. Faced with this threat of extradition, Sheridan remained defiant, declaring that he would remain in New York to face the allegations, rather than make for the American west as he had originally planned:

British Courts of law in Ireland are organised simply to convict. Victims are wanted. I know that if [Dublin Castle] *got me into its clutches I would certainly be hanged, even though I disproved, as I could easily disprove, every charge which informer Carey has sworn against me. My innocence or guilt would not affect the issue … I feel my trial here, should it come to that will result in giving the American people an opportunity of judging of the class of evidence on which innocent men are almost daily hanged in Ireland. Such an expose, I imagine, would be productive of good results for Ireland; therefore I remain.*[330]

THE
EXECUTIONS

15

JOE BRADY

I am the bold undaunted youth, Joe Brady is my name,
From the chapel of North Anne Street one Sunday as I came,
All to my surprise who should I espy but Moreno and Cockade,
Says one unto the other: 'Here comes our Fenian blade.'

I did not know the reason why they ordered me to stand,
I did not know the reason why they gave me such a command.
But when I saw James Carey there, I knew I was betrayed.
I'll face death before dishonour and die a Fenian blade.

They marched me up North Anne Street without the least delay,
They passed me on the path, it filled them with dismay.
My sister cried, 'I'll see you Joe, if old Mallon gives me lave,'
Keep your heart for Ireland, like a true born Fenian blade.'

It happened in the Phoenix Park all in the month of May,
Lord Cavendish and Burke came out to see some polo play,
James Carey gave the signal and his handkerchief he waved,
Then he gave full information against our Fenian blades.

It was in Kilmainham Prison the Invincibles were hung.
Mrs Kelly she stood there all in mourning for her son.
She threw back her shawl and said to all: 'Though he fills a lime pit grave,
My son was no informer and he dies a Fenian blade.'

Since the time of his court case, Joseph Brady had been imprisoned in Kilmainham Gaol, awaiting execution on 14 May. He was incarcerated in a cell once used by prison guards when working in the wing, today known as the McCann cell, a short walk from the yard where he would be executed. With Brady slept two prison warders, on single beds to either side of his, as was customary with prisoners awaiting execution. Outside, nearby his cell, was stationed a force of six constables, there to prevent any probable escape from the gaol by the leading Invincible.

The morning of Joseph Brady's execution, Whit Monday, 14 May, was marked by a remarkable calmness. The morning was fine and bright, the skyline indicating that the rising sun would bring a warm and bright day of public holiday. Yet outside Kilmainham Gaol's cold, grey walls, between 3,000 and 4,000 people had assembled from an early hour to pay homage to the passing of one of the Invincibles:

The whole neighbourhood was thronged and the crowd was densest on the bridge and in the Cherry orchard beneath the rear walls of the prison.[331]

Expecting large crowds, the authorities had stationed large numbers of police and soldiers around the perimeter of the gaol. Parallel to this, plain-clothes soldiers were planted within the assembled crowd outside the gaol, ready to help disperse the crowd in the event of a sudden rush on the gaol, an attempted rescue or violence breaking out. Inside Kilmainham Courthouse, a strong contingent of grenadiers was stationed, while adjacent to the Courthouse, near the entrance to the Royal Hospital, was a heavy detachment of dragoons. The forecourt facing the entrance to the gaol was sealed off by a combination of police and military, the assembled crowd restricted to an area beside a nearby bridge, and an area near the north wall of the gaol, where the black flag would be raised as soon as Brady was declared dead.

The Saturday before Brady's execution, his mother had visited him in the gaol, and they were seen to have a long discussion. Crying as she left Brady to his fate, she turned back to him and loudly exclaimed, 'Mind Joe, no statement!' She threatened to disown her son if he gave any information, and Brady replied steadfastly that he would refuse to give any statement to the State.[332]

On the morning of his execution, he was woken at 6am. He was allowed to attend mass in the Catholic chapel, presided over by Reverend Canon Kennedy. Receiving the sacraments, it was noted that the condemned man remained calm and resolute. Returning to his cell for a final time, William Marwood now arrived to prepare him for execution. As a final request, Brady was allowed to write a letter to his mother before being pinioned with leather straps. Joseph Brady

Joe Brady, photographed at Kilmainham Gaol.

244

was said to have remained silent throughout his pinioning, co-operating with Marwood. Near eight o'clock, he was summoned by prison guards, along with the gaol Governor James Gildea, Sub Sheriff Mr Ormsby and the prison Chaplain, Reverend Canon Kennedy. Making his way outside, Brady was recorded to be praying, clutching a Bible as he walked towards his execution. Brady had been led through the litany for the dying by the Chaplain, and was reported to be responding to prayers by Canon Kennedy.

Outside in the prison yards, Brady was confronted with a large wooden scaffold, about twelve foot square, standing in the southwest corner of the yard. Extending out from the gallows was a substantial timber platform, reached by wooden stairs, with two drop doors in the middle, opened by pulling a lever on the side. Brady was directed onto the platform by prison warders, the condemned man stopping briefly to look up at the cross from which the noose descended. Marwood directed him to stand atop the drop doors. Brady did as he was instructed, and the hangman now pinioned his legs together. This done, Marwood directed that a white cotton mask should be given to him, which he tied over the condemned mans head. Placing the noose over this, Marwood then walked to the lever and, at the stroke of eight o'clock, pulled it. Joseph Brady fell through the drop doors, eight feet eleven inches, and his neck broke and his spinal cord ruptured instantaneously. The first Invincible was now dead.

Up to the last moment Brady retained that animal courage he displayed in the deed itself. He slept until four o'clock in the morning and rose at six. Before seven o'clock the Roman Catholic Chaplains of the prison, the Rev. Canon Kennedy and the Rev. Mr Reilly, arrived and were immediately ushered into his cell. Brady had been very attentive to the instructions of his spiritual guides, and when Mr Kennedy and Mr Reilly arrived he received the last sacrament. He declined having anything to eat, and occupied himself with his devotions. When Marwood entered the cell to pinion him, he was still engaged in prayer, but immediately arose and met the executioner. He then presented the prayer book to one of the warders, saying 'take this.' Except his prayers these were his last words.[333]

Outside the prison the thronged crowds looked toward the unused flagpole on the southwest corner. At the time of Brady's death, as the black flag was raised to signify his execution, the crowd outside were recorded to shriek and pray for the soul of Joseph Brady.[334]

As the fatal hour approached, the elements had dramatically changed their character. The sky, a moment before unclouded blue, was streaked with cloudlets, and in the southern sky black masses of vapour, rolling upwards, were threatening a downpour of rain. Every moment added to the thousands of curious spectators who at every point from which a view of the flagstaff could be obtained, had their gaze steadily fixed toward upon the prison. Many of the men assembled were seen taking off their hats as a mark of respect, while others dropped to their knees, blessing themselves and praying for the repose of Brady's soul. Falling silent, the crowd then began to disperse, the only remaining people being the press, who had been promised entry to Kilmainham Gaol until a Coroner's Jury was obtained.

Near half past nine, pressmen were allowed enter the prison, under strict supervision and in possession of relevant tickets and credentials. They were taken to the debtors' wing of the prison, to the cell once occupied by Charles Stewart Parnell, where the Coroner's inquest would take place, chaired by Dublin District Coroner Dr Hearty. The jurors, having been sworn in, were taken to the yard where Brady was executed, to view his body. Having been left hanging for an hour, as required by law, Brady's body had been placed in a rough deal coffin, laying on a wooden trestle table. He wore the suit he was executed in, the suit he had worn since his arrest in January 1883, and on his feet were prison slippers rather than shoes. His face was recorded to look rather contented, indicating that death had come instantaneously, with no pain. Having viewed Brady's body, the Coroner's Jury came to the conclusion that death was by means of complete dislocation of the cervical vertebrae, rupturing his spinal cord and breaking his neck, resulting from hanging.

Brady's body was now lifted out of the coffin and placed on the wooden trestle. By order of Dr William Carte, Kilmainham Gaol physician, the executed prisoner was to be beheaded, his brain to be dissected and studied by craniologists at the Royal College of Surgeons in Dublin. Once more placed into his rough deal coffin, the lid securely fixed, Brady was quickly buried inside the prison walls, near to where he was executed. His body was covered with shovelfuls of quicklime.

John Mallon, present for the execution, was given the rather unpleasant job of delivering Brady's head to the College of Surgeons. The head was wrapped in a cloth and given to Mallon, who hurried out of the gaol on his ghastly task. As Mallon left Kilmainham Gaol, he was approached by a friend of his, French journalist Frederick Moir Bussy, who was covering the trials and executions of the Invincibles. Bussy noted that the policeman was white as a sheet, and rather curt. As Bussy approached, Mallon shouted at him, 'Don't speak to me!' Mallon was then driven away at speed in a waiting car, under a heavy police escort. Meeting Bussy years later, Mallon apologised for his curtness to the French reporter. Bussy replied that he had been a little hurt by his friend's behaviour, and Mallon told him that his intention was not to hurt Bussy or to be rude to a good friend:

> Did you notice that I had a parcel with me tied up in something white? Well that was Joseph Brady's head I had in a table napkin.[335]

In an interesting note, Bussy recorded that from then on, Mallon always kept a part of Brady's spine in his jacket pocket.

16

DANIEL CURLEY

Like Brady, Daniel Curley remained stoically resolute prior to his execution, refusing to make any form of confession or statement to the authorities. Inside Kilmainham, he was recorded as being angry about his trial, and continuing to highlight discrepancies in the Crown case, based as it was largely on the evidence of informers.

On the Thursday before his execution, the Chairman of the Invincibles was allowed to see his family. These final meetings were seen to weaken Curley's resolve, particularly when he said goodbye to his wife Jane and three of their children, in a meeting recorded as 'of the most affecting description'.[336]

Daniel Curley.

Before saying goodbye to her husband, Jane Curley was allowed to cut a lock of his hair as a memory. Leaving the cell, she broke down, crying loudly for her husband, and her three children were much affected as the cell door shut on their father, whom they would never see again. Comforted by the prison chaplain, Curley was finally given permission to write his wife a letter:

My dear and most ever-beloved wife and children,

I take this opportunity, the last on this deceitful earth, of saying a few words to you, hoping that you will forgive me for the step that I took with regard to my trial – I mean for not trying to save myself as others did; but I could not stoop so low or bring myself to do so. My dear wife, I will die as I have lived, faithful to my principles and to my country's cause. I will do as all honest men do, bring my secrets to the grave with me, and leave them that is at freedom to enjoy it.

Dear wife, I will say no more on this subject, as I have domestic business to speak upon. I request you to keep a vigilant watch on our dear children. Keep them to their school and religion and off the street, as you yourself know that I dread to see children getting the run of the street.

Dear Jane, do not think that because I say this I have no confidence in you. Yes, dear wife, I will die at rest; I know that you will do what is just to them. I will also request of you not to let them out of your sight or care to anyone as long as you can help it, my dear and faithful wife. Now about yourself. As I have told you before, I will not ask to restrict you in any manner. If you think it well to change your widowed life, you can do so with all my wish and blessing. I never like to see anyone tied I love. I love liberty.

But, my dear wife, if you ever change your life, be very careful in your choice of companion. Deceitful men! My dear and faithful wife, I love you. Excuse me, I cannot speak of this matter, as it was very hard to tear my trustful heart from you and offer it to God – what a trial! That the base and brutal deceiver should be the cause of separating two loving and trustful hearts but God's will be done.

That is my only consolation. My dear wife, I will ask you to be attentive to your religious duties. No matter how much you are engaged in the business of the world, never neglect that.

My reason for saying so is that I shall die with the hope that we shall meet in the Kingdom of Heaven, never to be parted by the power of man. Dear wife, I am sure you will be glad to hear that I die in peace with all men, forgiving enemies. May God give them the injury they have done me.

I am happy and at peace with God. Oh, may God protect you and the children in this deceitful world. Remember me to Frank, Peter and Nelly, Mr and Mrs. Hyland, Granny Misey, and all friends. Believe me to be your faithful and loving husband,

Daniel Curley

To his affectionate and faithful wife and dear children, Mary, Jane, Michael, Peter and Daniel. Pray for the soul of your dear husband. May the Lord have mercy on my soul.[337]

Daniel Curley would be executed on the morning of Friday, 18 May 1883, ironically the day on which the trials of the Invincibles officially ceased at Green Street Courthouse.

The day before the execution, State executioner William Marwood decided to take in the sights of Dublin, and leave the overbearing confines of the prison. Accompanied by plain-clothes policemen, he walked to the South Circular Road. The police who had been dispatched to protect him, however, were recognised, and word spread that someone important was walking up the road, many concluding that this was indeed Marwood the hangman. A large crowd began to assemble, protesting his presence in Ireland. His police escort quickly ushered him back to Kilmainham Gaol.[338]

Like for Brady's execution days before, the sun shone brightly on Kilmainham Gaol on 18 May, and large crowds gathered in solidarity with the condemned prisoner. Again, considerable security was placed surrounding the gaol, to marshal the public and to prevent any potential rescue attempt. However, compared with the security operation surrounding Brady's execution, the numbers of soldiers and police were much smaller. At the Royal Hospital gates, shut to the public, few soldiers could be seen. *The Irish Times* reported the following morning:

> *The troops chatting in the Courthouse where chatting away with as much animation and gaiety as if there was no such terror as death, and oblivious or regardless of the fact that a fellow creature in full breath and the very prime of his manhood, was at that moment walking toward the spot where his own grave had been dug and the arrangements for his burial perfected.*[339]

Among the crowd, numbering over 700 people, stood Curley's father. He was predicted to speak, but on the occasion, overcome by grief and dissuaded by his imprisoned son the day before, he declined the opportunity. The remainder of Curley's family had refused to attend the prison, choosing rather to go to morning mass in his memory at the time of his execution. Masses for the repose of Curley's soul were said throughout Dublin city, and the litany for the dying was recited at the gaol.

Curley slept badly the night before his execution. Waking at quarter to six, he was viewed at quarter to seven by Canon Kennedy and Father O'Reilly, who remained with him for a quarter of an hour, attending to his spiritual needs. Curley was next allowed to leave his cell for a final mass in the nearby prison chapel. After the mass, at half past seven, Curley was ushered back to his prison cell, in the Great Hall of the gaol.

William Marwood, in the company of prison Governor James Gildea, now entered the cell. Marwood began the process of pinioning the prisoner in preparation for execution. Curley was recorded to be emotional, yet struggled to maintain himself, exclaiming that he wished those present to give his love to his wife. He wore a fine, dark tweed suit and frock coat, with a crucifix pinned to the breast. Near eight o'clock, Curley and Canon Kennedy led the final procession out of his prison cell, with Governor Gildea, William Marwood and a number of prison warders, including Chief Warder Frederick Searle. The Canon recited the litany for the dying to the condemned man, who emotionally responded.

The procession slowly made its way to the small yard where Curley would be executed. Walking toward the scaffold, Curley would have seen the spot where Brady had recently been buried, understanding his fate to be the same. Stopping before the steps leading to the gallows platform, the condemned Curley turned around to Governor Gildea, thanking him and shaking his hand. Bidding him goodbye, he then walked up the steps to the scaffold.

Curley was directed to stand on top of the drop doors, as Brady had done a few days before. Standing in silence, fear in his eyes, Curley looked into space, making no statement. Marwood now directed a warder to give him a cotton mask, which he proceeded to place and tie over Curley's head. The mask secured, Marwood tied the noose around the prisoner's neck, and checked its tightness. Marwood slowly walked over to the lever, and pulled it. Daniel Curley fell eight feet and eleven inches through the drop doors, his spinal cord rupturing and death being instantaneous.

Left hanging from the scaffold for one hour, Curley's lifeless body was then cut down and placed into a rough deal coffin, on the same wooden trestle upon which Brady was beheaded. The mask being removed from his head, it was noted that his face was bloodstained, fresh blood having flowed from his nose, but despite this, there was no visible sign of pain on his face. The body had descended heavily and, from the steadiness of the rope, it appeared that death had been instantaneous.

At exactly eight o'clock, the black flag was again raised on the Kilmainham flagpole, signalling that another Invincible was dead. A great shriek arose in the crowd outside, with many falling to their knees, making the sign of the cross and praying for the soul of the departed. Curley's father was inconsolable, dropping to his knees, knowing his son had just died within yards of him, separated by the prison wall:

> *He was merely an object upon whom was bestowed the pity of everyone who saw his grey head bared in the sunlight, and his tearful eyes fixed upon the spot from which it would be announced to the outer world that all was over.*[340]

By law, Curley's body now had to be examined by a Coroner's Court. The court once more took place in the cell formerly occupied by Charles Stewart Parnell, in the presence of a jury and pressmen. It was found that Curley had died from hanging. With the Coroner's Court judgement reached, Curley's casket was closed and he was buried next to Joseph Brady, in the yard below the gallows.

17

MICHAEL FAGAN

Michael Fagan arose from bed at six o'clock on Monday, 28 May, the day of his execution. Like Brady and Curley before him, he was allowed to attend mass, accompanied by Reverend Canon Kennedy and Curate Father Thomas O'Reilly, the Canon afterwards recalling that Fagan had spent his entire time in the Kilmainham chapel on his knees praying, remaining there until ten minutes to eight. At this time, Thomas Flewett, the Deputy Governor of Kilmainham, and Ormsby, the Sub Sheriff, arrived to inform Fagan his time had come. Leaving the chapel, Fagan was given a crucifix, which he held tightly in his hands, refusing to relinquish it to prison officers.

Michael Fagan.

Matching the mood of the condemned prisoner, the weather was gloomy and dreary, with heavy rain pouring onto the crowd assembled outside the prison. So bad was the weather that the crowd was the smallest to date, estimated at between two and five hundred persons, many staying at home rather than brave the dismal conditions.[341] The majority of those who had gathered were of Dublin's working class, sheltering beside the lofty walls from the cold blasts of wind and rain. As on previous occasions, the crowds had assembled where the prison flagpole could be seen. They were under strict supervision, prevented from gathering at the front of the gaol by a cordon of police and soldiers, and entry to the gaol itself was refused to anyone without a ticket. Many of those assembled were saying prayers for Fagan, once more reciting the litany for the dying; others attended simply out of curiosity.

As these prayers were being said for the soul of Michael Fagan, on the other side of the prison walls, undeterred by the dreary weather, Marwood meticulously checked his gallows, especially the workings of the drop doors. He could not afford any hitch in his part in the proceedings, both for his professional reputation as a master hangman and out of courtesy to the prisoner, so as not to cause him to suffer more than necessary.

Like Brady and Curley before him, Michael Fagan made no statement prior to his execution. Pinioned by William Marwood, he remained quiet at all times, making no conversation and showing no emotion:

> ... a halt was made for Marwood, who came forward and pinioned the culprit. This process Fagan went through with firmness. Marwood unbuttoned the shirt collar and then surveying Fagan from head to foot, he passed over to the Yard, into which a few minutes later the procession emerged.[342]

The process completed, Fagan walked firmly up the steps to the gallows, as Brady and Curley had before him. Praying to himself, he took his last look at the world, registering the patch of uneven ground where his former comrades lay and where he was bound. Reaching the gallows platform, he was seen to tremble, but continued praying. Canon Kennedy once again repeated the liturgy for the dying, standing beside him briefly. Marwood, now taking his place, gently tied the cotton mask over his head and placed the noose, previously used to execute Brady and Curley, around his neck. Fagan, despite the mask covering his face, looked upwards towards the sky, audibly praying, as he only had seconds left to live.

The lever was pulled and the third Invincible plummeted through the drop doors. His spinal cord ruptured, and death was delivered instantaneously. While Fagan's death was no different to that of Brady and Curley who preceded him, his death left a vivid imprint on all assembled. The cotton mask that Marwood had so gently placed over his head fell off and blew away on the breeze. Fagan's lifeless body swayed left and right, his tragic face visible to all in a sight that few would forget. His face was overspread with colour around the eyes, and his neck was bleeding, having been cut by the rope.

Cut down from the rope at 9am, the dead man's body was placed on a table, to be examined by the jurors of the Coroner's Court, which concluded that he had died instantaneously of spinal rupture:

> ... *the body lay face uppermost on the table on which it had been placed on being released from the noose. Deceased was dressed in the grey tweed trousers, black vest and dark coat, which he had worn at the trial. The feet were encased in slippers. The neck was bare, the colour having been opened and turned down ... The facial expression was calm but the features were overspread with a livid colour particularly about the eyes and on the left side near the ear.*[343]

Michael Fagan's body was placed into a shell coffin and buried alongside Brady and Curley. It was noted that the crucifix Fagan had been given that morning was still tightly in his grasp.

When the black flag was raised over Kilmainham Gaol, signalling the death of Michael Fagan, the small crowd wailed and kneeled in honour of the executed man. A respectable-looking woman began a pre-arranged series of prayers and hymns in Fagan's honour, followed fervently by the assembled crowd. Among the crowd were Fagan's brother and brother-in-law, his brother overcome with emotion as the black flag signalled the death of his younger sibling. Fagan's mother, unable to attend the assemblage, had attended a mass said for Fagan in Dublin. As the black flag fluttered over Kilmainham Gaol, the clouds above heavily burst, scattering the gathering, leaving only a few remaining kneeling on the muddied grass and wet paths.

Michael Fagan was illiterate, and left no verbal or written testament before his execution. We are merely left with his final pronouncement to the courtroom, that he was a Fenian and would die a Fenian.

18

THOMAS CAFFREY

On 2 June 1883, Thomas Caffrey would be executed at Kilmainham Gaol. As with the previous executions, Caffrey was given permission to attend mass in the prison chapel, performed by Reverend Canon Kennedy around 6.30am. Like the other men, Caffrey took the Eucharist and receive

CAFFRY_ executed.

the rite of absolution for past sins. The condemned prisoner remained in the chapel until a quarter to eight. Ushered out, he was accompanied by Governor Gildea, Ormsby and several prison officers to the Great Hall. En route, Canon Kennedy recited the litany for the dying into the prisoner's ear, and Caffrey responded accordingly. At the Great Hall, a procession had assembled, including

Thomas Caffrey.

Dr Carte and Deputy Governor Thomas Flewett, and they proceeded to walk down a long, dark corridor out into the prison yards. In this corridor, they paused and Marwood pinioned Caffrey for execution.

> [Marwood] *raised the index finger of his left hand. At this signal the procession* *halted. Marwood stepped forward and placing his hand on Caffrey's shoulder,* *whispered in his ear. Caffrey raised both his arms, and the executioner circled* *his waist with a belt, to which the pinioning straps were attached. Into these* *he inserted the convict's wrists, and he also strapped both his arms, holding the* *strap from behind. He made a signal and the procession moved along in the* *same order, the Priests reciting the litany for the dying. Caffrey* [answering] *the* *responses in an audible tone.*[344]

As in the previous three pinionings, Caffrey remained silent throughout, but he showed much anxiety considering his final ten minutes in this world.

Entering the yard where he was to be executed, a tremor seemed to overcome Caffrey's body. Walking up the steps towards the gallows, Caffrey thanked Marwood and shook hands with Canon Kennedy, expressing his desire to be forgiven by God in the next life. Making no further statement, Caffrey stood on the drop doors of the gallows, as Marwood tied a cloth over his head, and then fixed the noose around his neck. The process completed, the hangman pulled the lever, opening the doors as the prisoner fell nine feet into an artificially constructed pit.

William Marwood always argued that his job was simply to carry out the order of the courts. He understood that if he miscalculated, the prisoner would suffer, dying a slow and painful death. On this occasion, he did miscalculate, and Thomas Caffrey did not die instantaneously from spinal rupture, but died from asphyxiation. Ironically, Caffrey was the only one of the executed Invincibles who had pleaded guilty to involvement in the Phoenix Park assassinations.

The execution of Caffrey attracted the least attention of the executions of the Invincibles, and for many this was accounted for by his guilty plea. Unlike the previous executions, only a handful of people had gathered outside the prison walls to see the raising of the black flag.

Twenty-four-year-old Caffrey was a widower, employed as a dock worker. He had been recruited into the Invincibles by James Carey, whose testimony partially led to his execution. Caffrey was survived by one child, a four-year-old boy. Meeting his brother for a final time, Caffrey had expressed a firm desire to be executed, rather than spend the remainder of his life in gaol. Seeing his sister for a final time, along with his son, he asked that he be remembered as seeking forgiveness, not only for himself, but for the informers who played so great a role in ending his life. He was given permission to write a final letter to his mother, on the eve of his execution:

Kilmainham Gaol, 1 June 1883, Half past 8 o'clock PM

Dear Mother,

I write you these few lines for the last time in this World, and hope you will offer up all your sorrows along with my sufferings in atonement for my crime, and all the sins of my past life. I hope you will forgive all who have done me harm in this World, as I forgive them from the bottom of my heart, as I expect to get forgiveness from my merciful father in Heaven.

Dear Mother, I am just after receiving the Holy Sacrament of Confirmation, and I am quite prepared with the help of God to go before the judgement seat of justice. Make sure to mind your religion, yourself and the child, and I hope to meet you one day in Heaven, where there will be no more parting for all eternity, and there in the company of our blessed Mother, and all the Saints, we will praise our blessed redeemer for evermore. Tell all inquiring friends that I hope no one will ever throw a slur on any Child or anyone belonging to me for the death I had to suffer; and I hope you will never have cause to blush when my

name is spoken, and I am paying the full penalty of my crime in this world and
I hope I will not have to suffer in the next. Whenever you see this letter pray
for me. No more in this World from your loving son, THOMAS CAFFREY. –
Larry, Mary, Catherine, Katey, Jemmy, Michael, and Sissy, pray for me! Lord,
have mercy on my soul!

Caffrey was left hanging for the requisite one hour, and was cut down at
9am, his body placed on a wooden trestle for examination and viewing. He
was then placed into a coffin and buried next to the scaffolding and the
three other Invincibles in the gaol yard.

19

TIMOTHY KELLY

An apprentice coachbuilder by trade, nineteen-year-old Timothy Kelly was the youngest of the Invincibles. He had taken a leading role in the Invincibles conspiracy, being intimately connected with Joseph Brady, and alongside Brady, was one of the actual assassins in Phoenix Park on 6 May 1882. The last of the Invincibles to be executed, Kelly was held in Kilmainham Gaol while the four other condemned men were being executed, the psychological strain of this weighing intensely on him.

Sentenced to be hanged at Kilmainham on Saturday, 9 June 1883, Kelly requested that the night before his execution he should be held in the prison cell previously

Nineteen-year-old Timothy Kelly, the last of the Invincibles to be executed.

occupied by his old friend Joseph Brady prior to his execution. His request was granted, and Kelly was moved to Brady's cell. That evening, with his last meal, Kelly was afforded the luxury of porter. As he neared the end of his meal, Governor Gildea entered his cell. The young Invincible rose, as was the prison regulation when the Governor entered a cell. Kelly quickly threw the contents of his porter glass over Gildea, sarcastically shouting, 'To your honour's health and a long life!'[345] As punishment for this act of insubordination, the remainder of Kelly's meal was withdrawn.

He sang into the night, his voice reverberating around the silent corridors as he sang 'Salve Regina' and 'The Memory of the Past'.

Sleeping badly, Kelly woke at 5am, dressing in a dark suit and a pair of gaol slippers. The condemned man was received by Canon Kennedy and Reverend Bernard O'Reilly, and attended a final mass and received the Eucharist in the prison chapel. The ceremony lasted for under an hour, and then Kelly was approached by Chief Warder Searle, informing him that his time had come. Kelly was recorded as being pale and nervous. Taken back to his cell briefly, he was then placed at the head of a procession consisting of Governor Gildea, the religious ministers, Searle and a number of prison guards, and they made their way to the execution yard. Descending the staircase from the chapel, the priests whispered the last rites into Kelly's ear. The procession turned left into the dispersals hall and walked along a long, narrow corridor, with prison cells on the left-hand side and a bare limestone wall on the right, with small windows of muff glass allowing little light through and no view of the outside world. Here Kelly was met by Marwood, who stopped the procession in order to undertake his grisly task.

Walking toward Kelly, with leather straps and belt in hand, Marwood asked him to hold out his arms. Beginning the process of pinioning the prisoner in preparation for his execution, Marwood wrapped the belt around Kelly's waist, locking the prisoner's hands in hoops attached to it. Using a further strap, Kelly's arms were pinioned tightly, making movement from the top of his body almost impossible. Marwood now placed his hands on Kelly's neck, feeling gently and discreetly, then removing his shirt collar, leaving his neck bare so as not to interfere with the noose. The process completed, Marwood signalled the procession to move once more. Moving through a smaller yard and then turning left, the imposing structure of the gallows became visible through the small gateway leading into the execution yard.

Recorded as nervous, Kelly paused to take cognisance of the gallows, and the rope tied through a solid metal buckle. Ascending the steps to the platform, Kelly was ushered by Marwood to the drop doors, standing on a spot marked by a chalk 'X'. Standing upon it, Kelly could not but have noticed the graves of the other four executed Invincibles, whom he would be joining shortly. Remarkably, standing atop the flagpole upon which the black flag was to be raised, was a black crow. It remained there, facing in the direction of the execution yard, from twenty minutes to eight until Kelly had been executed and the black flag was hoisted over Kilmainham Gaol.

Marwood continued the process of pinioning the prisoner in preparation for execution, as Kelly prayed loudly. Kelly was instructed not to move from the white X, as Marwood tied his legs together securely. Marwood reached over to a nearby table, taking up the white sack to be placed over the condemned man's head. Kelly stopped praying, and asked him if he could kiss the crucifix hanging around his neck before his execution. Marwood consented, indicating that Father O'Reilly could ascend the gallows and facilitate Kelly's final wish, as Kelly could not reach it with his pinioned arms. Withdrawing from the gallows, O'Reilly retook his place at the foot of the structure, overlooking the burial place of Brady, Curley, Fagan and Caffrey.

Marwood tied the sack over Kelly's head, positioned the noose and removed the safety pin of the gallows. He walked slowly over to the gallows' lever, examining the structure one final time. Checking his watch to see had it reached eight o'clock, Marwood pulled the lever, and Kelly fell nine feet to his death.

In the days before his execution, members of the Political Prisoners' Aid Society had sought to win a reprieve for Timothy Kelly. The Society had written a series of letters to Gladstone, urging an immediate reprieve of the death sentence, holding, as was testified at Kelly's trial, that he was at a meeting of the Society at the time of the assassinations, and therefore could not have been involved in the killings. These letters were ignored by Gladstone. A representative of the Society, Amos J Varian, had secured a meeting with Earl Spencer to examine Kelly's case and make a critical evaluation of the evidence that had led to his conviction. Amos left the meeting believing that Spencer would reconsider Kelly's case, but this was not to be. Varian recalled:

Alas in my simplicity of heart, I left believing in my own truthful statement and that it would have carried some weight in commuting the extreme penalty of the law, and not until I witnessed the fatal black flag this morning could I give up hope in the power of a true and faithful record of the facts, as I endeavoured even at the last moment to win a reprieve.[346]

Outside Kilmainham Gaol, thousands of people had gathered to pay their final respects. The largest group were gathered at the South Circular Road, facing the east side of the gaol, the immediate environs of the gaol being heavily protected by soldiers and police, there to prevent people from getting too close to the prison. Others stood near the entrance to the Royal Hospital, controlled by a cordon of soldiers. Directly in front of the prison, police and soldiers were stationed, and absolutely no public loitering or access was allowed. Further crowds thronged the streets surrounding the prison. With the raising of the black flag, the crowd is recorded to have fallen to its knees, praying for the soul of Timothy Kelly:

Many heads were already uncovered awaiting the dreaded signal. The hour
had barely struck when the black pennant was run up over the roof of the jail.
Simultaneously a groan like expression of 'oh' went up from the crowd and
several women and young girls burst into tears. There was no reading of prayers
or general engagement in religious exercises by the multitude – which by this
time had swollen to fully a thousand persons.[347]

Within minutes, the crowd had dispersed. Notably missing from the group
were members of Kelly's family and his friends. They had assembled at the
Catholic church on Francis Street, where a mass was offered for the soul of
the executed prisoner. The Kelly family were described as inconsolable and
broken with emotion. Under request from Mary Kelly, Canon Kennedy
cut a lock of her son's hair prior to his burial, and he presented this to her
following his death. At the family home, a large crape bow was tied to the
family door, bearing the message 'Timothy J. Kelly died June 9th 1883 –
may he rest in peace.'[348]

Kelly's mother Mary was left grief-stricken by the death of her son.
She was in continual correspondence with supporters in Irish-America. PJ
Sheridan – of the Land League and, if Carey is to be believed, a leading
figure in the Invincibles conspiracy – was certainly in regular contact with
her. Sheridan, with her permission, published a letter from Mary Kelly in
the *Irish World* newspaper. The letter lamented a broken family and a sorrowful state:

I think on the face of the Earth there is no one more desolate than I am at present.
I have lost the best boy ever a mother reared – my sole dependence in my old age.

My husband, through this great trouble that has fallen on us, has turned into
a harmless idiot. My eldest son I am after sending to the County Meath, to see
would a change of air restore him to his health again, but the doctors have little
hopes of him.

The house in which my children were born and reared sold over my head the day before my fine boy was hanged. Whose trouble can equal mine?

Had my boy spoken he could have saved his own life, but he was too noble for that.

I remain yours truly, Mary Kelly.

Accompanying Mary Kelly's letter was a short prayer for the soul of her son:

A prayer

Of your charity pray for the soul of Timothy Kelly

Who was executed at Dublin on June 9th, 1883

Today we mourn the loss of one who died for our land to save.

Keen sorrow lays a nation's tears upon the early grave:

Erin now weeps but still hopes on, and as she breathes the sigh,

Looks hopeful for her cause is safe, her sons fear not to die,

Lov'd land, tho' death be still the fate of those who for thee strive;

Yet from the fight there's no retreat while one remains alive.

GOD SAVE IRELAND!

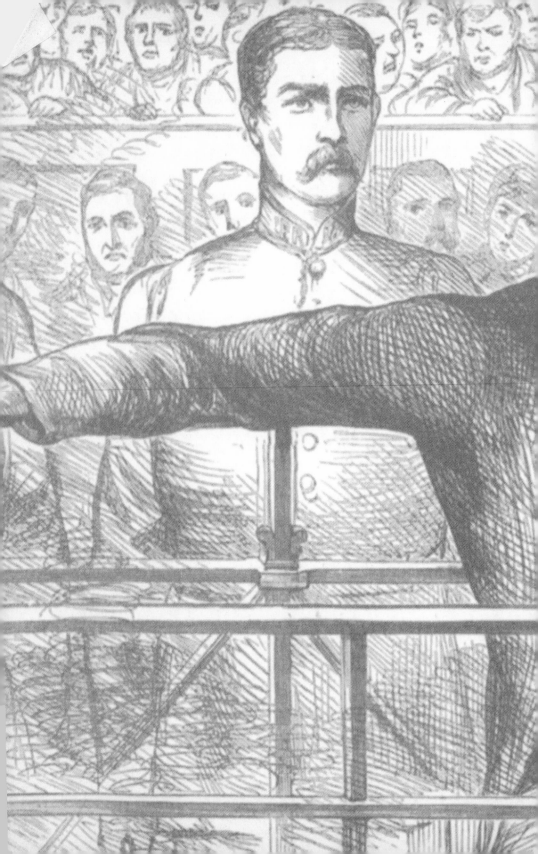

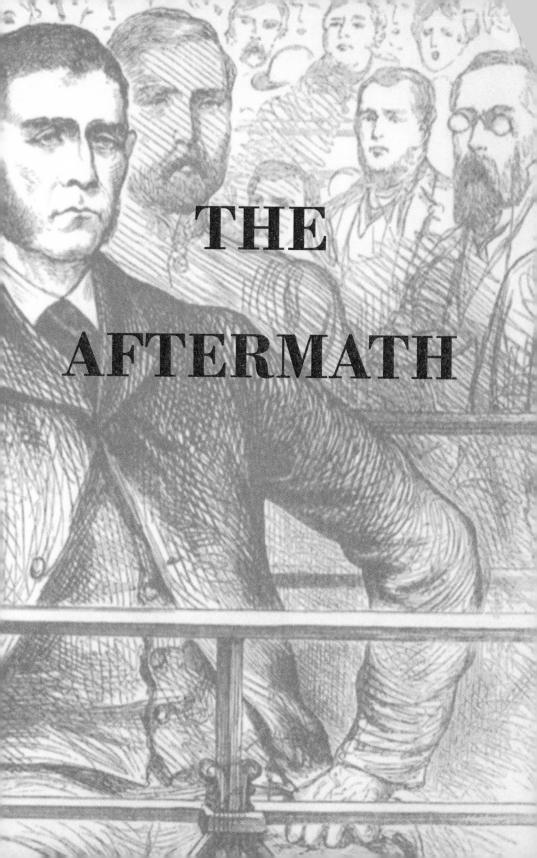

THE

AFTERMATH

20

CAREY'S FLIGHT

After the five executions had all been carried out, James Carey still languished in his cell in Kilmainham Gaol. He was very anxious to leave prison, having co-operated fully with the police investigation, at great cost to himself. Included in this cost was valuable revenue Carey had lost, with tenants refusing to pay rent on his sublet properties, while his family had difficulty selling any property Carey had claim to, as few would do business with the Carey family. Furthermore, there was a very real possibility that Carey could still be hanged for his involvement in the Invincibles conspiracy, his own evidence having been damning enough to secure his execution. He had not yet received his pardon from the State, as promised to him in exchange for his testimony, and was growing ever more bored of his time in Kilmainham, and anxious regarding his future. On the day following Tim Kelly's execution, Carey wrote to express his displeasure at his overall treatment, noting his desire to leave Ireland and to receive a full Crown pardon:

Kilmainham Jail, 10th June 83.

Sir,

The trials are over more than 3 weeks and I am here yet – I have seen Mr Mallon to speak to him only once since the trials began ten weeks ago. I have written 5 times to him and he was in Kilmainham 7 times and he never called to see me.

Also Sir I have asked for him to provide for me a written pardon and if possible a position that would suit me in Cape Town or Natal. I had to make a present of 2 houses to relations, as no one would buy anything belonging to me. I am ready to leave in 4 days when I give over those houses to my relations.

As I intend to bring my family I am going a few days before them. They would require an outfit. And before leaving a private visit as my wife does not know where I am going and 2 warders are present it would not be right to speak in their hearing.

If I am required again of course you [know] where I am ... I would wish to spend a few days in London before leaving, perhaps forever, I have got some clothes sent to me. I am hoping sir that you will settle my business soon.
I beg to remain yours most respectfully
James Carey TC.[349]

Carey would suffer a further blow while in prison. On 20 June 1883, it was reported that his title of Trades Councillor had been revoked. Carey was disqualified from standing in the Trinity Ward on the basis of felony, which incurred forfeiture of goods, and therefore bankruptcy. On the same day, the Collector General of the Rates for Dublin called in Carey's debts on premises he sublet at South Gloucester Street, Cumberland Street, Hamilton Row and Denzille Street. The State request, served on him personally at Kilmainham Gaol, was for £95.10s.7d, money which Carey could no longer afford to pay. A story now emerged publicly that Carey, despite his debts and his vilified status, was determined to maintain his office of Trades Councillor upon his release from Kilmainham. A letter had been smuggled out of Kilmainham for him, to be given to Charles Dawson, Dublin's Lord Mayor, asserting:

> It would have given me great pleasure to attend the meeting of the Municipal Council to be held on Monday next, especially as I see by yesterday's Times, that Alderman Meagher was selected to fill the high post which your lordship so worthily fills. But circumstances over which I have no control compel me to deny myself that agreeable and pleasing duty ... In conclusion I might draw your attention to the old and trite saying (nevertheless true) that no gentleman is as black as he is painted. When I give my account of making history to the council, my conduct will stand in its true light.[350]

How this would have been possible is extraordinarily hard to see, given the level of hatred towards Carey. Had he re-entered Dublin life in such a high-profile position, he would undoubtedly have been killed. Nevertheless, it distracted attention from the actual plans of the State to shuffle him away to the colonies:

> James Carey the informer still firmly asserts his resolution to take his seat in the Corporation and not to leave the Country. He has positively declared this to be his determination, and has furthermore demanded from the authorities his release from confinement ... he would not change his name under any circumstances – 'not being ashamed of himself or conscious of having committed any crime,' he was he said James Carey, a working bricklayer and a member of the Corporation, and was not ashamed of himself in the least.[351]

Despite these rather sensationalised stories of Carey's determination to rebuild his life in Dublin, he was in reality desperate to leave Ireland and

Kilmainham Gaol. The approver would, however, remain in the prison for several more weeks, the authorities judging that this was the most secure place for Carey until the State decided what to do with him. As Patrick Tynan would recall:

The police, detectives and the machinery of alien rule, had a white elephant on their hand in the person of James Carey. His protection was necessary for British prestige. The English no matter what their feelings toward Carey might be, knew that the duty of safely guarding him was imperative.[352]

Carey was thus held in Kilmainham Gaol, in a large cell formerly occupied by the great patriot Robert Emmet. This prolonged detention was maddening for him. Meanwhile, outside the prison walls, due to official silence, rumours were growing that Carey had already been spirited out of the country, in such heavy disguise that no one could have recognised him. Some speculated that Carey had been taken from the gaol by night, en route to Belfast, and would make for Canada. Others asserted that he was now in England, blending into the immigrant Irish community under an assumed name. Against this background, *The Irish Times* reported:

We are able to state that James Carey has not yet left his native city and that yesterday he was as safe in Kilmainham as bolts and bars could make him. He has become more tractable in his demeanour and is said now to acquiesce in the necessity of leaving the country. Arrangements are being made with that object, and in all probability the informer will be on his way aboard within the next fortnight. Where his destination will be is kept a profound secret – but that it has been fixed upon is certain.[353]

The Irish Times was correct – it had been decided when and where to move Carey. He was to be shipped to Natal in southern Africa. Within four days of the newspaper report, on 29 June, John Mallon would abruptly take him from his cell. Carey was told he was leaving the gaol, though where he was going remained unknown to him for the present. He was allowed take some materials with him, including an image of the Sacred Heart, with the medal and ribbon of the sodality of the Sacred Heart, which hung on the wall over his bed. Prior to his departure, for reasons of Carey's safety, he was washed and shaved within the gaol, to make him almost unidentifiable to the outside world. Mallon supervised the process, and would recall to Bussy:

> He was clean shaven, and his kinky hair was cut short and parted at the side instead of being divided down the centre as of old. He was a foreboding, objectionable looking person, with repulsively low forehead, on which the hair grew almost down to his eyebrows, and a large besotted red nose. The removal of moustache and beard had disclosed a peculiarly animal mouth that added to the sinister, cut throat suggestiveness of the whole.[354]

Carey was shuffled out of the gaol secretly and silently by John Mallon, aboard a low-key cab. Mallon and Carey made for Kingstown, briefly stopping in the Lower Castle Yard at Dublin Castle. Passing through James's Street into Thomas Street, the cab drove past a small tobacco shop run by Jane Curley, the wife of the executed Dan Curley:

> On the night of his release from Kilmainham, while he was faring by quiet ways to Kingstown, the arch informer chanced to look out the cab, as it passed the little tobacco shop kept by Curley's widow. Crossing himself he exclaimed, 'God save the soul of Dan Curley.[355]

Mallon, flabbergasted at this hypocrisy, commented on Carey's role in the death of Curley, to which Carey simply sat in the cab, silent.

Arriving in Dublin Castle, Mallon took Carey to his office. He gave him a revolver for protection, and some money to help him build a new life in the southern African colonies. They left the Castle in a new cab, and as they drove down Parliament Street, Carey drew the revolver on Mallon, threatening to kill him. Bluffing, Mallon looked him straight in the eyes and claimed to have a revolver in his pocket with his hand on the trigger. He called for the cab to stop, then opened the door and ordered Carey to get out. With nowhere to run, and people beginning to take notice of the fuss, Carey relented, claiming that he was merely teasing. Mallon ordered the cab to move on.

At Kingstown Harbour, Carey was accosted by detectives from Scotland Yard, there to escort him away from Ireland. Arriving in England, Carey was first taken to Scotland Yard, and then to Newgate Prison in London, where he would be detained until he left for Africa. Carey's family had been in London since his transfer from Kilmainham Gaol. They were holed up in London's East End, disguised as an immigrant Irish family and protected by an armed guard drawn from the Special Irish Branch, under Sergeant Patrick McIntyre.

On 3 July, the family were put aboard the steamer *Kinfauns Castle*, bound for the Cape of Good Hope. Carey joined his family at Dartmouth two days later, under the pseudonym of James Power.

By coincidence, also aboard the *Kinfauns Castle* was an Irishman, Patrick O'Donnell. O'Donnell was born in Gweedore, County Donegal, in 1835, and had previously been living in New York. He had travelled home, then on to London, and then set sail on the *Kinfauns Castle*. He planned to make his fortune in the diamond mines of southern Africa, and to start a new life with his girlfriend Susan Gallagher, whom he presented as his wife. A fellow Irishman, O'Donnell met and became acquainted with James Carey, becoming on intimate terms during the voyage, the O'Donnells regularly socialising with the 'Powers'. Such was the relationship between the two families that one of the Carey children looked upon Susan as an aunt.

On learning that O'Donnell was going to Cape Town, Carey persuaded him to follow them on to Natal, where the opportunities for getting wealthy were greater. Carey recommended to O'Donnell that he should pretend to be Scottish, and call himself MacDonald.

While Carey was en route to South Africa, news had broken back in Dublin that the approver had been spirited out of Kilmainham Gaol. *The Freeman's Journal* lamented:

> *Certain movements of the Kilmainham authorities yesterday favour the belief that James Carey had at last been removed from Dublin, his destination being, however, unknown. So far complete silence has been maintained in official quarters but there is good reason to suppose that Carey is gone probably to England for the present, pending the decision as to his permanent residence.*[356]

The Irish Times concurred, stating that with Carey's departure for the colonies, wherever he was bound, Kilmainham was rid of the last of its high-profile informers.[357] With Carey reportedly in England, the police actively watched Republican circles and clubs. Of particular interest was the arrival of Joe Brady's brother in London within two days of Carey's arrival in England. Special Irish Branch were alerted by Dublin police that Brady's brother may have been in London with the intention of killing Carey, and surveillance was placed on the Irishman upon his arrival in London's Euston Station. Brady never found Carey, and it is doubtful that he was looking for him.

The *Kinfauns Castle* arrived at Cape Town on Friday, 17 July 1883. The Powers and the O'Donnells disembarked, boarding a smaller ship, the *Melrose*, on 28 July, bound for Port Elizabeth and Durban, and a bright new future in a new land. Carey, however, had undermined this future by engaging in a drunken argument on the day the *Kinfauns Castle* had docked at Cape Town.

Robert Cubitt and his brother Frank were passengers aboard the *Kinfauns Castle*, acquainted with O'Donnell and Carey. Cubitt went into a wine and beer shop cum tavern, where the subject of James Carey came up in conversation with the attendant, who was an Irishman. The attendant was convinced that Carey was in the tavern, having seen a row between 'Power' and two men from the *Kinfauns Castle*. Power had grabbed a man, 'Scotty', by the throat, for saying that the Irish were savages who could never rule themselves:

> *[Carey] said the English were a people too base to live. If he had his way he would exterminate every one of them. 'Ireland for the Irish, that's my motto.' This nettled the Scotsman. So Scotty retorted, 'What would you do with it? Why, you would eat one another up.' 'Do you mean to say we are Cannibals?' shouted Carey in a violent passion; and his hand was on the throat of Scotty, who would have been choked but for Williams, who interfered. What Carey's object was in ventilating such opinions is difficult to say; perhaps he wanted to get on friendly terms with any Irishman who would be in the colony; but what is more probable they were his real feelings, which he could not repress.*[358]

Whatever Carey's motivations for this violent display, Cubitt said it was probably just idle drunken scuffling, and that Power, obviously with nationalistic tendencies, was drunkenly offended by the man 'Scotty'. The barman now withdrew from behind the counter an issue of the Dublin newspaper *The Weekly Freeman*, published on 5 May. The newspaper included a portrait of Carey, and despite the shaving off of his beard and the different combing of his hair, Power was almost identical to the notorious informer. Cubitt returned to the docks where the *Melrose* was moored and, seeing O'Donnell on the shore, he approached the Irishman and asked him if he had seen the newspaper and the portrait of Carey:

I produced it, and showed it to him – he said 'I will shoot him' – he asked me
for it, and I think he put it in his pocket – he went on board the Melrose, and I
believe she sailed about a quarter of an hour after the interview referred to.[359]

Parallel to Cubitt and O'Donnell becoming aware of Carey's identity, *The Cape Argus* newspaper stated that Carey was aboard the *Melrose*. With increasing alarm, Carey began to lay low aboard the ship, sending his son Thomas ahead to check for suspicious individuals when he went on deck. From the quays, men were seen to point at Carey.

O'Donnell planned to expose him aboard the *Melrose*, rather than kill him. He would tell him he wanted nothing more to do with such a vile character, and end their friendship. He met Maggie Carey in the ship's bar, and enquired where her husband was. Carey was summoned by his son Thomas, and within a couple of minutes joined O'Donnell in the saloon. Also in the bar were Thomas Carey and Susan Gallagher, while outside, near the bottom of the stairs leading from the deck, boatswain Tom Jones was playing with Carey's five-year-old daughter. A James Parish had just entered the saloon, and was to witness the notorious events that followed.

On entering the saloon, Parish saw Susan Gallagher with her arm around O'Donnell, who was freely chatting to Carey. It was clearly a conversation between friends, as they were laughing and acting jocularly. The conversation became more serious, however, when O'Donnell tested Carey's attitude to Irish politics. Carey took a militantly nationalist line. Now O'Donnell accused him of being James Carey the informer, and said he would have nothing more to do with him. Shocked, Carey asked, 'What do you mean, an informer?'[360] O'Donnell again asserted that he was James Carey the informer, responsible for the deaths of the five Invincibles in Kilmainham Gaol. Carey sprang to his feet immediately, reaching for the pistol that Mallon had given him. He clearly intended to kill O'Donnell, but O'Donnell was too fast. He drew his pistol on Carey and shot him three times. Parish recalled:

I noticed O'Donnell pulling his arm round from his pocket and holding it towards the deceased – he fired at the deceased and hit him in the neck – Power turned round and called out 'Oh! Maggie, I'm shot,' and as he was staggering towards the bottom of the saloon, having got about two yards from him, the prisoner fired two more shots at him, hitting him in the back – the prisoner was only two yards from the deceased and remained in the same sitting position – I was standing about five yards from the prisoner – Mrs. Carey came out of her cabin and caught the deceased as he was falling – they both fell together – I rushed past the prisoner to the deceased, and put my finger in the wound of the neck to stop the bleeding, and remained there until the doctor came – as I passed the prisoner I saw him putting the pistol into his left side coat-pocket.[361]

Perhaps in the heat of the moment, O'Donnell had initially shot Carey in self-defence. But then, as Carey stumbled across the floor, shouting for his wife, O'Donnell stalked him and shot the prime informer a further two times, with the intention of killing him. Hearing the gunshots, Maggie Carey must surely have known her husband had been attacked. As she opened the door to see the commotion, rather poignantly Carey fell into her arms, knocking her to the floor. Parish ran past O'Donnell and placed his finger on the wound in Carey's neck. Carey's eyes were blank, staring into space, then he looked towards his wife and then back again into nothingness. Maggie Carey was hysterical. Patrick O'Donnell was immediately arrested by crewmen.

Within a quarter of an hour, James Carey, the most notorious informer of the nineteenth century, was dead. His body was buried in an unmarked, unattended grave near Port Elizabeth, thousands of miles from his homeland, his name stained for generations. Five years later, an Irishman named George Duval visited Carey's grave, reporting home:

Carey's body lies in an enclosed graveyard on the Rise of a Hill near Port Elizabeth. None but coloured people and persons who have died in jail are buried in this miserable looking graveyard. Carey's grave is next to a 'kaner's, and on a large white stone at the head are written badly in lead pencil, James Carey, The Irish informer. [362]

21

THE REACTION

The news of Carey's death spread rapidly throughout the world, and proved a significant embarrassment to the British Government, considering the expense and special measures they had taken to protect Carey. It was clearly seen, in the extensive news coverage, that despite the immense resources of the British State, it could not protect an informant from the long arm of Fenian vengeance. One American newspaper lamented that 'the closest kept counsels of the authorities are open to the conspirators'.[363] This perception would clearly affect the British State's ability to recruit informers and intelligence assets in the future. Carey's killing was thus a harsh blow to the British authorities.

A popular story emerged that O'Donnell, supposedly a veteran Fenian and Invincible, had left America to stalk Carey in reprisal for the executions of his five comrades at Kilmainham Gaol. In this increasingly popular narrative, O'Donnell was re-written as a veteran of the Fenian Rising of 1867, who fought with distinction at the Battle of Tallaght, in South County Dublin. Another story spread that Patrick O'Donnell was engaged in the Fenian dynamite campaign then raging across Britain. O'Donnell was increasingly credited with involvement in an attempted explosion at the Mansion House in London, reportedly escaping in the aftermath to the safety of Irish-America. Once in America, according to this narrative, O'Donnell had been dispatched by a council of avengers to hunt Carey down, making his way to Dublin where he was met by a network of dedicated and retributive Fenians.

The story increasingly proliferated that, despite the secrecy of the British Government, and the measures they had taken to protect James Carey, 'an Invincible knew of it and kept on the track of the fugitive, and accomplished his purpose'.[364] This popular story was propagated by Irish-America, with Patrick O'Donnell portrayed as an avenger, a member of 'a committee of blood'[365] seeking justice for the Kilmainham five. Images of an 'order of Avengers'[366] were summoned up, shadowy figures who had dispatched O'Donnell to hunt down the notorious informer, dogging him across the world unhindered by the forces of the British Empire. The media tended to exaggerate the role of the Invincibles in Carey's death, one newspaper contending:

> [The British Government] *appear to be somewhat dazed at the completeness of the information possessed by the Invincibles, of which this assassination furnishes complete proof.*[367]

From Boston, Patrick Ford of radical newspaper *The Irish World* echoed this theme, saying that O'Donnell had travelled across the world with the support of the Fenian network, to stalk Carey and eventually execute him for his betrayal of the Kilmainham five. Ford's propaganda contended that Carey's killing would act as a warning to all existing and potential informants. He declared that there was no safety in their counsels, and that they would meet a similar fate. He published the following verse, in the shape of a cross:

Commemorative to all

Carey's Editor Irish World:

Arch traitors and diabolical informers, who disgrace their manhood for safety or

reward of blood money, by the fate of the cold blooded wretch Carey will learn

that their miserable shameful lives are not worth much in the nineteenth century.

Let Irish traitors fear the wrath of Ireland, and ponder well the following lines

commemorative to their accursed treachery: –

'Oh, for a tongue to curse the slave,

Whose treason, like a deadly blight,

Comes over the councils of the brave,

And blasts them in their hour of might!

May life's unblessed cup for him,

Be drugged with treachery to the brim,

With hopes that but allure to fly.

With joys that vanish while he sips,

Like dead sea fruits that tempt the eye,

But turn to ashes on the lips,

His country's curse, his children's shame,

Outcast of virtue, peace and fame,

May he at last, with lips of flame,

On the parched desert thirsting die,

While likes that shine in mockery nigh,

Are fading off untouched, untasted,

Like the once glorious hopes he blasted,

And when from the Earth his spirit flies,

Just profit, let the damned one dwell,

Full in sight of paradise,

Beholding heaven and feeling Hell!

The idea that O'Donnell had set out to kill Carey, carrying out an elaborate plan of vengeance, was, of course, a complete fabrication, initially invented by newspapermen to sell their titles, and then built upon by Fenianism for propaganda purposes. That O'Donnell had booked his ticket for the *Kinfauns Castle* one month before Carey had been dispatched by Dublin Castle for his services, and before a decision had been made to send him abroad, was written out of the O'Donnell narrative, replaced by sensationalist tales

How Parnell came to be viewed by some sections of the media in the years following the Phoenix Park assassinations – a sort of puppet-master, his throne made of the skulls of, among others, Cavendish and Burke.

St. Stephen's Review Presentation Cartoon, Decr 15 th, 1888.

THE FIGHT WITH APOLLYON.

Parnell portrayed as Apollyon, the Destroyer or Angel of Death from the Book of Revelations.

referencing committees of avengers. Further undermining the conspiracy theory, O'Donnell was on intimate terms with Carey on the voyage to southern Africa prior to finding out who 'James Power' actually was.

The news of Carey's killing was greeted with manifest joy among Irish nationalists. In Cork, the news was initially greeted with incredulity, but when it was confirmed, many expressed immense delight, feeling that the informer 'deserved his fate'.[368] In London, among Irish circles, the news was broadly welcomed, with many praising the speed in which the killing took place, given the elaborate precautions to prevent Carey's whereabouts becoming known. In Dublin, thousands of people took to the streets to cele-brate the death of the informer, with effigies of Carey burned throughout the city streets. At Mary Street, Abbey Street, Clarendon Street and Townsend Street, locals gathered to light bonfires. It was noted that following confirmation of Carey's death, money was solicited around Dublin by ordinary people to buy materials to burn in celebratory bonfires, the popular call being recorded as, 'Give a penny, sir, to burn James Carey.'[369]

At Townsend Street, Dublin, such was the crowd that gathered that police, attempting to disperse the crowd and put out their jubilant bonfire, were attacked by a riotous throng throwing stones and bottles, a police officer named Dunne being briefly hospitalised. At Moore Street, a street populated by street vendors and butchers near to Dublin's main thoroughfare, O'Connell Street, materials including cutting blocks were freely volunteered to be burned on the celebratory fires. In Denzille Street, where Carey had lived, six bonfires were lit and large crowds openly paraded in the street, cheering. At Marlborough Street, an enormous bonfire included tar barrels and large crates, along with an effigy of the informer. In Dublin, ultimately eighty people would be fined in connection with lighting bonfires celebrating Carey's death.

In Limerick, similar scenes were witnessed. An effigy of Carey was hurled through the streets, and then burned amid great cheers, the effigy subjected to every indignity and its residue then kicked and stomped upon mercilessly by the boisterous crowd.[370] In Belfast, similar effigies were burned in nationalist areas throughout the city. On Shankill Street in Lurgan, effigies were burned amid cries of, 'God bless the man who shot Carey.'[371] In New York, similar scenes were witnessed in nationalist circles. One newspaper lamented:

> For [Carey] *there can be neither pity nor regret. It is, however, to be regretted that Irish indignation was not sufficiently self respecting to have allowed the arch-traitor to linger out a wretched fragment of existence with the brow mark of Cain upon him, or to emulate his prototype Judas and go out and hang himself.*[372]

Immediately following the killing of Carey, the *Melrose* was boarded by John Cherry, the Chief Police Inspector of Port Elizabeth, and O'Donnell was taken ashore for questioning. O'Donnell was overheard to shout that he did not murder James Carey, but had killed him in self defence. Cherry seized O'Donnell's luggage, discovering the portrait of Carey given to him by Cubitt, and a number of naturalisation papers. Cherry also took possession of his father's revolver, importantly noting that while it was a six-chambered revolver, only five chambers were loaded.

O'Donnell had killed Carey at the Cape of Good Hope, and the question of where he would stand trial was a matter of some debate. The *Melrose* was a registered British vessel, meaning that O'Donnell could be deported to stand trial in England, which would inevitably result in his execution. However, the killing took place at sea, and international law stipulated that any country within three miles would have exclusive sovereignty over the matter, so that O'Donnell could equally be tried in the colonies and potentially avoid execution. The technicality that O'Donnell's life thus depended on was whether the assassination took place less than three miles from the shore, in which case he would not be extradited to Britain to stand trial.

However, crimes committed at sea, regarding British colonies, fell within the jurisdiction of the High Court of the Admiralty. When the Central Criminal Court was established in London, the Admiralty Judge was made a Judge of the Court, having jurisdiction over crimes committed on the high seas. The Jurisdiction of the Central Criminal Court within the colonies was weak, however, and under existing law, crimes committed within the jurisdiction of the Admiralty could legally be tried in local courts. The question was ultimately whether the British Government wished to force the issue. They did, and jurisdiction for the trial of Patrick O'Donnell was granted to London's Central Criminal Court.

The trial was heard in London before Mr Justice George Denman, and O'Donnell was defended by the Liberal MP Charles Russell, the Irish MP AM Sullivan and Rodger A Pryor, paid for by Irish-Americans through *The Irish World*. The defence contended that Carey's killing was a matter of self-defence:

> What would the most likely thing for a coward like Carey to do, armed as he was with a weapon, that the Government had furnished him with? Of course it would be to produce it, either for the purpose of a show of violence to deter the other man from further violent acts, or for the purpose of deadly use to give effect to the show of violence. If that were the true statement of the case, the prisoner's life ought not to be forfeited to the law.

On behalf of the Government, illustrating the enormity of the O'Donnell case, the Crown was represented by Sir Henry James, British Attorney General, and Henry Poland, solicitor to the Treasury. Seeking to have O'Donnell executed for the assassination of James Carey, the State argued that, while no evidence existed of O'Donnell's desire to kill James Carey, and he had not boarded the *Kinfauns Castle* to do so, he had killed James Carey upon seeing the rough sketch of the informer shown to him by Robert Cubitt. Henry James thus implied that the killing of Carey was premeditated and wilful, an act of deliberate retribution, refuting O'Donnell's claim of self-defence.

The first witness against O'Donnell was James Parish. He recalled that O'Donnell was sitting down as he shot Carey, and said he had not seen any gun except O'Donnell's pistol. Parish said he had only heard through hearsay that Carey was armed with a revolver. Parish was sure O'Donnell had killed Carey around 3.45 on the afternoon of 28 July 1883. He testified that he saw O'Donnell placing the pistol into his left-side inner jacket pocket, and claimed he declined to intervene for fear of his own life:

On Saturday, 28th July last, I sailed in the Melrose from Cape Town to Natal. I was employed as servant to three of the officers – on Sunday, the day after we sailed, I was in the second-class saloon, where my cabin is, at the bottom of the stairs in the fore part of the vessel [plan produced] *– I was in the 'peak,' to the right of the cabin stairs, where the officers' servants and the steward slept, about 3.30 in the afternoon – I was in my own cabin and came out into the second-class saloon, on both sides of which there are berths with tables in the centre and settees – I saw the prisoner, his wife, and another passenger called James Power – the prisoner and his wife were sitting on the settee with their backs to the table and near the prisoner's berth on the left side of the saloon going aft – James Power was standing at the corner of the prisoner's berth, and was about a yard from O'Donnell with his face towards him – the woman had her arm round the prisoner's neck and resting on his shoulder – I noticed O'Donnell pulling his arm round from his pocket and holding it towards the deceased – he fired at the deceased and hit him in the neck – Power turned round and called out 'Oh! Maggie, I'm shot,' and as he was staggering towards the bottom of the saloon, having got about two yards from him, the prisoner fired two more shots at him, hitting him in the back – the prisoner was only two yards from the deceased and remained in the same sitting position – I was standing about five yards from the prisoner – Mrs. Carey came out of her cabin and caught the deceased as he was falling – they both fell together – I rushed past the prisoner to the deceased, and put my finger in the wound of the neck to stop the bleeding, and remained there until the doctor came – as I passed the prisoner I saw him putting the pistol into his left side coat-pocket – Dr Everett attended Carey, who died a quarter of an hour afterwards – about a quarter of an hour previously I saw them drinking together; that was about 3.30 – after the shots were fired I picked up a bullet under the table in the saloon where the deceased died – it was about two yards from the spot where the shots were fired* [The bullet was here produced] *– that is the bullet – I noticed other persons in the saloon at the time, Carey's son, the boatswain Jones, and the little girl Carey – Jones was playing with the little girl at the bottom of the stairs – young Carey was also at the bottom of the stairs, but I did not notice him go anywhere.*[373]

The defence argued that Parish had not seen any other pistol due to poor visibility, stating that Carey had a pistol upon his person at all times for personal safety. Charles Russell cited the discovery of the same pistol in Thomas Carey's possession, saying that the son had taken the weapon to make it look like his father had been shot while defenceless. A witness for the defence, Walther Young, a cab driver at Port Elizabeth, testified that Thomas Carey had told him that he had tried to get the revolver from his father:

> I remember one day meeting Thomas Francis … I went to get a drink of water, and he came and took the mug out of my hand before I took it from the lion's mouth, and I said to him 'You are a fine fellow; why did you not shoot O'Donnell when he shot your father?' – he said 'I had not the revolver, but I went for to get it in the cabin, and when I got there it was gone, because my father had it' – I said 'It is a bad job, quite likely you will have to go to England, if you had shot him there might be no more about it' – this was after the inquiry before the Magistrate at Port Elizabeth – I spoke of this on the cabstand among all the cabmen.[374]

As this evidence was being given, Judge Denman theatrically examined O'Donnell's pistol and the bullets used to kill Carey, halfway across the world. Thomas Carey of course denied making the statement testified to by Young, asserting that O'Donnell had killed his father in cold blood. The younger Carey testified that O'Donnell and his father had been good friends throughout the voyage, and no one had suspected his father's true identity until their arrival at the Cape. He had been in the saloon no longer than three minutes, hearing no 'high words' passing between his father and O'Donnell, when his attention was drawn by the sound of gunfire. He claimed to have seen O'Donnell taking his gun out of his pocket and firing randomly at his father, O'Donnell sitting down as he did so. Following the shooting of his father, Thomas ran to his mother's cabin, hoping to get

James Carey's revolver. He did so, he claimed, not with the intention of killing O'Donnell, but to give it to his father to defend himself. The fifteen-year-old emotionally testified:

> *Up to the beginning of July I had lived in Dublin – my father had been in prison some time before he left Dublin – on 4th July I went on board the Kinfauns Castle in London with six younger children and my mother – we all went in the name of Power, except one, who was called M'Kenna – on 6th July my father joined the vessel at Dartmouth – he also went by the name of Power, and we all went to the Cape of Good Hope – I saw the prisoner on the voyage; I think he came on board in London – he was accompanied by a young woman – I recollect arriving at the Cape on Friday, July 27th, and on the 28th we all went on board the Melrose as steerage passengers – my mother and sisters slept*

Patrick O'Donnell in the dock at London's Central Criminal Court.

in the second-class cabin, and my father and three of us boys in the steerage – the steerage is all open – on Sunday afternoon I was in the second-class saloon – I went down from deck at 3.30, and when I came down my father, Mr Jones the boatswain, and my little sister were there, and O'Donnell was sitting on the settee, and Mrs. O'Donnell was sitting close to him – my father was standing at the corner of O'Donnell's berth; I was near the staircase, where Jones and my sister were – I had been about five minutes in the cabin before a shot was fired – during that time my father and O'Donnell were speaking together – I heard no high words between them – I saw the prisoner draw a revolver out of his pocket and fire at my father, and the cartridge, or a bullet, hit my father in the neck – he was standing and O'Donnell was sitting – I was near the staircase – when the bullet struck my father I think he did not speak, but I saw him stagger towards my mother's cabin at the end of the saloon on the left-hand side – I ran towards my mother's cabin to get my father's revolver – I went round the tables – my mother was in her cabin and I took the revolver from the bag produced – I had seen my father with a revolver when he came on board at Dartmouth, and I saw it when my father went on shore at Madeira, and when he came back he put it into the bag – I knew it was there because I afterwards saw my father and mother go to it to get money – I think it was on the bedstead – that was between Madeira and Cape Town – I knew the bag was in my mother's cabin, because I had taken it from the Kinfauns Castle myself – when I ran to the cabin I wanted to give the revolver to my father – it was unlocked and I took it out – there was only one pistol, and, to the best of my belief, this is the one produced – I then went back into the saloon – my mother had gone out before me – after I got out of the cabin O'Donnell fired the second shot – my father was running towards my mother, crying out 'Oh, Maggie, I'm shot' – I then heard a third shot fired – my father was then in my mother's arms, standing with his back towards O'Donnell – I kept the pistol in my pocket – I did not give it to my father, because I saw he would not be able to use it – my father and mother fell together, and he died within a quarter of an hour afterwards

– during the whole time I was in the cabin before the shot was fired I did not hear anything like a quarrel or see any struggle – I did not see my father with any pistol, I did not pick one up off the ground – I carried the pistol in my pocket until it was taken away from me, shortly after my father's death, by the second officer – there was a good deal of excitement at the time – I saw my mother go towards O'Donnell, who put out his hand and said 'Shake hands, Mrs. Carey, your name is not Power,' or something like that – I am not sure whether O'Donnell said 'I was sent to do it' or 'I had to do it' – I am not positive as to the words used – my mother, I believe, did not shake hands with the prisoner – Mrs. O'Donnell said 'No matter, O'Donnell, you are no informer' – I had seen O'Donnell using a pistol on the voyage – he was shooting flying fish with it, but I cannot say whether it was the one with which he shot my father.[375]

The young Carey's testimony, however, was riddled with inconsistencies. Whereas he had previously asserted that having heard the shots, Parish had entered the bar, he was then forced to admit that this was untrue, claiming he had misunderstood the earlier question. Thomas Carey said that O'Donnell had shot his father using his left hand, yet in earlier evidence he had asserted that he had used his right, forcing Carey's son to admit that he was unsure of the exact details of the killing. He acknowledged that he had taken his father's pistol, later taken off him by the second officer of the *Melrose*, but said that this was to take it out of his mother's way. He denied ever having met Walther Young, and therefore telling him that his father had had the pistol on him.

The contradictions in Thomas Carey's evidence were seized upon by Sir Charles Russell, particularly his relationship to his father's pistol. Russell asked Carey's son whether the case containing the gun was locked. Thomas Carey said it wasn't, as he couldn't then have got the pistol. Russell next asked how and when the pistol was taken from him, to which the younger Carey recalled surrendering the gun to the ship's first officer, saying he told him he had taken it to get it out of his mother's way. Russell now cleverly asked Thomas Carey, 'But I thought you said you wanted to give the gun to your father?' Carey answered clearly and audibly, confirming this statement. Russell asked him, 'Now, which was true?'[376]

The question of the gun was central to the defence examination of Thomas Carey, and showed up several inconsistencies in his testimony. It emerged that Thomas Carey had initially denied having his father's pistol upon his person, and only when he was searched a second time was it discovered in his trouser pocket. The idea that the young Carey had taken the gun from a box in his mother's berth was seen to be most improbable, as the box was continuously locked. Russell contended that James Carey would not have allowed himself to be without his gun for his own safety, and that the young Carey had removed the gun from the scene.

Maggie Carey next took the stand, dressed in a widow's black dress. She recalled that the O'Donnells and the Careys had become great friends aboard the *Kinfauns Castle* and the *Melrose*, and that it was on her husband's suggestion that the O'Donnells had decided to head for Natal. Maggie Carey recalled that:

> *I left London on July 4 on the* Kinfauns Castle *with my children, and was joined by my husband at Dartmouth on the 6th – on the way out we made the acquaintance of the prisoner and a woman who passed as his wife – we became very friendly, and played at draughts and chatted together – at Cape Town we did not sleep on shore, but were transferred to the* Melrose *on the Saturday of our arrival – the prisoner was to have stopped at the Cape, but he joined the* Melrose *for Natal – on the Sunday he was in the second-class saloon with his wife – my husband was on deck – the prisoner said to me 'Where is Mr Power?' – I said 'On deck' – he said 'You had better call him down' – my husband was called down … the prisoner asked my husband to have a bottle of ale, and he said he was just coming down to have one – my husband took the baby from me*

*and put it in our cabin; but it awoke, and I went to it – I went into the cabin,
and in five or ten minutes I heard the first shot, which I thought was a ginger-
beer bottle gone – before I went away I saw the men with ale before them
– O'Donnell and his wife were on the settee, and my husband too – I heard
a second shot – then I put down the baby and went out, and I heard a third
shot, and my husband met me and fell into my arms, crying 'Oh, Maggie, I am
shot, O'Donnell has shot me' – my son rushed into my cabin as I was coming
out – I saw my husband was bleeding from the side of his neck – he fell and
I fell with him – I remember going up to the prisoner, upon whose shoulder
the woman had her hand – I said 'O'Donnell, did you shoot my husband?' –
he said 'Shake hands, Mrs. Carey; don't blame me; I was sent to do it' – the
woman said 'No matter, O'Donnell, you're no informer' – up to that time we
had gone by the name of Power – up to the time I left the cabin my bag was
there – I knew my husband had a revolver; but I had not seen it – I heard
from the prisoner that he had sold a revolver in Cape Town for £3.10s – this
had come up in conversation.*[377]

Like her husband's earlier evidence in Kilmainham Magistrates' Courthouse in Dublin, Maggie Carey's testimony was greeted with absolute silence, with all present listening intently to every word. In her narrative, O'Donnell had claimed he was sent to assassinate Carey, and the saloon meeting was well planned. Maggie Carey's evidence could not be debunked by AM Sullivan, who moved onto the next witness – Dr Frederick Ensor, a surgeon from Port Elizabeth who had seen Carey's body. Dr Ensor said that Carey was a pow-erful, corpulent man, capable of grappling with O'Donnell. Describing his wounds, Ensor said that Carey had been shot three times by a man standing up, once more contradicting Thomas Carey's evidence.

Following Frederick Ensor, the defence sought to use John Mallon to ben-efit O'Donnell's case. Mallon testified that he had given Carey a revolver prior to his departure from Dublin. Seeking to besmirch Carey's already infamous character, the defence asked John Mallon a rather leading question as to his opinion of the assassinated informer. Charles Russell described Carey as a desperate and scandalous individual, to which Mallon had no choice but to agree, stating that Carey was 'a desperate man utterly regardless of human life, but always took care of his own'.[378] Russell was characterising Carey as quite capable of drawing a pistol on O'Donnell, bulwarking the defense of self defense. The Attorney General replied that while Carey was undoubtedly reckless, he had never openly displayed his reckless streak 'without carefully preparing a way for his own escape'.[379] Mallon said that, 'coward as he was',[380] Carey would not have hesitated to shoot the man who exposed him as an informer. On this evidence, Russell would contend:

> All this went to show that it would be more likely that a man like O'Donnell should have taken Carey's life ... but the Jury must bring their own common sense to bear, and ask themselves whether a man with deadly intentions would not, in the selection of time and place, have shown some desire to shield himself from the consequences of his act. Did it appear likely that without any previous quarrel or disturbance, O'Donnell would under such circumstances, have selected a time when there were seven persons present, when he was within 48 hours of Natal, and within reasonable distance of the security and secrecy of the bush?[381]

Judge Denman told the jury that they faced a sombre decision regarding O'Donnell's fate, as he had killed James Carey on the high seas aboard an English-registered vessel, within the Admiralty of England. The question they needed to consider was whether the killing of Carey was premeditated or self defence. Denman instructed the jury that if there was any reasonable doubt as to O'Donnell's motives for killing James Carey, he should be given the benefit of the doubt. The jury retired at seven o'clock on Saturday, 1 December 1883. Though there was no need for O'Donnell to remain in court, he insisted on remaining in the dock until the verdict had passed.

At half past seven, the jury returned, having been unable to reach a verdict. They requested clarification from Judge Denman on the law relevant to the case. Denman informed the foreman that if the jurors believed that O'Donnell was about to be shot by Carey, as asserted by the defence, then O'Donnell had killed him in self defence, and it was neither murder nor manslaughter. Denman reminded them, however, that O'Donnell had fired three shots at Carey, the final shot killing him, having followed him outside the saloon. At twenty minutes to eight, the jury once again retired. Denman was now challenged by O'Donnell's counsel, AM Sullivan, who accused the judge of effectively making a suggestion to the jury.

Within three quarters of an hour, the jury sent a paper to Denman, seeking clarification on the meaning of malice aforethought. Summoning the jury to Court, Denman defined malice aforethought as understanding that if a man killed another man wilfully, the law presumed malice, and the offence was then murder, unless it could be proven that circumstances justified a verdict of manslaughter. According to Denman, if Carey had pulled his pistol on O'Donnell first, and O'Donnell had acted in self defence, he could not be found guilty of murder, but of the lesser crime of manslaughter.

Returning to Court for the final time, the jury had now come to a decision. Patrick O'Donnell, in the dock, was recorded as looking tense and pensive, staring at the foreman of the jury. The verdict was guilty. O'Donnell immediately jumped to his feet, crossing his arms and looking coldly at Denman. Asked if he had anything to say before sentence of death was passed upon him, Patrick O'Donnell declined. Almost theatrically, like at the trials in Dublin earlier in the year, Denman put on the black cap, signalling the imminent passing of the sentence of death. Addressing O'Donnell, Denman said that Carey was hypocritical, abominable, reckless, wicked and cowardly, but that this did not justify O'Donnell's killing of the informer. Passing the sentence of death, he concluded:

> *I trust you will repent towards God before you die. But in order that it may be thoroughly understood what peril and misery are brought upon people who allow themselves to be brought into horrible doctrines of this kind. I have now to pass sentence upon you. The sentence of the Court is that you be taken hence to a lawful place of execution, there to be hanged by the neck until you be dead and may God have mercy on your soul.*[382]

Denman instructed officials to take O'Donnell from the Court, but the condemned Irishman now asked to speak. Denman refused the request, as the offer had already been made. O'Donnell now struggled with the court attendants, trying to shake them off and audibly declaring: 'Three Cheers for Ireland: Good bye to the United States: To hell with the bastard British Government and the perjurers who found me guilty!'[383] As he was being led down to the cells, the sound of scuffling was loudly audible to the Courtroom, along with O'Donnell's loud shout of, 'It is a plot made up to destroy me.'[384]

Patrick O'Donnell was taken to the imposing fortress of London's Newgate Gaol, which would be his home for the remaining days of his life. In the gaol, O'Donnell maintained his indignation against the justice system, continually using strong language as he 'anathematised England, her people and her laws, declared himself to be a victim of an infamous plot, and called for "Auld Ireland" ...'[385] O'Donnell was to be hanged at the prison on 17 December 1883.

22

THE EXECUTION OF PATRICK O'DONNELL

n Newgate Gaol, Patrick O'Donnell built up a rapport with a Father Fleming, a Catholic priest from Moorfield's Finsbury Circus, who acted as Newgate's unofficial Catholic chaplain. Father Fleming had a calming effect on O'Donnell in the days leading up to his execution, meeting him regularly for spiritual guidance and friendship. In his remaining days, O'Donnell was often observed chatting to prison officers. Never once did he accept the verdict of the court, although he commented that he was not surprised by it, though he did expect to receive the lighter verdict of manslaughter. As the days rolled by, O'Donnell remained stoically indifferent to his impending execution. State executioner William Marwood had by now retired, and had been replaced by Bartholomew Binns, his former assistant.

The execution of O'Donnell would be more difficult than those of the Invincibles several months previously. The British Government was looking at a possible diplomatic nightmare – Patrick O'Donnell, despite having been born in Donegal, was a naturalised American citizen. In Irish-America, intensive lobbying of political representatives was underway to intervene to prevent O'Donnell's death. On 8 December, over twenty congressmen called for Presidential intervention on his behalf. The congressmen informed President Arthur that the case against O'Donnell was unfair, and that his trial was a 'mockery' and a 'scandal of justice'. The President was presented with a Clan na Gael petition in defence of O'Donnell:

The act for the commission of which our fellow citizen Patrick O'Donnell, now awaits execution is that of having dared to defend successfully his life against an attack made upon him by a wretch who had already betrayed and bounded to death several of his own associates. The conduct of O'Donnell is regarded as not only justifiable but meritorious by hundreds of thousands of American citizens of every origin, as is proved by their liberal contributions to the fund for his defence.

We request your prompt aid to relieve him from his impending fate, not for these reasons alone, but also because it is acknowledged even by his prosecutors that not only was he unconnected with any society, but that he was quite ignorant of the identity of his assailant until a very short time before the affray. Therefore the essential elements of deliberation, premeditation and malice aforethought, necessary to establish a charge of murder are totally wanting. Because the Colonial authorities at the Cape of Good Hope insisted that he had committed the alleged offence within their jurisdiction, and ought consequently to have been tried in their courts, notwithstanding which they were compelled by the British Government to yield him up that he might be tried in the centre of its power; because he was not tried at 'the first port of the nation' whose laws he was said to have transgressed, according to legal usage and requirement; and because the judge who presided at his 'trial' contrary to law and precedent undertook to decide the question of fact – the very purpose for which a jury is empanelled and without which the sacred right of trial by jury becomes a mockery.

We are confirmed in the conviction that it can not be considered unbefitting

that even executive action should be requested in the present instance, by the

fact that in several cases – one notably of quite recent date – such a course has

been adopted at the solicitation of friends of the accused. The question is simply

whether an American citizen shall, by a foreign Government, be put to death by

illegal and foul means without remonstrance, without an effort to save him?

We rely confidently upon your sense of justice and national spirit to render

such help as may be in your power in this matter and request such action as may

lead to the desired result.[386]

Acting upon instructions from his Government, James Russell Lowell, the American Minister (Ambassador) in London, wrote to the British Home Secretary, William Vernon Harcourt. Russell Lowell, as instructed by President Arthur,[387] requested that the British Home Office undertake a careful re-examination of the case, allowing O'Donnell's counsel to present any alleged points of error in the judicial proceedings.[388] Furthermore, without dissent, the United States House of Representatives was resolved to bring O'Donnell's case and an appeal for a stay of execution to the President, in order to ascertain his naturalised American citizenship parallel to a careful re-examination of the case.[389] Charles Russell would similarly plead on O'Donnell's behalf, outlining seven reasons why O'Donnell should not be executed and urging a 'serious consideration'.[390]

Russell reminded Harcourt, as had been asserted at the Central Criminal Court, that O'Donnell had not engaged in a premeditated quest to assassinate James Carey, and had not been aware of his identity until alerted by Cubitt at Cape Town. Cubitt believed that O'Donnell was not serious when he said he would swing for Carey upon learning his identity, and in all probability the act was 'the result of sudden impulse caused by some altercation, and probably proceeded by some show of violence by James Carey, otherwise it is difficult to believe the prisoner would risk his life when detection was certain where so many opportunities of comparative safety were at hand'.[391] This was further evidenced by O'Donnell's remark to Maggie Carey that he had had to kill her husband, which Russell contended was in view of apprehension of danger to himself. This danger was due to Carey's possession of a pistol upon his person, as denied by his son, in testimony that Russell described as 'unworthy of intelligent acceptance', and 'discredited'.[392]

Recommending leniency, Russell reminded the Home Secretary of the dangers to Britain from Irish-America, a nation in exile outside of its jurisdiction. He said that a commutation of O'Donnell's execution in favour of a life sentence would have a 'salutary and soothing influence in America', rather than exacerbate existing Irish-American political grievance.[393] While O'Donnell should be punished, he pleaded to Harcourt, 'spare his life'.[394]

In Ireland, opinion was growing that O'Donnell should not be killed. A Ladies' Committee, representing the families of men charged with conspiracy, similarly appealed to the Home Secretary for some degree of clemency. The Ladies' Committee, like Lowell and Russell, questioned the evidence supplied by the young Carey as to the whereabouts of his father's gun. Highlighting O'Donnell's plea of self defence, the Committee noted Denman's concluding remark that James Carey was an 'infamous, abominable and wicked man'.[395] If Judge Denman had come to this conclusion, was it really so improbable that, with his true identity exposed, Carey would have tried to murder O'Donnell? The Ladies' Committee asked for mercy, and a royal intervention:

> We therefore earnestly appeal to you – as the advisor to the Queen and ask you whether this is not a case for expressing the prerogative of mercy on behalf of the condemned man – that the extreme penalty of the law may not be carried out.[396]

In a further appeal for clemency, a number of residents of Glin in County Limerick sent a petition to the British Queen, seeking an immediate reprieve for Patrick O'Donnell from the sentence of death. It was again noted that O'Donnell had not set off from America with the express purpose of assassinating James Carey, but had left for the Cape on legitimate business, having purchased a ticket for the *Melrose* prior to the departure of Carey and his family under the alias of Power. The petition argued that O'Donnell had had ample opportunity to kill James Carey prior to 29 July – had he actually planned to kill Carey with malice aforethought, as suggested, he would surely have waited till the *Kinfauns Castle* arrived at Natal, where the unsettled country would have facilitated his design and escape without detection.[397] This argument was supported by French playwright Victor Hugo, who also pleaded with Queen Victoria for clemency on O'Donnell's behalf:

> *The Queen of England has shown more than once her greatness of heart. The Queen of England will grant the condemned man O'Donnell his life, and will accept the unanimous and profound thanks of the civilised World.*[398]

Lionel Sackville West, the British Consul at Washington, was approached by Congressman Abram Stevens Hewitt. Hewitt noted the existence of a sizable Irish community in his district and expressed a need to appease them.[399]

These appeals for clemency fell on deaf ears. On 16 December, Harcourt responded to Russell's letter, stressing the importance of O'Donnell's execution, despite American opposition and the several points raised by Russell and others. A similar communication was sent to James Russell Lowell for the elucidation of the American Government. Harcourt stated that the Government could find no grounds upon which they would be justified in interfering with the sentence of the law and its execution.[400]

The day before his execution, O'Donnell was given permission to see his brother one final time. The two men spoke in Irish, although Patrick O'Donnell was aware that one of the officers could understand Irish, and warned his brother to say nothing controversial in his presence. O'Donnell remained cool with his brother until, saying goodbye, he asserted that he intended to state from the gallows that he had killed James Carey the informer, and was proud of it. Thinking of his wife and family in America, he was happy that the money raised for his defence would be used to take care of them, and would not leave them wanting in his absence. Finally, to comfort his brother, Patrick O'Donnell said that he was 'dying for Ireland and would die like a brave man'.[401] The prison staff, who had grown fond of the condemned man, also believed he would die courageously.[402]

O'Donnell's brother sought the return of his body for burial in a consecrated area, but his request was refused, and so he would never see his brother again. Before leaving the condemned prisoner, his brother said that he would wait as near as possible to the gates of the prison on the morning of his execution, to be as close to him as possible. Breaking down, his brother now left Patrick O'Donnell.

Rising at 6.30 on the morning of 17 December 1883, O'Donnell spent most of his remaining few hours with Father Fleming. The weather outside perhaps mirrored O'Donnell's mood, the sky overcast and gray, while a powerful wind bellowed through the empty prison yards. For the first time, O'Donnell's indifference appeared to fade, as the gravity of his situation became increasingly apparent.

Shortly before eight o'clock, the bell of the prison chapel began to toll, indicating that the procession for O'Donnell's execution had formed. O'Donnell's cell was opened to receive Gaol Governor Captain Kirkpatrick, accompanied by Sheriff's Lieutenant Colonel Cowan and Clarence Smith, with the Gaol Doctor Philip Francis Gilbert. Bartholomew Binns, who had been staying in the gaol since Friday, entered O'Donnell's cell, where Father Fleming sat in conversation with the condemned prisoner. O'Donnell stood and greeted the executioner. Binns began the process of pinioning O'Donnell in preparation for his execution, supervised by prison officers and Father Fleming. O'Donnell remained silent, and did not resist.

Outside the prison, a sizable crowd had gathered, largely out of voyeurism, but partly out of sympathy for the Irishman. O'Donnell's brother was in the crowd by himself, and was seen to move to and fro, avoiding conversation with those who tried to make it. He was recorded to be inconsolable.

Working up the courage to address the crowd, O'Donnell's brother said, 'My brother has died as bravely as any man ever did!'[403] The death of Patrick O'Donnell was lamented by AA Walls in verse, in a memorial card:

> Long, long shall his name in our memory remain,
> And the words that he uttered, our hearts will inflame.
> The shot that he fired, caused traitors to shake;
> He dearly loved Ireland, and died for her sake.
> While they pinioned his arms, he smiled on the slave,
> And his cruel executors admitted him brave.
> Oh! had we ten thousand such heroes as he,
> Our country no longer in bondage would be.
> Cursed be the Saxon! how could they deny,
> The remains of our hero in Ireland to lie.
> And in the grave of his Fathers, why not let him rest,
> In the land of the Shamrock, with those he loved best.
> But O'Donnell has gone! He has died for our cause!
> He was brutally murdered by England's vile laws.
> May his soul rest in Heaven with the Angels of Light,
> Is the prayer that we offer up, morning and night.

Patrick O'Donnell was buried within Newgate Prison in an unmarked, unattended grave. His remains rested there until 1902, when he was reinterred in the London City Cemetery in a mass grave of former Newgate prisoners. Despite extensive research by the National Graves Association in the twentieth century, it has been impossible to locate the exact spot where O'Donnell was buried. As a result the Association placed a bronze plaque in O'Donnell's honour atop the mass grave. The greatest legacy to O'Donnell's memory remains, however, a large cenotaph erected in his honour by Irish-America in Dublin's Glasnevin Cemetery. It simply reads:

In Memory of Patrick O'Donnell. Who heroically gave up his life for Ireland in London, England 17 December 1883. Not tears but prayers for the dead who died for Ireland.

AFTERWORD

One of Shane Kenna's ambitions in life was to see the remains of the Invincibles exhumed from Kilmainham Gaol and given a dignified burial in Glasnevin Cemetery. In 2013, Shane wrote to the Minister of State with responsibility for the Office of Public Works, requesting that the Government consider exhuming the bodies of the executed men. He got an acknowledgement that his letter had been received, which also stated that once enquiries had been completed in the matter, he would receive a substantive response. There has been no further correspondence from the Minister's office.

I worked closely with Shane on the 1916 Centenary Committee of the National Graves Association (NGA), and during this time, we discussed the Invincibles case many times. We made a pledge that post the 2016 celebrations, we would campaign with the NGA to have the remains of Joseph Brady, Daniel Curley, Michael Fagan, Thomas Caffrey and Timothy Kelly exhumed from the prison yard where they have lain since 1883.

Shortly after Shane's passing in 2017, the NGA wrote to the Minister of State with responsibility for the Office of Public Works. The NGA stated its belief that the five members of the Irish National Invincibles buried in Kilmainham Gaol should be exhumed and re-interred in consecrated ground. The Minister's reply was lengthy, but can be summarised in one sentence contained in the letter: 'I have consulted with the Commissioners of Public Works and I concur with their view which is not to support your request.'

Undeterred by this negative response from Government, the NGA formed a sub-committee for the sole purpose of campaigning for the exhumation and re-interment of the Invincibles. One of our first tasks was to locate descendants of the five men, and get their support for the campaign. Some of these relatives were already known to the Committee, and with several online appeals, relatives of the others were identified within a few months. Descendants of all of the men have given their support to the campaign.

A number of public figures have also given their support to the Invincibles Re-interment Campaign, including Lord Mayor of Dublin Nial Ring. In October 2018, the Lord Mayor wrote to the Minister for Culture, Heritage and the Gaeltacht, expressing his full support for the campaign and requesting that a meeting be held with the Committee to discuss how to bring this proposal forward in a positive way. We are currently awaiting a reply from the Minister.

Watch this space.

Aidan Lambert
Secretary of the Invincibles Re-interment Committee
November 2018

EDITOR'S NOTE

The political assassinations in Phoenix Park by the Irish National Invincibles, thirty-five years after the famine and thirty-four years before the 1916 Rising, sent shockwaves through the establishment, crystallising and shaping attitudes and politics for years afterwards. The Invincibles seem to occupy a prominent place in the Irish psyche, and they have popped up in all sorts of places in literature and song ever since:

James Joyce was born in the same year as the Phoenix Park assassinations, and *Ulysses* is full of references to the Invincibles. In the 'Lotus Eaters' chapter, the informer James Carey pops into Leopold Bloom's mind as he strolls past All Hallows Church on Westland Row, though he gets Carey's name wrong. Stephen Dedalus discusses the Invincibles at length with a bunch of newspaper men in 'Aeolus'. They get all sorts of names and dates wrong, which may be a comment by Joyce about journalism, or perhaps about people generally. There is a mention, of the X-rated variety, of Joe Brady's execution in the 'Cyclops' chapter and later, in 'Eumaeus', Dedalus and Bloom stop at a cabman's shelter, for a chat with a man they believe to be 'Skin the Goat' Fitzharris, one of the getaway drivers at Phoenix Park.

Joyce's sequel, *Finnegans Wake*, also seems to be about some terrible crime committed in Phoenix Park.

THE INVINCIBLES

Frank O'Connor and Hugh Hunt's play *The Invincibles* first opened in the Abbey theatre on 18 October 1937, starring Cyril Cusack as Timothy Kelly.

Another great Irish writer, Brendan Behan, mentioned in an article in the *Irish Press*, 18 June 1955, that he was '… ever proud to know that I had Invincible blood in me'.

As well as the 'Fenian Blade' song quoted on pp. 242–243 of this book, the Invincibles feature in the satirical 'Take Her Up to Monto', by George 'Hoddy' Hodnett and a big hit for The Dubliners in 1966. The second verse begins, 'Have you heard of Buckshot Forster, The dirty old imposter' – the first target for assassination by the Invincibles. 'Monto' itself is also immortalised as 'Nighttown' in *Ulysses*. And they get the whole fourth verse to themselves:

When Carey told on Skin the Goat
O'Donnell caught him on the boat
He never should have been afloat, the dirty skite
It wasn't very sensible to tell on the Invincibles
They stood up for their principles, day and night
And you'll find them all in Monto, Monto, Monto …

Eoin O'Brien
January 2019

ENDNOTES

1. Hoppen, Theodore K., *Ireland since 1800: Conflict and conformity* (New York, 1992) p.95.

2. Moody, T.W., *Davitt and the Irish Revolution* (Oxford, 1982) p.564.

3. Hoppen, Theodore K., *Ireland since 1800: Conflict and conformity* (New York, 1992) p.95.

4. House of Commons debates, third series, 30 June 1876, cols 807–808 (London, 1886).

5. John Daly's recollections of Fenianism, *Irish Freedom*, April 1913, p.2. *It must be noted that Daly's recollections were written 40 years after the actual event, and he confuses dates and events. The meeting with Parnell, according to Daly, took place in 1873; Thornley asserts this could not have happened until 1874 or afterwards. This point is pedantic, and by no means casts doubt on the occurrence of the meeting. Daly had absolutely no reason to lie 40 years afterwards.*

6. Devoy, John, 'Fragments of Fenian history I.X. Davitt, Parnell and the Fenians – the story of the new departure I.V.,' *Irish Freedom*, November 1913, p.6.

7. Moody, T.W., *Davitt and the Irish Revolution* (Oxford, 1982) p.390.

8. Devoy, John, *The Land of Eire: The Irish Land League, its origin, progress and consequences* (New York, 1882) p.42.

9. 'New Departure explained', *New York Herald*, 27 October 1878; Devoy, John, 'Fragments of Fenian history I.X. Davitt, Parnell and the Fenians – the story of the new X.I.,' *Irish Freedom*, January 1914.

10. Ibid.

11. Ibid.

12. Devoy, John, 'Fragments of Fenian history I.X. Davitt, Parnell and the Fenians – the story of the new X.I.', *Irish Freedom*, November 1914.

13. O'Brien, William, & Ryan, Desmond (eds.) *Devoy's Post Bag* Vol. 1 (Dublin, 1948) p.401.

14. Kee, Robert, *The Green Flag*, Vol. II (London, 1972) pp. 72–73.

15. As a veteran of the 1867 rebellion, Lomasney had been involved in the seizure of Ballyknocken barracks. He would later play a prominent role in the dynamite war.

16. William Mackey Lomasney to John Devoy, in O'Brien, William, & Ryan, Desmond (eds.) *Devoy's Post Bag* Vol. II (Dublin, 1948) p.40.

17. Henri Le Caron to John Devoy, 18 June 1881, in O'Brien, William, & Ryan, Desmond (eds.) *Devoy's Post Bag* Vol. II (Dublin, 1948) pp. 89–90.

18. The Times Special Commission report, XII, pp. 49–50.

19. Parnell, John Henry, p.127.

20. Lyons, F.S.L., *Charles Stewart Parnell* (Dublin, 1977) p.79.

21. Brown, Thomas, *Irish-American Nationalism 1870–1890* (New York, 1966) p.96.

22 O'Brien, William, & Ryan, Desmond (eds.) *Devoy's Post Bag* Vol. 1 (Dublin, 1948) p.370.

23 Ibid.

24 *The Freeman's Journal*, 29 August 1877.

25 'New Departure Explained', *New York Herald*, 27 October 1878.

26 Moody, T.W., *Davitt and the Irish Revolution* (Oxford, 1982) p.564.

27 Sullivan, A.M., *New Ireland* (London, 1877) p.439.

28 Ibid.

29 Ibid.

30 *The Illustrated London News*, 8 January 1881.

31 *The New York Times*, 7 January 1881.

32 Quoted in O'Brien, William, & Ryan, Desmond (eds.) *Devoy's Post Bag* Vol. 2 (Dublin, 1948) pp. 41–42. See also text of an untitled and unreferenced speech written by John Devoy, undated, in notes and drafts for John Devoy's recollections, NLI Ms 18,014.

33 Wilson, Robert, *The Life and Times of Queen Victoria* (London, 1900) p.612.

34 Ibid.

35 *The Illustrated London News*, 12 February 1881.

36 O'Brien, William, *The Parnell of Real Life* (London, 1926) pp. 17–19.

37 Tynan, Patrick, *The Irish National Invincibles and Their Times* (London, 1894) p.215.

38 Ibid., pp. 217–218.

39 Ibid., p.18.

40 Ibid., p.218.

41 Ibid., p.220.

42 Ibid, p.224.

43 Comerford, R.V. 'The Land War and the Politics of Distress,' in William Vaughan (ed.), *A New History of Ireland* (Oxford, 2010) p.49.

44 Ibid.

45 The arrest warrant for Charles Stewart Parnell MP, *Parnell: Kilmainham Gaol Document Pack* (Dublin, ???).

46 *The Freeman's Journal*, 14 October 1881.

47 Ibid.

48 O'Shea, Katherine, *The Uncrowned King of Ireland* (Dublin, 2005).

49 *The Irish Times*, 22 October 1881.

50 Ibid.

51 Ibid.

52 Ibid.

53 Ibid.

54 Ibid.

55 Ibid.

56 Ibid.

57 Ibid.

58 Ibid.

59 Ibid.

60 Browne, Malcolm, *The Politics of Irish Literature* (University of Washington Press, 1972) accessed on astonisher.com/archives/mjb/irish-lit/irishlit_ch17.html (10 December 2009).

61 *The New York Times*, 21 October 1881.

62 Davitt, Michael, *The Fall of Feudalism in Ireland* (London, 1904).

63 Ibid.

64 The evidence of James Carey before John Adye Curran, Kilmainham Gaol, Dublin, 2 March 1883 TNA HO 144/98/A25908C.

65 Ibid.

66 Text of the Invincibles' oath, handwritten by PJ Sheridan, undated, private collection.

67 Tynan, Patrick, *The Irish National Invincibles and Their Times* (London, 1894) pp. 429–430.

68 Corfe, Tom, 'Political Assassination in the Irish Tradition', in Yonah Alexander and Alan O'Day (eds.), *Terrorism in Ireland* (Kent, 1984) p.114.

69 The evidence of James Carey before John Adye Curran, Kilmainham Gaol, Dublin, 2 March 1883 TNA HO 144/98/A25908C.

70 William Henry Joyce, quoted in Leon O'Brien, *The Prime Informer* (London, 1971) p.30.

71 Now the residence of the American Ambassador.

72 The evidence of Peter Carey taken before John Adye Curran at Kilmainham Gaol, Dublin, 3 April 1883, *Depositions of the Witnesses at the Trial of the Invincibles* (Dublin, 1883) p. 232, Kilmainham Gaol Museum & Archive 1C35-10.

73 The evidence of James Carey before John Adye Curran, Kilmainham Gaol, Dublin, 2 March 1883 TNA HO 144/98/A25908C.

74 The evidence of James Carey before John Adye Curran, Kilmainham Gaol, Dublin, 2 March 1883 TNA HO 144/98/A25908C.

75 The evidence of James Carey before John Adye Curran, Kilmainham Gaol, Dublin, 2 March 1883 TNA HO 144/98/A25908C.

76 The evidence of Joseph Smith to John Adye Curran, 10 March 1883, *Depositions of the Witnesses at the Trial of the Invincibles* (Dublin, 1883) p.101, Kilmainham Gaol Museum & Archive 1C35-10.

77 O'Shea, Katherine, *The Uncrowned King of Ireland* (Gloucestershire, 2005).

78 *The Irish World*, 13 May 1882.

79 Davitt, Michael, *The Fall of Feudalism in Ireland* (London, 1904) p.356.

80 Ibid., p.360.

81 Curran, John Adye, *Reminiscences* (London, 1915) p.132.

82 Tynan, Patrick, *The Irish National Invincibles and Their Times* (London, 1894) p.254.

83 Corfe, Tom, *The Phoenix Park Murders* (London, 1968) p.176.

84 Brown, Malcolm, *The Politics of Irish Literature* (London, 1972) p.271.

85 *The Irish Times*, 7 May 1882.

86 O'Broin, Leon, *The Prime Informer* (London, 1971) p.31.

87 The examination of Nicholas Brabazon by Nicholas C. Whyte, H.M. Coroner for the county of the city of Dublin, 8 May 1882, *Depositions of the Witnesses at the Trial of the Invincibles* (Dublin, 1883) p.93, Kilmainham Gaol Museum & Archive 1C35-10.

88 The evidence of James Carey before John Adye Curran, Kilmainham Gaol, Dublin, 2 March 1883 TNA HO 144/98/A25908C.

89 The information of Joseph Smith to John Adye Curran, 10 March 1883, *Depositions of the witnesses at the trial of the Invincibles* (Dublin, 1883) p.107, Kilmainham Gaol Museum & Archive 1C35-10.

90 *The Irish Times*, 7 May 1882.

91 Ibid.

92 Ibid.

93 *The Northern Echo*, 8 May 1882.

94   Tynan, Patrick, *The Irish National Invincibles and Their Times* (London, 1894) pp. 429–430.

95   Ibid., p.55.

96   Tighe Hopkins, *Kilmainham Memories* (London, 1896) p.50.

97   Police memorandum by Constable John Burke, 17 May 1882 NAI CSO Crime and Police reports, box 1.

98   Tighe Hopkins, *Kilmainham Memories* (London, 1896) p.54.

99   The evidence of James Carey before John Adye Curran, Kilmainham Gaol, Dublin, 2 March 1883 TNA HO 144/98/A25908C.

100   John Mallon to Edward George Jenkinson, 30 August 1882 NLI Ms 31, 369.

101   John Mallon's police report of the Phoenix Park assassinations, 30 August 1882 NAI CSO Police and Crime reports 1882.

102   The examination of Samuel Watson Jacob by Nicholas C. Whyte, H.M. Coroner for the county of the City of Dublin, 8 May 1882, *Depositions of the Witnesses at the Trial of the Invincibles* (Dublin, 1883) p.208, Kilmainham Gaol Museum & Archive 1C35-10.

103   The statement of William Dawson, 4 June 1882, NAI CSO Crime and Police reports, box 1.

104   John Mallon to Edward George Jenkinson, 30 August 1882 NLI Ms 31, 369.

105   John Mallon's police report of the Phoenix Park assassinations, 30 August 1882 NAI CSO Police and Crime reports 1882.

106   John Mallon to Edward George Jenkinson, 30 August 1882 NLI Ms 31, 369. This was confirmed by Thomas Foley, who had noted the getaway cab was red in colour, the examination of Thomas C. Foley by Nicholas C. Whyte, 8 May 1882, *Depositions of the Witnesses at the Trial of the Invincibles* (Dublin, 1883) p.94, Kilmainham Gaol Museum & Archive 1C35-10.

107   John Mallon to Edward George Jenkinson, 30 August 1882 NLI Ms 31, 369.

108   John Mallon's police report of the Phoenix Park assassinations, 30 August 1882 NAI CSO Police and Crime reports 1882.

109   John Mallon to Edward George Jenkinson, 30 August 1882 NLI Ms 31, 369.

110   John Mallon's police report of the Phoenix Park assassinations, 30 August 1882 NAI CSO Police and Crime reports 1882.

111   Ibid.

112   The deposition of George Godden, to John Adye Curran, 20 December 1882, *Depositions of the Witnesses at the Trial of the Invincibles* (Dublin, 1883) p.192, Kilmainham Gaol Museum & Archive 1C35-10.

113   The statement of Mary Sharpe, 4 June 1882, NAI CSO Crime and Police reports, box 1.

114   RIC Memorandum by George Hillier, 12 May 1882 NAI CSO Crime and Police reports, box 1.

115   *The Illustrated Police News*, 13 May 1882.

116   The examination of George Hornidge Porter, Surgeon, to N.C.

Whyte, H.M. Coroner for the county of the City of Dublin, 8 May 1882, *Depositions of the Witnesses at the Trial of the Invincibles* (Dublin, 1883) p.97, Kilmainham Gaol Museum & Archive 1C35-10.

117 Ibid., pp. 97–98.

118 Nicholas C. Whyte, 8 May 1882, *Depositions of the Witnesses at the Trial of the Invincibles* (Dublin, 1883) p.89, Kilmainham Gaol Museum & Archive 1C35-10.

119 Anon, *The Mysteries of Ireland* (London, 1883) pp. 202–203.

120 Ibid., p.202.

121 Curran, John Adye, *Reminiscences of John Adye Curran* (London, 1914) p.142.

122 *The Prevention of Crimes (Ireland) Bill.*

123 The Secretary of State for the Home Department, Sir William Vernon Harcourt, to the Viceroy of Ireland, Earl Spencer, 20 May 1882, Ms Harcourt papers, Bodleian Library Oxford, 39.

124 Lord Northbrook to Earl Spencer, 7 May 1882, in Peter Gordon (ed.), *Red Earl: The papers of the fifth Earl Spencer 1835–1910* (Northampton, 1981) p.193.

125 Earl Spencer to W.E. Gladstone, 7 June 1882 in Peter Gordon (ed.), *Red Earl: The papers of the fifth Earl Spencer 1835–1910* (Northampton, 1981) p.205.

126 Hutchinson, Martha Crenshaw, 'The image of terrorism and the Governments response to terrorism,' in David C. Rapoport (ed.), *Terrorism: Critical Concepts in Political Science*, Volume II (Oxfordshire, 2006) p.266.

127 Earl Spencer to William Vernon Harcourt, 11 May 1882, in Peter Gordon (ed.), *Red Earl: The papers of the fifth Earl Spencer 1835–1910* (Northampton, 1981) p.196.

128 W.E. Forster, Irish Chief Secretary, to the Secretary of the Treasury, 20 June 1881, NAI CSO LB 279.

129 Earl Spencer to W.E. Gladstone, 7 May 1882, in Peter Gordon (ed.), *Red Earl: The papers of the fifth Earl Spencer 1835–1910* (Northampton, 1981) p.190.

130 Brackenbury, Sir Henry, *Some Memories of my spare time 1856–1885* (Edinburgh, 1909) p.312.

131 Ibid., p.313.

132 John Mallon's police report on the Phoenix Park assassinations, 30 August 1882 NAI CSO Police and Crime reports 1882.

133 Davitt, Michael, *The Fall of Feudalism in Ireland* (London, 1904) p.358.

134 Parnell, Katherine, *The Uncrowned King of Ireland* (Gloucestershire, 2005) p.151.

135 Ibid., p.358.

136 Tynan, Patrick, *The Irish National Invincibles and their Times* (London, 1894) pp. 272–275. This statement by the executive of the IRB was reputedly by Charles Kickham and John O'Leary of the IRB Supreme Council, indicating that there may have been disagreement within the IRB as to the legitimacy of the assassinations.

137 John Mallon's police report of the Phoenix Park assassinations, 30 August 1882 NAI CSO Police and Crime reports 1882.

138 John Mallon report, 20 May 1882, NAI CSO Police and Crime reports 1882.

139 John Mallon report, 17 November 1882, NLI Ms 31, 649.

140 Anon, *The Mysteries of Ireland* (London, 1883) p.213.

141 Joseph Poole was executed for the assassination of John Kenny. His brother-in-law, William Lamie, gave evidence against him. Poole was a leading Fenian centre, strongly connected to James Mullet, Daniel Curley and Michael Fagan, alongside Caffrey, all leading Invincibles.

142 Quoted in Tom Corfe, *The Phoenix Park Murders* (London, 1968) p.232.

143 *The Freeman's Journal*, 15 August 1882.

144 *The Freeman's Journal*, 14 August 1882.

145 *The Freeman's Journal*, quoted in Tynan, Patrick, *The Irish National Invincibles and their Times* (London, 1894) pp. 293–294.

146 *The New York Times*, 17 August 1882.

147 George Otto Trevelyan MP, Chief Secretary for Ireland, House of Commons debates, 13 November 1882 vol 274 cc1316–7.

148 *The Pall Mall Gazette*, 13 November 1882.

149 Tynan, Patrick, *The Irish National Invincibles and their Times* (London, 1894) p.304.

150 *The Freeman's Journal*, 27 November 1882.

151 Tynan, Patrick, *The Irish National Invincibles and their Times* (London, 1894) pp. 506–507.

152 *The Freeman's Journal*, 29 November 1882.

153 The information of Denis J. Field examined by John Adye Curran [undated], *Depositions of the Witnesses at the Trial of the Invincibles* (Dublin, 1883) p.208, Kilmainham Gaol Museum & Archive 1C35-10.

154 Ibid.

155 Anon, *The Mysteries of Ireland* (London, 1883) p.252.

156 Ibid.

157 *The London Times*, 29 November 1882.

158 Tynan, Patrick, *The Irish National Invincibles and their Times* (London, 1894) p.508.

159 *The Dublin Gazette*, 28 November 1882.

160 *The New York Times*, 30 July 1882.

161 Curran, John Adye, *Reminiscences of John Adye Curran* (London, 1914) p.143.

162 Ibid, p.156.

163 Curran, John Adye, *Reminiscences of John Adye Curran* (London, 1914) p.157.

164 The deposition of Mary Brophy before John Adye Curran, 4 December 1882, *Depositions of the Witnesses at the Trial of the Invincibles* (Dublin, 1883) pp. 185–186, Kilmainham Gaol Museum & Archive 1C35-10.

165 Curran, John Adye, *Reminiscences of John Adye Curran* (London, 1914) p.160.

166 McCracken, Donal P., *Inspector Mallon* (Dublin, 2009) p.104.

167 Tighe Hopkins, *Kilmainham Memories* (London, 1896) p.63.

168 Curran, John Adye, *Reminiscences of John Adye Curran* (London, 1914) p.160.

169 Bussy, Frederick Moir, *Irish Conspiracies – Recollections of John Mallon* (London, 1910) p.86.

170 O'Broin, Leon, *The Prime Informer* (London, 1971) p.33.

171 Bussy, Frederick Moir, *Irish Conspiracies – Recollections of John Mallon* (London, 1910) p.86.

172 Robert Farrell, examined by John Ayde Curran, 29 December 1882, *Depositions of the Witnesses at the Trial of the Invincibles* (Dublin, 1883) p.208, Kilmainham Gaol Museum & Archive 1C35-10.

173 Ibid., p.205.

174 Bussy, Frederick Moir, *Irish Conspiracies – Recollections of John Mallon* (London, 1910) p.88.

175 Ibid., pp. 84–85.

176 The Statement of Robert Farrell to Inspector Kavanagh, 3 January 1883, *Depositions of the Witnesses at the Trial of the Invincibles* (Dublin, 1883) p.211, Kilmainham Gaol Museum & Archive 1C35-10.

177 Curran, John Adye, *Reminiscences of John Adye Curran* (London, 1914) p.164.

178 The Statement of Robert Farrell to Inspector Kavanagh, 3 January 1883, *Depositions of the Witnesses at the Trial of the Invincibles* (Dublin, 1883) p.211, Kilmainham Gaol Museum & Archive 1C35-10.

179 Ibid.

180 Ibid., pp. 211–212.

181 The sworn statement of Robert Farrell, made before John Ayde Curran, 12 January 1883, *Depositions of the Witnesses at the Trial of the Invincibles* (Dublin, 1883) p.214, Kilmainham Gaol Museum & Archive 1C35-10.

182 Ibid., p.215.

183 Ibid., p.216.

184 Ibid., p.214.

185 Curran, John Adye, *Reminiscences of John Adye Curran* (London, 1914) p.166.

186 Ibid., p.179.

187 *The Freeman's Journal*, 13 January 1883.

188 *Reynolds's Weekly Newspaper*, 21 January 1883.

189 Tighe Hopkins, *Kilmainham Memories* (London, 1896) p.66.

190 *The Irish Times*, 22 January 1883.

191 *The Irish Times*, 29 January 1883.

192 Ibid.

193 Tighe Hopkins, *Kilmainham Memories* (London, 1896) p.66.

194 Ibid., pp. 67–68.

195 Tynan, Patrick, *The Irish National Invincibles and their Times* (London, 1894) pp. 310–311.

196 Bussy, F.M., *Irish Conspiracies – Recollections of John Mallon* (London, 1910) p.89.

197 Ibid., p.156.

198 Anon, *The Mysteries of Ireland* (London, 1883) p.264.

199 *The New York Times*, 11 February 1883.

200 *Reynolds's Weekly Newspaper*, 11 February 1886.

201 Tighe Hopkins, *Kilmainham Memories* (London, 1896) pp. 67–68.

202 Bussy, F.M., *Irish Conspiracies – Recollections of John Mallon* (London, 1910) p.96.

203 Tynan, Patrick, *The Irish National Invincibles and their Times* (London, 1894) pp. 313–314.

204 Bussy, F.M., *Irish Conspiracies – Recollections of John Mallon* (London, 1910) pp. 97–96.

205 Tynan, Patrick, *The Irish National Invincibles and their Times* (London, 1894) p.313.

206 O'Broin, Leon, *The Prime Informer* (London, 1971) p.33.

207 Curran, John Adye, *Reminiscences of John Adye Curran* (London, 1914) p.181.

208 Tighe Hopkins, *Kilmainham Memories* (London, 1896) p.69.

209 Tynan, Patrick, *The Irish National Invincibles and their Times* (London, 1894) p.314.

210 Bussy, F.M., *Irish Conspiracies – Recollections of John Mallon* (London, 1910) p.94.

211 Hall, J.B., *Random Records of a Reporter* (Dublin, 1928) p.177.

212 *The Penny Illustrated Paper*, 24 February 1883.

213 Anon, *The Mysteries of Ireland* (London, 1883) p.266.

214 *The Leeds Mercury*, 21 February 1883.

215 *The Penny Illustrated Paper*, 24 February 1883.

216 Sullivan, T.D. *Recollections of Troubled Times in Ireland* (Dublin, 1905) p.380.

217 *Report of the trials at the Dublin Commission Court April and May 1883 of the prisoners charged with the Phoenix Park murders* (Dublin, 1883) pp. 26–27.

218 Anon, *The Mysteries of Ireland* (London, 1883) p.266.

219 *The New York Times*, 18 February 1883.

220 *The Freeman's Journal*, 19 February 1883.

221 *The Graphic*, 24 February 1883; and Anon, *The Mysteries of Ireland* (London, 1883) p.271.

222 The statement of Sergeant Stephen McInroy, Dublin Metropolitan Police to John Adye Curran, 2 March 1883 TNA HO 144/98/A25908C.

223 The warrant for the arrest of Patrick Joseph Tynan, 2 March 1883 TNA HO 144/98/25908C.

224 Hansard's Parliamentary Debates, third series, Vol. CCLXXVII, the House of Commons 20 February 1883 (London, 1883) Col. 414.

225 Ibid., Col. 415.

226 Hansard's Parliamentary Debates, third series, Vol. CCLXXVII, the House of Commons 22 February 1883 (London, 1883) Col. 618–619.

227 Wilson, Robert, *The Life and Times of Queen Victoria* (London, 1900) p.656.

228 Hansard's Parliamentary Debates, third series, Vol. CCLXXVII, the House of Commons 23 February 1883 (London, 1883) Col. 716–720.

229 Ibid., Col. 722.

230 Wilson, Robert, *The Life and Times of Queen Victoria* (London, 1900) p.656.

231 Hansard's Parliamentary Debates, third series, Vol. CCLXXVII, the House of Commons 22 February 1883 (London, 1883) Col. 724–725.

232 *The Freeman's Journal*, 20 March 1883.

233 Ibid.

234 Ibid.

235 *The Graphic,* 24 February 1883; see also *The Leeds Mercury,* 13 April 1883.

236 *The Irish Times,* 9 April 1883.

237 Hall, J.B., *Random Records of a Reporter* (Dublin, 1928) p.179.

238 *The New York Times,* 12 April 1883.

239 Hall, J.B., *Random Records of a Reporter* (Dublin, 1928) p.181.

240 *The Special Commission Act, 1888, Mr Charles Stewart Parnell, MP and others, evidence of Farrell, Carey and others in the Phoenix Park trials* (London, 1888) p.15. Kilmainham Gaol Museum, 09 MS 1D46 16.

241 Ibid.

242 Ibid., p.17.

243 Ibid., p.23.

244 Anon, *The Mysteries of Ireland* (London, 1883) p.270.

245 Ibid.

246 Ibid.

247 *The Leeds Mercury,* 13 April 1883.

248 Ibid.

249 Ibid.

250 *The Special Commission Act, 1888, Mr Charles Stewart Parnell, MP and others, evidence of Farrell, Carey and others in the Phoenix Park trials* (London, 1888) p.33. Kilmainham Gaol Museum, 09 MS 1D46 16.

251 Ibid., p.5.

252 Ibid., p.9.

253 *The Leeds Mercury,* 13 April 1883.

254 *The Irish Times,* 14 April 1883.

255 *The Daily News,* 14 April 1883.

256 Hall, J.B., *Random Records of a Reporter* (Dublin, 1928) p.181.

257 Ibid.

258 *The Irish Times,* 17 April 1883.

259 *The Freeman's Journal,* 17 April 1883.

260 Ibid.

261 Ibid.

262 Ibid.

263 Ibid.

264 Ibid.

265 Ibid.

266 Peter Carey, examined by John Ayde Curran, 3 April 1883, *Depositions of the Witnesses at the Trial of the Invincibles* (Dublin, 1883) p.239, Kilmainham Gaol Museum & Archive 1C35-10.

267 *The Freeman's Journal,* 18 April 1883.

268 *The Freeman's Journal,* 19 April 1883.

269 Ibid.

270 *The Irish Times,* 20 April 1883.

271 *The Glasgow Herald,* 21 April 1883.

272 *The Irish Times,* 20 April 1883.

273 *The Freeman's Journal,* 20 April 1883.

274 *The Penny Illustrated Paper,* 28 April 1883.

275 *The Irish Times,* 20 April 1883.

276 *The Freeman's Journal,* 20 April, 1883.

277 Ibid.

278 Ibid.

279 *The Glasgow Herald,* 21 April 1883.

280 *The Northern Echo,* 21 April 1883.

281 *The Leeds Mercury,* 26 April 1883.

282 The deposition of John Fagan to John Adye Curran, *Depositions of the Witnesses at the Trial of the Invincibles* (Dublin, 1883) p.167, Kilmainham Gaol Museum & Archive 1C35-10.

283 *The Leeds Mercury,* 26 April 1883.

284 The evidence of Peter Carey taken before John Adye Curran at Kilmainham Gaol, 3 April 1883, *Depositions of the Witnesses at the*

Trial of the Invincibles (Dublin, 1883) p.234, Kilmainham Gaol Museum & Archive 1C35-10.

285 The evidence of Peter Priestly taken before John Adye Curran at Kilmainham Gaol, 3 April 1883, *Depositions of the Witnesses at the Trial of the Invincibles* (Dublin, 1883) p.234, Kilmainham Gaol Museum & Archive 1C35-10.

286 *The Irish Times*, 27 April 1883.

287 Ibid.

288 *The Northern Echo*, 1 May 1883.

289 The evidence of Joseph Neill, 19 February 1883, *Depositions of the Witnesses at the Trial of the Invincibles* (Dublin, 1883) pp. 255–256, Kilmainham Gaol Museum & Archive 1C35-10.

290 *The Birmingham Daily Post*, 17 May 1883.

291 *The Pall Mall Gazette*, 20 August 1897.

292 Anon, *The Mysteries of Ireland* (London, 1883) p.285.

293 *The Irish Times*, 3 May 1883.

294 Ibid.

295 Ibid.

296 Bussy, F.M., *Irish Conspiracies – Recollections of John Mallon* (London, 1910) p.129.

297 *The Irish Times*, 3 May 1883.

298 Bussy, F.M., *Irish Conspiracies – Recollections of John Mallon* (London, 1910) p.130.

299 *The Irish Times*, 3 May 1883.

300 *The Freeman's Journal*, 9 June 1882.

301 *The Pall Mall Gazette*, 9 June 1882.

302 Campbell, Fergus, *Land and Revolution: Nationalist Politics in the West of Ireland, 1891–1921* (Oxford, 2005)

pp. 175–176.

303 Bussy, F.M., *Irish Conspiracies – recollections of John Mallon* (London, 1910) p.133.

304 Anon, *The Mysteries of Ireland* (London, 1883) p.287.

305 *The Irish Times*, 4 May 1883.

306 Ibid.

307 Anon, *The Mysteries of Ireland* (London, 1883) p.287.

308 *Lloyd's Weekly Newspaper*, 6 May 1883.

309 *The Leeds Mercury*, 3 May 1883.

310 Bussy, Frederick Moir, *Irish Conspiracies – Recollections of John Mallon* (London, 1910) p.134.

311 Ibid. p.135.

312 Ibid., p.134.

313 *The Freeman's Journal*, 8 May 1883.

314 The evidence of Joseph Hanlon taken before George Bolton, Crown solicitor, at Kilmainham Gaol, 3 April 1883, *Depositions of the Witnesses at the Trial of the Invincibles* (Dublin, 1883) pp. 255–256, Kilmainham Gaol Museum & Archive 1C35-10.

315 *The Freeman's Journal*, 8 May 1883.

316 Ibid.

317 *The Freeman's Journal*, 10 May 1883.

318 Ibid.

319 Ibid.

320 Ibid.

321 *The Belfast Newsletter*, 10 May 1883.

322 *The Freeman's Journal*, 11 May 1883.

323 The deposition of Thomas Scallon, 12 March 1883, *Depositions of the Witnesses at the Trial of the Invincibles* (Dublin, 1883) p.157, Kilmainham Gaol Museum & Archive 1C35-10.

324 The deposition of William Lamie, 27 January 1883, *Depositions of the Witnesses at the Trial of the Invincibles* (Dublin, 1883) pp. 25–27, Kilmainham Gaol Museum & Archive 1C35-10.

325 The deposition of Acting Inspector Joseph Warmington, 5 February 1883, *Depositions of the Witnesses at the Trial of the Invincibles* (Dublin, 1883) p.41, Kilmainham Gaol Museum & Archive 1C35-10.

326 *The Freeman's Journal*, 11 May 1883.

327 Ibid.

328 Ibid.

329 Ibid.

330 *The San Francisco Daily Evening Bulletin*, 23 February 1883.

331 Tighe Hopkins, *Kilmainham Memories* (London, 1896) p.80.

332 *The New York Times*, 15 May 1883.

333 *Lloyds Weekly newspaper*, 20 May 1883.

334 Tighe Hopkins, *Kilmainham Memories* (London, 1896) pp. 80–81.

335 Bussy, Frederick Moir, *Irish Conspiracies – Recollections of John Mallon* (London, 1910) p.156.

336 *Lloyd's Weekly Newspaper*, 20 May 1883.

337 *The Belfast Newsletter*, 19 May 1883.

338 *The Irish Times*, 18 March 1883.

339 *The Irish Times*, 19 May 1883.

340 Ibid.

341 *The Freeman's Journal*, 29 May 1883.

342 Anon, *The Mysteries of Ireland* (London, 1883) p.299.

343 *The Belfast Newsletter*, 29 May 1883.

344 *Aberdeen Weekly Journal*, 4 June 1883.

345 Tighe Hopkins, *Kilmainham Memories* (London, 1896) p.79.

346 *The Irish Times*, 11 June 1883.

347 Ibid.

348 Ibid.

349 James Carey to unknown, Kilmainham Gaol, 10 June 1883 TNA HO 144/1538/4.

350 *The Irish Times*, 11 July 1883.

351 *The Irish Times*, 21 June 1883.

352 Tynan, Patrick, *The Irish National Invincibles and their Times* (London, 1894) p.332.

353 *The Irish Times*, 25 June 1883.

354 Bussy, F.M., *Irish Conspiracies – Recollections of John Mallon* (London, 1910) p.149.

355 Tighe Hopkins, *Kilmainham Memories* (London, 1896) p.79.

356 *The Freeman's Journal*, 28 June 1883.

357 *The Irish Times*, 29 June 1883.

358 Tynan, Patrick, *The Irish National Invincibles and their Times* (London, 1894) p.334.

359 Proceedings of the Central Criminal Court, 19 November 1883 (London, 1883) p.148 OBP t18831119-75.

360 *The Freeman's Journal*, 3 December 1883.

361 Proceedings of the Central Criminal Court, 19 November 1883 (London, 1883) p.138 OBP t18831119-75.

362 *The New York Times*, 16 July 1888.

363 *The North American*, 31 July 1883.

364 Ibid.

365 *The Bristol Mercury and Daily Post*, 18 December 1883.

366 *The Milwaukee Sentinel*, 31 July 1883.

367 Ibid.

368 *The Freeman's Journal*, 31 July 1883.

369 *The Belfast Newsletter*, 2 August 1883.

370 *The Freeman's Journal*, 31 July 1883.

371 *The Belfast Newsletter*, 2 August 1883.

372 *The North American*, 31 July 1883.

373 Proceedings of the Central Criminal Court, 19 November 1883 (London, 1883) p.138 OBP t18831119-75.

374 Ibid, p.155.

375 Proceedings of the Central Criminal Court, 19th November 1883 (London, 1883) pp. 141–142 OBP t18831119-75.

376 *Lloyd's Weekly Newspaper*, 2 December 1883.

377 Proceedings of the Central Criminal Court, 19 November 1883 (London, 1883) p.145 OBP t18831119-75.

378 *Birmingham Daily Post*, 1 December 1883.

379 *The Daily News*, 1 December 1883.

380 *The Freeman's Journal*, 3 December 1883.

381 Ibid.

382 Ibid.

383 Ibid.

384 Ibid.

385 *The New York Herald*, 9 December 1883 TNA HO 144/122/A30424.

386 Ibid.

387 James Russell Lowell, United States Minister at London, to Earl Grenville, Secretary of State for the Foreign Office, 12 December 1883 TNA HO 144/122/A30424.

388 Philip W. Currie to Earl Grenville, Secretary of State for the Foreign Office, 12 December 1883 TNA HO 144/122/A30424.

389 James Russell Lowell, United States Minister at London, to Earl Grenville, Secretary of State for the Foreign Office, 12 December 1883 TNA HO 144/122/A30424.

390 Charles Russell to Sir William Vernon Harcourt, 10 December 1883 TNA HO 144/122/A30424.

391 Ibid.

392 Ibid.

393 Ibid.

394 Ibid.

395 The Ladies' Committee, to Sir William Vernon Harcourt, Secretary of State for the Home Department, 12 December 1883 TNA HO 144/122/A30424.

396 Ibid.

397 The Petition of the undersigned inhabitants of Glin Co. Limerick and vicinity to Her Most Gracious Majesty Queen Victoria, [undated] TNA HO 144/122/A30424.

398 The Petition of Victor Hugo to Her Most Gracious Majesty Queen Victoria, pray for the reprieve of O'Donnell, *The Irish Times*, 17 December 1883.

399 Lionel Sackville West, to the Earl Grenville, 12 December 1883, TNA HO 144/122/A30424.

400 Home Office memorandum by Sir William Vernon Harcourt, Secretary of State for the Home Department, 14 December 1883 TNA HO 144/122/A30424.

401 *The Birmingham Daily Post*, 17 December 1883.

402 *The Irish Times*, 17 December 1883.

403 Ibid.

ACKNOWLEDGEMENTS

The O'Brien Press have asked me to write an acknowledgement for this book by my dear son, Dr Shane Kenna, who sadly passed away on 28 February 2017, at the age of thirty-three.

Shane was a great historian, author, lecturer and broadcaster, and was awarded a PhD in Trinity College, Dublin. He wrote many books in his short life, including *War in the Shadows: The Irish American Fenians Who Bombed Victorian Britain, Conspirators: A Photographic History of Ireland's Revolutionary Underground, Jeremiah O'Donovan Rossa: Unrepentant Fenian* and *16Lives: Thomas MacDonagh.*

Shane was an excellent researcher, travelling widely to investigate facts for his books. He had such a love of Irish history, and one of his real passions was the Invincibles. Shane had great drive to see the Invincibles removed from Kilmainham Gaol and reinterred in Glasnevin Cemetery in consecrated ground. He was part of the campaign to have them moved, and this campaign continues to this day.

On Shane's behalf, I would like to thank the Lord Mayor of Dublin for offering to host the launch of Shane's book in the Mansion House. Something that Shane would have been very proud of. I would also like to thank Ruan O'Donnell, Senior Lecturer at the University of Limerick, who wrote the introduction to this book. Both Shane and Ruan have the same passion about our history.

I would like to thank my son John Kenna. John found this completed book on Shane's laptop after he passed away, and without him this book would not have been printed. John brought it to fruition – thank you, John.

I would like to thank Michael Kenny, Chairman of the Invincibles Reinterment Campaign Committee, as well as other Committee members, including Aidan Lambert, Peggy Galligan, Eva Ó Cathaoir, Gearóidín Ní Caha, Gerry Shannon, Mícheál Ó Doibhilín, Liz Gillis and Séamus Ó Mídheach.

I would like to thank all of Shane's friends and colleagues for keeping his memory alive. You are all wonderful, and I thank you from the bottom of my heart.

Liz Gillis – a great friend to Shane, who wrote the remembrance for the book.

Gerry Shannon – another great friend, who wrote the bibliography.

Aidan Lambert – a dear friend, who wrote an Afterword for the book and also helped me to put this together.

Mícheál Ó Doibhilín, owner of Kilmainham Tales, for keeping Shane's memory alive so well. Shane wrote two books for Kilmainham Tales – thank you, Mícheál.

I would also like to thank the National Graves Association, especially secretary Matt Doyle and chairman Sean Whelan.

Shane was a wonderful human being, kind, caring, loving and thoughtful. A true gentle giant. We love and miss you, my Pal.

Signed Mam xxx (Olive Kenna)

INDEX